THOUGHTS OF HANOVER

THE PARENTS WE CHOOSE

TANYA R CHAMBERS

THOUGHTS OF

HANOVER

THOUGHTS

OF

HANOVER

The Parents We Choose

TANYA R CHAMBERS

A Memoir

OLD MAN TREE PRESS

A Memoir. The names have being changed for various reasons.

Disclaimer: May contain adult languages and graphic details.
For age 18 and over.

THOUGHTS OF HANOVER:
The Parents We Choose

Author: Tanya R Chambers
Cover design by Tanya Chambers of lGSS-P&T LLC
Cover by Tanya Chambers of lGSS-P&T LLC
Editing: Yaya Oluwubarunla

This paperback edition of THOUGHTS OF HANOVER: The Parents We Choose, published by Old Man Tree Press, is an imprint of LAZY GAL SWOFIYAH SELF PUBLISHING & THINGS LLC.
Rochester, NY 14609

Published and printed in the United States Of America

Old Man Tree Press.
www.oldmantreepress.com

Designed by Lazy Gal Swofiyah Self-Publishing & Things LLC

ISBN 979-8-9989798-0-4
Library of Congress Control Number: 2025913339

To My Sister, Karen

TABLE OF CONTENT

Paper dolls and cardboard slippers

PROLOGUE

I t had never once occurred to me, not even for a fleeting moment, to entertain the dreadful idea of killing my mother. The thought had simply never entered my mind, and that's precisely how deeply conditioned I was throughout my upbringing. At church, the pastors would tirelessly drum into our heads the importance of obedience, especially when it came to our mothers. Sunday evenings at Sunday school received yet another layer of conditioning, where the teachers would use the Bible to reinforce the messages the pastor had already instilled within us. Even during moments of intense discipline, when our parents were mercilessly beating us and we dared to look at them with any hint of rebellion, the Bible scripture from Ephesians 6:1 became the scripture of choice to justify their actions while administering those abuses.

Jamaica has churches at nearly every corner of its vibrant streets, and it has more than fifty-one percent of unmarried women serving as head of households, a striking statistic that highlights the unique sociocultural dynamics at play. Really, these statistics alone should compel us to realize that, perhaps, Jesus wasn't truly working in our society the way one might hope or expect. Unfortunately, children raised in poverty were not taught to critically think about their situations or the underlying reasons contributing to such circumstances. Instead, we were conditioned to just accept the reality of our lives and make the best of it, regardless of how dire our situations might be.

Janet's particular brand of cruelty was even more profound and troubling because of her ongoing mental illness. I should have been smarter and more resilient, though. I should have thought about defending myself against her relentless torment. I should have considered the dark and drastic idea of chopping her up when I was learning the ways of a killer. It truly would have been so easy to have sliced off her head, just like I did to the chickens in our backyard, while she was asleep, shifting the blame onto Crotchless Wayne and his posse. Instead, I turned everything she did to me inward, allowing her to use me as her emotional stress management tool, while been the victim of her abuse and instability.

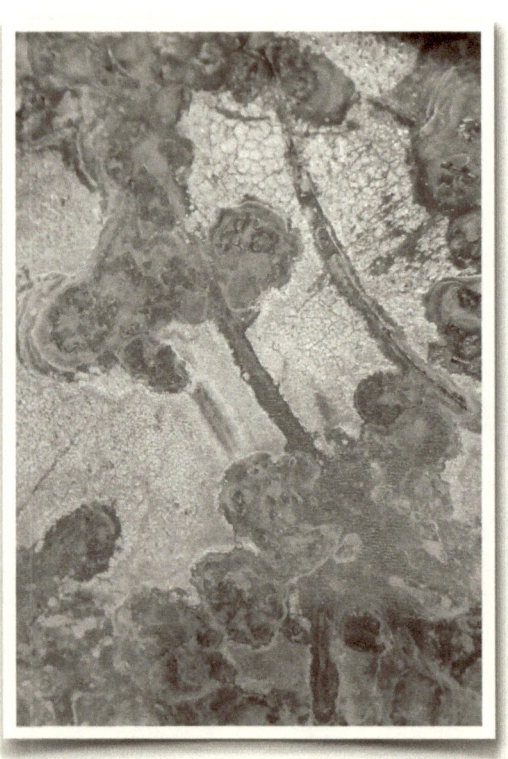

1. My Tyrant Of A Mother

A mother who had nothing meaningful to tell her children other than, "Don't guh fuck and breed, oonuu guh fuck and breed oonuu can't stay in here," really should reevaluate her warped mentality and life choices. This was especially critical, considering she began drumming this alarming message into our heads by the time the oldest reached a tender age of six, the second one was only five, and the third was a mere four years old. But that was tragically how we were brought up in our household.

My mother completely lacked the sensibility and patience needed to genuinely care for us. Every other word that tumbled out of her mouth was a curse word, followed by a sharp slap across the face, punctuated by her heartfelt wish that she had remained childless.

Growing up in Bower Bank, Kingston, Jamaica, alongside two sisters and three brothers could have been a wonderful experience, regardless of the dire poverty we faced, if only we hadn't had such an oppressive tyrant for a mother.

Janet, my mother, was unemployed, uneducated, and unskilled. She was a true hustler, fiercely determined, and utterly unafraid to utilize her body as a means of survival. When her body's earnings fell short of the funds needed to support our family, she sought out day labor, washing people's clothes and meticulously cleaning their houses. There were always individuals in the community who required their laundry done, and Janet had a knack for it, handling the work with a practical efficiency. She dedicated herself to washing clothes primarily on Thursdays and Saturdays, while on the other days, she focused her energy on cleaning houses. Some days, she would even take Klam with her, allowing her to contribute and learn from her.

Day's work also served as a necessary supplement to her habitual ganja smoking and frequent Lotto ticket purchases. However, when that source of income couldn't meet the demands of feeding all of us, she ultimately made the decision to pack up my three brothers and ship them off to live with their father.

As we grew older and the financial pressures mounted, Janet increasingly relied on Klam and me as her makeshift stress relievers. This was especially true during the moments when she couldn't find the money to fund her ongoing ganja addictions. During those times— which occurred far too often— we would sadly go to bed with gnawing hunger in our stomachs, a stark reminder of the challenges we faced as a family.

Ganja was her god. Her love. The one thing she claimed would never fail her, no matter the circumstances. It would always be there, endlessly providing solace when everything else seemed to crumble around her. It was the only power that felt tangible in her chaotic life, a small comfort amid her struggles. She had given up on God the very day my father left her, casting her to drift in a sea of despair, so she resorted to smoking ganja to drown her overwhelming sorrows and calm her frayed nerves. This she would sometimes confide to my aunt when my aunt, concerned for her well-being, told her with a sense of urgency, "Yuh smoke too bloodclaat much."

When Janet's supply of ganja ran out, Klam usually bore the brunt of her accumulated anger, which often overflowed in destructive ways. Klam was raised to be a hard worker—we all were taught the value of perseverance and hard work. Yet, she had an escape when the beatings became too much to bear and the mental abuse felt utterly unbearable. In those desperate moments, my grandmother became her refuge, a sanctuary from the turmoil of our home. When Klam had finally had enough of the relentless abuse, she would often flee to our grandmother's house, leaving Deidre and me to endure the harsh reality while suffering in silence.

Out of the six of us, Klam was the only one I shared the same father and mother with, a bond that was both sacred and complicated. She was the first of my mother's children, the disappointment in our tangled family tree. Janet's resentment often seemed directed most fiercely at Klam because she represented everything my mother didn't want for herself. To begin with, Klam faced numerous challenges due to her mental disability. And according to my father, she was deemed too black and unfortunately looking—to put it mildly—and not the gender he wanted. As a result, the marriage my mother so desperately craved, the one she had been dreaming of with my father, ultimately never materialized.

I was the second disappointment, a re-try at gaining a male that resulted in yet another gender failure. However, my father couldn't disown me; I was a chip off the old block, undeniably bearing his imprint. Deidre was the youngest girl of my mother's children and, without a doubt, the biggest disappointment of us all. Janet, in her desperate quest to finally birth a male child for my father, made the fateful decision to go with Deidre's father, hoping for a different outcome. But alas, it didn't work out as planned—Deidre came into this world with a punaney too.

Janet, in her profound stupidity, truly didn't understand that she was not responsible for determining the sex of the child she carried. She was blissfully unaware that whatever seed was planted within her womb was what was destined to grow and flourish.

My father, being the self-serving person he was, had promised to marry her if she ever managed to give him a son, even though he was already living with another woman who had borne him six children—five girls and one boy.

After the arrival of their third daughter, my father abandoned her, leaving her bitter and heartbroken. In her bitterness and anguish, she turned on her three daughters with a furious vengeance, a rage so intense that it made the neighbors afraid to come to our aid.

A year after Junior left her, my mother met a man named Danny, who gave her three boys over the span of just four years. Unfortunately, it didn't work out for them either, and Danny eventually left her, leaving behind the three boys.

The bitterness that Janet had developed towards my father had not dissipated over time; instead, it had only grown and transformed into something more insidious and consuming. Many people speculated that this festering resentment was the driving force behind my mother's secret mental breakdown, which became more apparent to those who were close to her.

~~~~~~~

I was chronically anaemic, battling an ongoing struggle that seemed to define my existence. I was the most fragile, physically vulnerable of all my mother's children. My skin was constantly breaking out in painful sores, festering with pus, while my weak limbs seemed unable to hold my frail body upright. I fell a lot, often landing ungracefully on the ground. With such evident fragility, my mother chose not to pick on me too much, perhaps out of concern, I would like to think.

I was also the smallest of the three girls, which contributed to my quiet demeanor. In moments of solitude, I would suck my fingers, sometimes sticking one up my nostril, while my other hand absentmindedly twirled my hair as I observed the world unfolding around me.

Janet, on the other hand, was a very large and hefty woman, known for her imposing presence and her heavy-handed hits. When she felt anger stir within her, her solid hand, which delivered a strike that felt like getting hit with a brick, would unceremoniously land on Klam. This was true even for the simplest of offenses, such as playing joyfully in the dirt or engaging in a sweet melody while singing.

At the tender age of nine, Klam's favorite song was "My Man," performed by the legendary Billie Holiday. One particular day, as the song played on the radio, Klam was busy sweeping the yard and dancing exuberantly with the broom in her hand. She sounded like a parrot on crack, full of life and delight, lost in the rhythm and joy of the moment.

Janet came out and immediately saw Klam standing there, before Klam knew what was happening, Janet had swiftly given her a hard kick with her hefty foot. Klam was sent sprawling and landed unceremoniously five feet away from her in the dusty yard.

Klam, who struggled with dyslexia and a slight speech impediment, took the abuse with much pain and tears, yet at the end of the day, however, she would still go and curl up next to Janet, somehow forgetting what Janet had done to her earlier. My mother, in her cruelty, would then kick her like a ball, casually stepping over her as if she were nothing more than a mere obstacle.

I had grown to intensely fear our mother, her unpredictable nature leaving me anxious and unsettled. Deidre, on the other hand, had managed to figure out how to navigate around her volatile moods. But she had a distinct advantage that Klam and I lacked. She had a father who genuinely wanted her, a father who was actively taking care of her needs. She was the only daughter that he had, the special one, the jacket my mother had given to my father.

It wasn't always good for Deidre, though. She possessed the biggest body and the lightest color of all the children, standing out in stark contrast. She looked just like her father, which added to the tension at home. Janet would often tauntingly refer to her as "mongoose color gal" before resorting to beating her red whenever she felt angry or frustrated. I believed that deep down, sometimes Janet would beat Deidre simply to see how many different shades of red her skin could turn, like it was some kind of twisted game to her.

Janet took considerable pleasure in mercilessly beating Klam and Deidre. Klam was the "ugly bloodclaat" who prevented Junior from marrying her. And as for Deidre, she was referred to as "that mangoose color raas," who, in Janet's eyes, didn't come through with a cock when it mattered.

When Deidre reached the tender age of seven, her real father, having come to a startling realization, decided that he wanted her in his life. He already had two sons, and she was his only precious daughter, a fact he could no longer ignore.

Although Janet passionately denied any claims that Deidre was his, she was more than happy to accept the generous money he was providing her for child support. The beatings directed towards Deidre ceased abruptly once Janet realized the financial benefits of having a cash cow at her disposal.

As the money began to flow in steadily from Deidre's father, she was elevated to princess status, significantly changing the dynamics of the relationship between the two for the better.

~~~~~~~

My grandmother was acutely aware of the numerous abuses Klam was enduring at the hands of Janet. So, on the weekends and during holidays, when there was no school to attend, she took it upon herself to instruct Klam to come and stay with her. Granny lived in a charming little house in Spanish Town, which was about an hour and a half drive away from our home in Kingston. Occasionally, Klam would remain with Granny for extended periods and even attend school from there.

As Deidre became more acquainted with her new family dynamics, she began to spend increasing amounts of time with them. There were times when she and Klam would be absent for months on end, leaving me to assume the challenging role of stress management for Janet. Eventually, after much consideration, they decided it was in their best interest to stay away, leaving me alone in the cramped one-room house with our monstrous mother.

My ganja-smoking mother would blatantly disregard the fact that I was far too delicate and sickly to endure the same kind of abuse she inflicted on the others. To her, it simply did not matter. As long as I was living under her roof, consuming her food, and sleeping in the bed she had prepared for me, I was subjected to her unwarranted and unrelenting wrath.

~~~~~~

Been the only one there with her during those chaotic times, I witnessed her gradual mental decline in heartbreaking detail, but I was far too young to truly understand the depth of what was happening. Janet, sometimes engulfed in her own madness and grappling with THC withdrawal, would often take the Dutch pot and swing it toward my head with force, like someone striking a drum—my head being the unfortunate drum. Usually, her outbursts would be over something as trivial as my desperate need for a little milk when I was hungry and there was nothing else in the house to eat. Later, when the smoke had taken over her senses and the THC effects began to wear off, she'd return, completely unhinged, wielding a machete and started beating the living daylights out of me—quite literally—for the same minor infraction, leaving long, stinging cut marks with blood running down my little body. In her confusion, she had forgotten that she had already punished me for the same thing just a moment before. She would then leave me in a haze of unconsciousness while she went off on her quest to find her elusive god. The neighbors, having witnessed the chaos, would start to whisper into my Aunty Norma's ear, planting the seeds of worry. Aunty Norma would come rushing to my rescue, always ready to clean up my little body, carefully sew up some of the worse cuts, apply salve to my painful sores, and nurse me back to life with all the love she could muster.

2. A Killer With Laugh Lines

Janet and I were the only ones living in her small, one-room house when she made the decision to bring a new man home into our lives. He was the very first man she had introduced to us since Danny had left, leaving a noticeable void. She would often go out at night to engage in her body spreading activities and she would come back home quite drunk. On some occasions, she would forget to return home altogether, leaving me alone in the house.

I guess she was finally ready to embark on a serious relationship, something she had been missing for quite some time. I was only eight and a half years old when I was first introduced to him. Wayne was a skinny man with a tall lanky body, possessing large, thick lips, big hands, and very large, deformed feet that made me wondered. To my innocent perspective, my mother appeared to be happy whenever he was around, and that realization made me feel happy too.

During the initial two weeks of having him stay in our small one-room house, the senseless beatings that had once plagued my life suddenly stopped. For that reason alone, I began to like him and appreciate his presence. He was providing her with everything she ever wanted and needed—food, clothing, ganja, and a little bit of money here and there. Those were the only things that truly mattered to her in life. With his support, she no longer had to rise early in the morning to go out and wash other people's "dirty clothes" or clean their "dirty houses."

She started getting up at six in the early mornings, when the community was still shrouded in a gentle haze of sleep. She gave God thanks—for she had rediscovered the deep solace of prayer again—while indulging in her big ganja spliff, the rich aroma filling the air around her. Accompanying her peaceful ritual was her off-key singing to her favorite Bob Marley songs, always playing joyfully in the background on her well-loved cassette player.

When the ganja spliff was halfway finished, she would expertly extinguish it, tucking the remaining portion behind her right ear as if it were a prized possession. She would begin to chant the psalms at the top of her voice, allowing the spirit of the words to fill her heart while simultaneously cursing out the hypocrite, busybody neighbors in the same breath; this was especially true as she focused on washing down the large slab of concrete flooring, which we affectionately referred to as our veranda.

Quoting psalms, for her, was the most effective means of casting her words towards her neighbors.

They were her chosen weapons in her daily one-sided battle with them. She knew most of Psalms word for word, and she had a knack for picking which ones to chant at specific times, based on her mood and the perceived slights of the day.

Once she finished washing down the veranda with soapy water and the sweet-smelling essential oil of rosemary, she would then turn her attention to sweeping the yard, an additional time-consuming chore that had once been assigned to Klam but had now fallen into my list of responsibilities. But in her irie mood—like she was in right now—she didn't seem to mind taking on this task at all. With the unsmoked piece of ganja spliff still perched safely behind her ear, the chanting would grow more fervent and energetically loud, echoing through the quiet morning air.

During her fervent chanting sessions, she would be uttering the neighbors' personal business onto the unsuspecting neighbors. How she possessed such intimate knowledge of their personal affairs, given that she didn't often go around gossiping with them or making any genuine friends, was a mystery only God could unravel. Once she was finished meticulously sweeping, she would take the extra step to sprinkle the newly swept yard with a fragrant mixture of

Rosemary oil combined with water. This particular kind of behavior typically occurred only when she was feeling particularly awesome or empowered. As a result, the neighbors harbored an innate fear of her. They were convinced that she was engaging in the mysterious practice of obeah.

~~~~~~

Although Janet no longer had to go out into the world to do the various things she used to do to earn a living, I still had to take up the responsibility of cleaning our small, cramped one-room house, washing the dishes, and laundering our clothes, including Wayne's, while also disposing of our biological waste. She had made the decision to stop us from using the communal bathroom a considerable time ago. This led us to the uncomfortable situation of having to pass our stools in old newspapers and then emptying that into the garbage out back. In addition to these tasks, I was also responsible for taking out the garbage every single morning without fail.

The chamber pot, a makeshift vessel we used for peeing, was kept hidden under the bed. We all relied on the chamber pot to relieve ourselves at night— well, they all did, while I never really got the chance to because I was considered a regular "piss-a-bed." I had to take on the unpleasant task of emptying the chamber pot in the yard the following morning, washing it afterward, then placing it back under the bed for its next required usage that very night. Most of these chores used to be Klam's responsibility. Deidre was assigned to wash the dishes, while my chore was to focus on cleaning the house. Now that I found myself as the only individual left residing in the house, all the chores had been handed down to me, increasing my burden significantly.

Janet did the cooking, and she truly excelled in the kitchen. She was a very good cook. Wayne adored the way her food tasted, so much so that he would often slip her additional money to ensure that the delicious cook food kept coming in plentiful supply. Although he was a skinny man, he had a voracious appetite and could eat enough for an entire army. Janet didn't mind cooking for him at all, as long as the money was rolling in, that was really all that mattered to her.

At the tender age of eight and a half, I was an obedient little domestic worker. It was all I knew how to do, and I was actively getting better at it every day. I had to improve, not just for my own sake, but to avoid enduring Janet's intimidating hefty-handed slaps that could loosen my teeth faster than their natural demise. Even the new ones that were rapidly growing in did not stand a chance against her ferocious bitch slaps. She was indifferent to my pain, entirely focused on her own frustrations.

When it came to homework, I often found myself doing those assignments at school before I got home. I learned this strategy quickly because of the heavy cloud of ganja smoke that would typically greet me upon arriving back from school. I was remarkably a heavy marijuana smoker at the age of eight and a half, and I didn't even realize it.

I was always a sickly child, and unfortunately, that unfortunate situation didn't change as I grew up. Janet's cruel way of coping with my constant sickliness was to beat the shit out of me, which only made things worse. So, in response, I learned to hide the fact that I was even sick whenever I was around her. Now that my sisters were no longer there to share the burden of the abuse, I had to learn to be strong and resilient on my own. Sometimes, however, it was incredibly difficult to mask my illness and not show her that I was suffering. I vomited frequently, especially after I finished forcing down the large quantities of food she would insist on piling on my plate while threatening me mercilessly if I didn't eat it all.

I fell down a lot, too, often injuring myself in the process. I frequently broke out in rashes that would quickly turn into painful, purulent sores. When I stumbled and fell, I usually hurt my knees in the same spots, so my knees were constantly covered in large, round sores, leaking water and pus that made me wince in pain.

The beatings would irritate the sores so badly that they'd become even more infested and deep, making it hard to recover. After taking me to the clinic on Giltress Street a couple of times, only to be told that they didn't know what had caused the rashes, Janet eventually gave up on the idea of seeking medical help at the clinic. Instead, she attempted to create her own healing salve, using the remedies her grandmother had taught her. It helped a little at first, only until the next dreaded beating.

Overtime, I learned to take care of myself, especially the longer I had to endure the pain while feeling utterly alone and bleeding. I also learned, without a doubt, to never go to her while crying when I fell down and hurt myself, or any such nonsense that could elicit her wrath. I had to be my own nurse and take care of myself, no matter how challenging that may have seemed.

~~~~~

Wayne was a hustler, a title he wore like a badge of honor. Like many Jamaican men who found themselves in similar predicaments, he was uneducated, unskilled, and sadly unemployed. However, what he lacked in formal education, he made up for with a keen sense of street smarts that guided him through the complexities of life. It was this remarkable ability to hustle and to swiftly evade the police that ultimately put much-needed money into his pocket. Janet was enamored with it all. This lifestyle kept her out of the clutches of the streets and, for a brief moment, provided a reprieve from the surrounding madness that often engulfed her.

I almost got my first bout of molestation after Wayne had settled in comfortably during his third week of living in our house. It was a typical Saturday, early in the late morning light, casting a warm glow over everything. Janet had taken it upon herself to visit the market to purchase food with the money Wayne had generously loaded her up with.

On Saturdays, she made it a point to arrive at the market as early as six in the morning. To accomplish this, she would wake up even earlier to perform her morning rituals, which included smoking, washing down the veranda, sweeping, and sprinkling the yard. All the while, she would be singing, chanting, and sometimes cursing out the neighbors who were all conveniently within earshot. By ten minutes to six, with a sense of purpose in her steps, she was out of the house, with Wayne tugging behind her. He too was preparing to carry out what he did best.

It was surprisingly peaceful for a moment, the third Saturday of his moving in, a brief oasis of tranquility amidst the changes. This was the third most peaceful Saturday morning I had experienced in a long, long time. I happily slept in until seven, feeling refreshed and content. Given that I didn't expect her to return anytime soon, I took my time leisurely completing my household chores.

I have always found joy in cleaning the house, especially relishing the sight of my face reflected in the gleaming floor, so I dedicated more time and care to ensure it sparkled just right. I carefully dyed the floor with a rich red-oak stain for added color, then rubbed smooth wax on it to prepare it for the thorough coconut brush shine that was to follow. I lovingly shined it three times with the specially designed brush made from dried coconut fibers, working meticulously until it met my high expectation. Due to my sore knees, I avoided kneeling on the floor as much as possible. Instead, I mainly squatted and deftly used my hands to achieve the shine. When my little arms grew tired, I would switch techniques and use my feet —one foot at a time, of course.

As for our furnishings, we didn't have much to call our own. There were two double beds, one designated for her and the other for me. When my sisters were around, however, the bed often became ours. A brand new eighteen-inch television that Wayne had recently purchased for her sat prominently on her elegant mahogany English-style dresser, adding a touch of modernity to the room. In the corner on the other side, a medium-sized refrigerator that Danny had bought during their time together stood, a remnant of what once was. We didn't possess any table or chairs, and thus the floor and the beds served that practical purpose of seating, creating a simple yet functional living environment.

In the kitchen area was a traditional Jamaican coal stove, a small wooden table, and a little shelf she utilized to neatly organize her seasonings, flour, sugar, and various other essential items. Underneath the kitchen table, she kept a large five-gallon white bucket filled with water, a sturdy box containing her collection of utensils, and an old pot of coal to fuel the fire for cooking. Outside on the breezy veranda, she had another small table designated specifically for washing dishes after meals. The large metal pans used for doing laundry were stored in the same corner, tucked away and neatly arranged beneath the table.

Each night, we would typically bring the pans inside, as Janet wanted to ensure that the neighbors would not inadvertently throw anything unwanted into them.

My mother held firm beliefs against accumulating excessive material possessions. Instead, she preferred to spend her money on ganja, convinced that possessing too much was detrimental to our well-being. She often expressed that we should lead a simple life, embracing poverty much like Jesus did during his time.

~~~~~

I was meticulously putting the final touch on our spotlessly clean one-room house, when I suddenly heard the unmistakable sound of someone approaching the veranda. No one dared to come near our house. The neighbors were far too intimidated by my mother, who was rumored to be "obeah working," to even consider stepping foot onto our property. Unlike the others, I was never afraid of strangers coming into the house with the intention to harm me. For me, the true monster was already living inside, the same one lurking in the shadows of my mind.

Wayne walked in just as I was adjusting the pillows on my perfectly made-up bed, which was positioned nearer to the entrance of the house. He was carrying a white plastic shopping bag in his right hand, and he was looking at me with a rather peculiar expression. I was far too young to fully comprehend the nature of that strangeness. He had been my savior for the past three weeks, or so, and his presence made my mother inexplicably happy. That fact alone was more than enough for me to like him.

Without acknowledging my presence, he passed right by me and walked over to my mother's bedside, which was situated near the other entrance that led to the back of the house. He didn't even bother to take off his shoes, leaving a trail of dirt prints on the clean, shiny floor. That had me fuming with frustration. I started pouting my little lips and blowing air into my cheeks, trying to suppress my irritation while grappling with the conflicting emotions swirling within me.

"Janet don't like it when people come in here with them shoes," I said to him, putting my hands firmly on my hips, trying to project my displeasure.

Him know that, but him still come in here with them, anyway, completely ignoring the rules. Now me have to go clean there again. I looked at him with an angry glare, but my frustration began to dissipate quickly when he held out the bag to me with a grin.

"Me buy you something, go turn the door," he said, looking very happy with that strange, look still shining in his eyes.

All thoughts of a clean floor and my irritation evaporated from my mind. No one had ever given me a bag with anything inside of it before, and the moment felt special. The disappointment melted away, and my heart began to race with excitement.

"A mine this?" I asked, hardly able to contain myself as curiosity bubbled within me.

I slowly opened the white plastic bag, the sound of rustling filling the air, and he took out the beautifully designed white frilly dress, complete with delicate green straps and a charming green bow neatly tied at the back. He held it up proudly in front of me, the fabric swaying gently as he showcased it. I realized, with a rush of emotion, that I had not received a new dress, as lovely as this, in such a long time; the colors of green and white were absolutely my favorite. My heart swelled with joy, and I truly adored it.

"Take off yuh clothes, let me put it on yuh," Wayne commanded, his voice laced with an unsettling authority, the creepy glint shimmering brightly in his eyes.

"Awright," I replied happily, feeling a flicker of excitement, and swung the tight, dirty, and torn frock I was wearing over my shoulders, eager to try on my new dress.

"And take off yuh panty tuh," he added, his tone firm.

"Yuh buy me new panty?" I asked excitedly, my eyes scanning the empty bag for any sign of something new.

I so desperately needed these things. Janet usually waited until she went to wash other people's dirty clothes to come home with their discarded garments for us to wear. I had never received anything fresh or new from her; only old, torn panties with the crotch and butt worn out, which she had to painstakingly reconstruct. If it wasn't for Aunty Norma, I would forever be stuck wearing strangers' reconstructed underwear and clothing, which was a constant source of embarrassment.

"No, me didn't buy yuh any panty, but me want to see yuh little pumpum," he said, his gaze unsettling and invasive.

"Oh, then me not taking off me panty, why you want me to take it off for?"

I was being quite facetious with the question, my tone laced with defiance. Just then, the door flew open with a loud bang, and my aunt burst in like a whirlwind, wielding a sharp machete in her hand, her expression a mix of alarm and determination.

"Aunty Norma, him buy me a new dress and tell me to take off me clothes so him can put it on me, but him didn't buy me any new panty, and still, him want me to take off my panty so him can see me little pumpum." I was feeling quite hurt and deeply disappointed by the whole situation. I really wanted some new panties to show off to my sisters, Deidre and Klam, who always wore such pretty panties to school. The disappointment was so overwhelming that huge teardrops had begun rolling down my cheeks, leaving crimson stains on the floor as they fell, emphasizing my misery.

3. Her Eyes

My aunt had seen him sneaking back two hours later, after he had left with Janet for what seemed like a perfectly ordinary outing. She was acutely aware that Janet wasn't back from her lengthy trip to the market yet, since she had to walk through the entire marketplace to find the absolute cheapest items available. My aunt also had a clear understanding of Wayne and his notorious badness; she knew that he harbored deeply disturbing tendencies, including an inclination toward harming little girls and burning them in the house whenever their mothers were conveniently away. For quite some time now, she had been vigilantly watching for him to make a move, her concern for my safety becoming increasingly palpable. She was genuinely worried for me, and thus, she felt compelled to stay vigilant and keep a watchful eye.

She was a big and hefty woman, much like my mother, sharing a striking resemblance that made them appear almost like twins at first glance. However, where my aunt possessed a kind, cheerful smile and gentle eyes with laugh lines surrounding them, my mother presented a stark contrast with her serious, no-nonsense demeanor, featuring a crazed, ominous look in her eyes, and a perpetually severe frown that rested on her lips.

Aunty Norma was very big in the chest, boasting a generous and prominent figure, while Janet was very big in the butt and thighs, exuding a curvaceous presence that turned heads. She liked to wear long, flowing blond cornrow extensions that added some height to her already impressive five feet, seven-inch frame. Given her stature, she stood a couple of inches taller than my mother, which always made her feel a bit proud. My aunt was deeply saddened that she couldn't protect me from her sister's wrath, but in the face of any other threat, she was not the least bit afraid and was quite prepared to chop them up if necessary.

"Yuh a go take yuh bloodclaat out a this house!" she declared firmly yet calmly, drawing the dangerously sharp-looking cutlass and pointing it directly at him with unwavering resolve.

"Swofiyah, put on back yuh clothes," she ordered with authority. "And take the dress tuh," she added as an afterthought, waving the menacing cutlass at the discarded garment with a fierce determination.

As I forced myself back into my tight, dirty dress, which clung uncomfortably to my skin, I heard her say to Wayne in a voice that brooked no argument, "Give me yuh money!"

"A what kind a money yuh a talk bout? A don't have any mmmmoney," he stuttered, his voice filled with nervousness and fear.

He had certainly heard of her reputation. Contrary to the whispers in the shadows, she was known as the relentless killer in their small community. Nobody dared to come into the vicinity and lay a hand on her own. However, he just didn't realize she was intricately connected to Janet, a name that stirred both fear and intrigue. Janet had never chosen to speak openly about her, opting instead for silence. As the realization struck him, he understood the enormous mistake he had made by sneaking back with the intent to kidnap the pretty little girl. She was, in fact, the catalyst for his entanglement with Janet, a web he had been slowly weaving over time while keeping a close eye on her. Later that day, when he discovered her alone—her two sisters mysteriously absent from her side—he decided it was the perfect moment to make his move.

"Next time, I have to be more careful," he promised himself, the weight of his actions bearing down on him.

I looked at my aunt's furious face, and within her steely gaze, I could see Janet reflected, fierce and unwavering. That Saturday morning, all traces of laughter had vanished, leaving only a potent need to inflict pain on this disgusting scoundrel who had nearly escaped the consequences of his vile deeds. She was determined to make sure he felt the full brunt of her wrath. Wayne, in that moment, was on the precipice of losing control, his fear palpable. I just hoped it wouldn't be me tasked with cleaning up the mess afterward. I glanced over at Wayne, taking in the sight of his thick lips twitching nervously, betraying the dread that had gripped him.

Before I fully comprehended the rapid series of events unfolding before my eyes, my aunt swung her arm with unexpected strength and slapped him sharply across his skinny cheekbones using the blunt side of the cutlass.

"Me say yuh must give me yuh bloodclaat money," she articulated slowly, each word dripping with intensity.

I could only surmise that she, too, found herself in dire financial straits. A swell of relief washed over me knowing that it was not I who was on the receiving end of that cutlass. She was truly terrifying, and I felt a deep-seated fear of the violent rage emanating from her being. Janet had unleashed similar brutal beatings on me, so I was all too familiar with the pain and the overwhelming sense of dread. However, Aunty Norma did not pull back her arm the way Janet had. Instead, she let her anger fuel her actions, every ounce of it radiating from her like a hurricane. The sheer force of steel colliding with soft flesh and fragile bones was nothing short of devastating.

"This little deformed bumboclaat did a go come and try to push him nastiness in my little niece and burn up her body like him duh the other pickney dem, with him bloodclaat deform self," she exclaimed, a measure of disbelief tinged in her voice. "Make me see what yuh a go do when yuh have no cock!"

With mounting anger coursing through her veins, she fiercely grabbed hold of his manhood and pressed the sharp edge of the cutlass against it while demanding that he hand over the money without delay. By that moment, my stomach churned with anxiety, and I could smell the unmistakable odor of shit, making me consider the mess I thought I was going to have to clean up afterward.

Wayne, clearly shaken, reached into his right pocket and pulled out a large roll overflowing with thousand dollar bills. Aunty Norma seized the pile from him with the hand that was holding onto his crotch, granting him a moment of relief, all the while stuffing the fat wad of money into her bra, still aiming the cutlass at his privates with her other hand.

"Swofiyah, guh bring Chris come!" she commanded forcefully. Chris was her youngest child and only son, who was around twenty-seven years old. Much like his mother, he held a notorious reputation as the gunman in the community, feared and respected in equal measures.

"Oh, gaad!" Wayne exclaimed in despair, and then began bawling like a helpless little girl.

I truly didn't understand what was unfolding in front of me, the chaotic scene leaving me bewildered. The tears began rolling down my cheeks as well, blending with my confusion and fear.

"Pickney, me said to go call Chris!" My aunt shouted at me with urgency as I tried to processed the chaos surrounding us.

She had never done anything quite like that before. A sense of fear gripped me, driving me to run as fast as I could toward Chris. My heart was beating furiously in my chest, a relentless rhythm that echoed my anxiety, and I desperately hoped I wouldn't fall down on my way to reach him.

~~~~~

Aunty Norma didn't live very far from us at all. Just two blocks away, on the opposite side of the street, her home was a familiar landmark. The house that she occupied was built by none other than

Michael Manley, the Prime Minister at the time, known for his ambitious housing initiatives. These houses were supposed to have been merely a temporary solution to the ongoing housing shortage and to help address the widespread issue of poverty in the surrounding area. Constructed from very sturdy wood, they were designed to withstand the test of time. Each module was made up of four single rooms, which provided basic living space for families in need. Each room boasted two exits; one at the back and another at the front, ensuring that occupants could navigate easily in and out. There were two modules to a block, and nestled between them was another building featuring four shower stalls, four water closet stalls—two of each on opposite sides—and two very large kitchens that served the modules.

In fact, one room on the modules could sometimes be occupied by a bustling family of six, as the need for housing often outweighed the comfort of personal space. Some fortunate families were lucky enough to have been given two rooms, in addition to one shower stall and a water closet stall, which offered them slightly more privacy and convenience. The large kitchen area was often partitioned into four small sections to accommodate the cooking needs of multiple households. Alternatively, some residents chose to add their own makeshift shanty kitchens, constructed from aluminum zincs, to improve their privacy. Additionally, there was a communal pipe stand that served as the washing area for everyone living on the block, fostering a sense of community despite the cramped living arrangements.

My aunt was one of the fortunate individuals who was able to occupy two separate rooms, affording her a bit more personal space than many others. In addition to her sleeping area, she had the luxury of a shower stall and a separate water closet stall, which was quite a convenience. To ensure her much-needed privacy, she creatively partitioned off a part of the huge communal kitchen to create her own little sanctuary. She had a strong aversion to having strangers intrude upon her personal space. Although her section of the kitchen was relatively small, it was very compact and efficiently organized, making it functional for her needs.

On the other hand, my mother's solitary room was constructed by Danny, situated on land that was unfortunately known as squatters' land. Numerous squatters occupied various parcels of land that had been left over from the project, creating a unique but challenging living situation. Danny chose not to build a bathroom for us, as we were expected to share facilities with the nearest neighbors, who were just a stone's throw away. Although we had sufficient space in the large single room to incorporate a kitchen, Danny never managed to complete that project either, leaving us to navigate our cooking arrangements without it.

When we first moved into what was then a very impoverished community, the situation had its perks, as we were fortunate enough to receive all utilities free of charge—light, water, and even the sewer removal system. However, as time went on and more families began to move in, the atmosphere transformed, and unfortunately, the community became increasingly violent and chaotic.

~~~~~~

My aunt loved flowers with a passion, and it really showed the instant I swung open her beautiful gate. It was like stepping into a little paradise bursting with color and life. Beautiful tropical flowers were blooming everywhere, creating a vibrant atmosphere, along with a small, well-tended vegetable garden that was loaded with calaloo, plump tomatoes, hearty pumpkin, juicy watermelon, and a delightful variety of mints perfect for tea. Additionally, there were fiery habanero peppers, colorful bird peppers, and a couple of tall banana trees, their branches heavy with clusters of ripe bananas hanging from them. These were not only pretty to look at but also some of her favorite ingredients to cook with, so she grew them herself, nurturing them with love.

Sometimes, when Janet was out and I needed a moment of respite, I would sneak over here just to use the bathroom.

"Chris!" I yelled out, my voice ringing through the air loudly.

"Yes," he answered back, a hint of surprise in his tone.

"Aunty Norma said yuh must come quick," I said, struggling to contain the hiccups that were now attacking me, making my words a bit disjointed.

He must have sensed the urgency in my voice, because he quickly came to the window, squinting to block out the bright sun as he peered at me, and then he vanished inside for a moment. Soon, he reappeared with his hand tucked behind his back, clearly hiding something. Not bothering to lock the door, he knew full well that no one would dare enter without his permission, anyway.

As I started to follow him, he suddenly turned around and ordered with an authoritative tone, "Stay!" He said it with an expectation that I would immediately obey his command.

I halted in my tracks, feeling a mixture of defiance and compliance, but as soon as he turned the corner and out of sight, I quickly decided to take a shortcut through Ms. Violet's yard to make my way back to our house. With determination, I reached the line of shrubs that divided Betty's yard from ours. Despite the occasional mishaps, I was quite the fast runner when I wasn't tumbling down. I crouched down quietly behind the bushes just as Chris walked into our modest single-room house, firmly locking the door behind him with a definitive click. I dashed to the back of our house, which wasn't fenced off yet, leaving me with an open view and an undeniable urge to uncover the mystery within. My curiosity was absolutely consuming me, and I was desperate not to miss a single moment of whatever was unfolding. I carefully peeped through the narrow opening between the wooden boards of our house to catch a glimpse of Aunty Norma, who seemed to be pulling quite forcefully on Wayne's pants front while the cutlass swung back and forth. She was animatedly explaining to Chris what had just happened, her expression a mix of urgency and concern.

Wayne seemed to have been in a desperate struggle against her, as evidenced by the numerous painful chop marks all over his arms where he had attempted to block her relentless advances. But of course, he was no match for her immense strength and formidable skills.

Chris, revealing his intimidating prowess, delivered a big man slap across Wayne's right cheek, targeting the very same spot where he had taken a brutal slap from the cutlass earlier. It was a jarring moment, and I truly thought his neck might crumple from the impact. A couple of Wayne's teeth flew out in the aftermath, scattering like small white projectiles. Instinctively, Wayne's right hand shot to his cheek, desperately trying to shield it from further injury.

In a shocking turn of events, Chris brandished a gun from behind his back and expertly aimed it at Wayne's crotch, sending a chill of horror down my spine as I witnessed blood beginning to drip onto the floor where they stood. Aunty Norma, fueled by a newfound energy, continued to saw through the front of Wayne's pants, while he still struggled to protect his dignity and manhood. With Chris standing there, gun aimed steadfastly at him, Wayne was reduced to a meek figure who could do nothing but tremble like a fragile leaf in the wind.

I observed my cousin close the distance, pushing his gun threateningly against Wayne's neck, and began to pat him down with an unsettling calm. To my surprise, he uncovered another substantial roll of five hundred dollar bills tucked away on Wayne. This discovery appeared to ignite a surge of anger within Aunty Norma, her expression twisting with discontent.

"Give me that!" she demanded forcefully, her voice echoing with authority, and Chris, without a moment's hesitation or question, promptly handed over the roll of cash.

"Look in his back pocket if yuh see any more," she suggested, glancing at Wayne with a mix of determination and urgency.

Chris sighed and patted down Wayne's backside, feeling for any hidden treasures, and to his surprise, he found a couple more hundred dollar bills tucked away. Those, he swiftly pocketed for himself. By this time, Aunty Norma's hand was soaked with blood, a stark contrast to the floor below, which had transformed into a chilling puddle of pee mixed with blood that surrounded Wayne's feet, creating a gruesome scene that was hard to ignore.

4. My Bad Aunt

Wayne's body wracked with violent tremors, and he was emitting a raw, animalistic noise that echoed through the room. I found myself shaking uncontrollably as well, my own body betraying my emotional state. Tears streamed down my cheeks as I cried for Wayne, completely unaware that I was making any sound at all. In a desperate attempt to stifle my cries, I covered my mouth, but I couldn't look away as horror gripped me tightly.

My aunt, with a final, brutal push, forced the cutlass to sever its gruesome connection, and it came off in her hand. The severed part of Wayne was wiggling grotesquely, long, stiff, and bleeding profusely. The front of his cut-off pants was now a flattened mass, bright red and spurting blood onto the surface of Janet's bed and splattering onto the floor beneath. My aunt, seemingly unbothered, stood off to the side, carefully avoiding the spray of warm blood that erupted from him.

"This will teach yuh not to fuck no more pickney," she declared coldly, shoving the bloody cut-off cock into his mouth, allowing the scrotum to dangle grotesquely from his thick, trembling lips. It was an effective means of silencing his loud, pitiful moans, at least for the moment.

THOUGHTS OF HANOVER

"Don't faint, yuh bloodclaat," Chris told Wayne, his voice commanding, as he noticed Wayne's frail state teetering dangerously close to collapse on the floor. "If yuh raas faint, me a go shoot yuh," he warned, his tone nonchalant as if discussing the weather.

I guess the pain coursing through Wayne's body was simply too much to bear, for he fainted anyway.

"This little bloodclaat, how much pickney you rape and burn up?" Aunty Norma demanded, her eyes filled with a steely anger as she poked the bloody cutlass into Wayne's belly, now limp and unconscious. "A shoulda take him outside and put him on fire." "Come!" She ordered, her voice rising in irritation as she turned angrily to her son. "Help me pack up him things them."

There was a makeshift closet situated snugly between the two beds, and some of Wayne's clothes were haphazardly hung up alongside my mother's garments. In an impatient and furious motion, she took them down and threw them onto the floor in the bloody mess that had accumulated. Utilizing some of the clothing to wipe up the gruesome remnants, she subsequently stuffed them into the very bag he had brought the dress in.

With a determined flick of her wrist, she threw a white silk shirt at Chris and ordered sharply, "Tie this around his mouth; I want the cock to stay in for when they find him."

Chris, without hesitation, tied the luxurious white silk shirt securely around Wayne's head to prevent the sawed-off penis and scrotum from falling out of his mouth. The fabric became soaked with blood almost instantly, yet they took no notice of it. My aunt, frantically scanning the room, was searching for more plastic bags to stow the remainder of his messy shirts in. When she couldn't find any, she resorted to spreading them out on the floor, layering them beneath the unconscious body, before rolling him onto them. His body began to convulse violently. She didn't seem to notice his distress as she hastily tied the shirts around his waist to hold everything in place.

They both worked with unsettling familiarity and alarming precision. I watched in horror as the vivid red liquid spread rapidly through the fabric. A wave of nausea assaulted my chest, but I dared not make a sound or draw attention to myself. I saw Chris hunched down by Wayne's head, tapping him lightly with the tip of the revolver against his forehead as if it were a mere game. They didn't care that he was bleeding out; their focus remained fixed on their grim task.

"Hey, me no tell yuh me a guh shoot yuh if yuh faint?" he asked the motionless, unconscious body lying on the floor, his voice barely above a whisper as he attempted to instill fear.

Wayne started to moan softly as he began to regain consciousness. It registered in his mind that this horrifying scenario was not just a bad dream; reality set in, and he began to shake uncontrollably. His eyes glazed over with agony as he watched Chris methodically put a silencer on the mouth of his menacing revolver.

"How much pickney you rape and burn up, eee?" Chris asked, his voice calm as if he was having a casual conversation.

Wayne was unable to provide any answer at all, as his cut off penis and attached scrotum had been violently shoved into his mouth. Blood was now soaked through the fabric of the shirt that had been cruelly tied around his face, a grim attempt to keep the penis from falling out of his mouth. Wayne was still sprawled out helplessly on the cold floor, his hands and feet flapping erratically like a fish floundering out of water.

In a calculated move, Chris pressed the gun with the silencer against Wayne's skinny left knee and mercilessly pulled the trigger. Wayne's body convulsed violently in response, and he let out a muffled grunt of pain, blood gushing freely as it pooled around him.

I stood frozen in place, listening intently to the gruesome details of what he had done to the other innocent children, my mind racing with horrifying thoughts, imagining the same gruesome fate awaiting me if my aunt hadn't arrived just in time. I still couldn't process the fact that this monstrous individual was the very one committing these atrocities. My nausea was almost overwhelming, threatening to consume me completely.

I had heard about it during a heated discussion Janet was having with Wayne not long ago. She was expressing utter disbelief and disgust at such a horrendous monstrosity. Wayne, with an intensity I had never seen before, was emphatically saying that whosoever was committing such an atrocious act should have his penis cut off, and both he and his offending appendage should be set ablaze in a fiery spectacle.

Imagining that alarming scenario! I thought I should tell Aunty Norma to light him on fire. But then

I paused, remembering that I was supposed to be over at her house at that very moment. I felt a wave of anxiety wash over me as I was breathing very hard, desperately willing the bad feelings away from my mind and heart. Still, I continued to peek through the window, mesmerized by the chaotic scene unfolding before me, and I suddenly heard my aunty fiercely threatening Wayne.

"If you ever set yuh pussyclaat foot them back in a this neighbourhood again, me a go chop yuh up in a little pieces and throw yuh in a the sea!" she declared, her voice a potent mix of anger and authority.

She was incredibly intimidating in that moment. I had never seen her like this before. My little eight-and-a-half-year-old eyes were widening, finding this formidable woman to be an absolute super badass. And deep inside, I prayed she would never turn against me like Janet did.

In contrast to my mother, who was monstrously evil in her own right, my aunt was dangerously scary. She was a killer wrapped up in the guise of a woman who still had laugh lines around her eyes, making her all the more enigmatic.

Wayne, nodding his head like a bobblehead doll, watched with wide eyes as she expertly angled the cutlass between his shoulder blade and the side of his head. He was trembling terribly, with eyes still glazed over from shock. The leg with the bullet hole was doing the 'della move,' a peculiar shake that seemed to mock his plight. He was trying very hard not to faint again, summoning all his strength just to remain upright.

"Throw him through the gate!" she ordered Chris sharply, flashing her right hand with authority. Her tone dripped with disgust, making it clear that her patience was running thin.

Chris quickly tucked the revolver back into the waistband of his pants. He grabbed Wayne's hand firmly and, with a sudden jerk, dragged him to his feet. Wayne had no choice but to move, gritting his teeth against the pain as Chris pulled him by his collar out of the house and through the wrought iron gate. Without a second thought, Chris threw him onto the street, uncaring that Wayne was shaking like a leaf in the wind.

Chris seemed completely indifferent to the fact that some of the neighbors were now curiously watching the chaotic scene unfold. He picked up the bag that Wayne had dropped amidst the chaos and tossed it out the gate after him. He stood by and watched as Wayne struggled to drag himself up the road, each movement a testament to his determination despite the pain.

Wayne, with his two legs spread apart for balance, was moving slowly and shakily, the shot-up left foot remarkably still doing the 'della move.'

~~~~~

My aunt didn't go out with Chris, whom I had hoped would at least offer some distraction. Instead, she simply stopped at the door, standing there quietly watching them until they disappeared from view, then, after a moment of hesitation, she came back inside. Turning to where I was, she locked her gaze onto mine and said, "Come here little gal, yuh raasclaat, peeping tom."

My heart started to beat furiously at the thought of being caught. "How long she know I was there watching her?" I asked myself as I slowly rose to my feet, full of dread, and walked hesitantly toward her.

I was uncertain whether I should be afraid of her in that moment. I didn't really want to feel fear, but the horrifying scene I had just witnessed loomed in my mind. My hands were trembling uncontrollably as I took each step closer to her. I worried that she might take out her frustration on me with the cutlass she still held firmly in her hand. The closer I got to her, the more my nerves escalated and twisted inside me like a coiled spring. Tears began streaming down my cheeks in huge, uncontrollable droplets.

My aunty, noticing the fear etched across my face, recognized that she was scaring me with the cutlass and quickly placed it down on the floor. I was nearly at the door when she rushed toward me and lifted me up in her big, hefty arms, squeezing me close against her warmth. The feeling was unlike anything I had ever experienced before; my mother had never held me in that way. I cried uncontrollably into her neck, letting all of my fear and confusion spill out.

"Hush, don't cry, me dear, yuh awright now, me not going to make anything do yuh, awright?" she whispered softly, reassuring me. She began patting my back gently while bouncing me up and down in her arms, treating me as if I were a newborn baby. It was a warm embrace that provided both comfort and protection in a moment that had felt terrifying just minutes before.

"Now, me want you to stop the crying and really listen," she said, looking deeply into my eyes, still holding me close. I rubbed my eyes with my dirty hands, which were still stained red from cleaning the floor earlier with the red oak. It felt like it happened a lifetime ago, yet the memory was vivid in my mind. I nodded my head at her, and she gently set me down on my bed to sit for a moment.

"Pickney, a time yuh smart up. Any man at all come in here and tell yuh to take off you clothes, them up to no good—so come call me when that happens, yuh understand?" Her gaze was intense, piercing right into my very soul as she asked me this important question.

I nodded my head at her, though I wasn't really grasping what she was saying at all. I suppose it was because of all the beatings I had received to my head with the dutch pot, which had seriously impaired my level of comprehension.

She must have noticed the blankness in my eyes, she let out a loud sigh of frustration. Her eyes darted around the room, searching for the bloody mess left behind. It was only on Janet's bed now, as she had wiped up the rest with Wayne's clothing, leaving the room in disarray.

"Me have to go buy yuh mother back a sheet like this, cause she a go definitely miss this one when me throw it out," she said thoughtfully, contemplating the situation.

"She buy it at the pharmacy," I replied helpfully, struggling to suppress my hiccups as I spoke, hoping to make some sense in this chaotic moment.

"If yuh mother ask yuh if yuh see Wayne, what yuh must tell her?"

"Me don't see him!"

"Good! Yuh mustn't tell her anything at all about today," she said gently, her tone filled with an unspoken urgency. "As a matter of fact, don't say anything about today to anybody, yuh understand?"

I nodded my head at her again, still quite surprised that she hadn't reacted more harshly. Janet would have quickly reacted by bitch slapping me down already for this kind of behavior. She absolutely hated it when we looked her directly in the eyes and calmly nodded our heads at her. She often called us "dry eye and bare face" whenever we did, which was meant to shame us into submission. But my aunt was just gazing at me with bright kind eyes, patiently waiting for me to show her that I truly understood the gravity of what she was saying. I nodded my head at her once more.

"Me not going to tell her, or anybody nothing, Aunty Norma," I said, attempting to sound like a responsible grown-up. "Me know that him was a bad man and that's why you cut off him buddy, so me not going to tell her."

It was very difficult to maintain that adult-like tone when you're speaking through fast-paced and overwhelming hiccups.

"This is for yuh, make sure yuh hide and save it," she insisted in a serious tone, as she handed me the money.

"Yes, Aunty Norma," I replied, utterly shocked, as I carefully took the money from her hand, overwhelmed by the unexpected gesture. "A my share this?" I asked in disbelief, my mind racing with thoughts of what I could possibly do with such a large sum.

"Yes," she answered firmly, casually putting the rest of the pile back into the depths of her bosoms.

I had never in my life received so much money at once. I certainly was going to make sure it was well hidden and kept safe.

"Save it and don't tell anybody anything!" she warned me with a knowing look.

"Me not going to tell anybody," I promised her earnestly, feeling a weight of responsibility settle on my young shoulders.

She was still gazing deeply into my soul, and she must have discovered something significant hidden within me. With a slight nod of her head, she glanced around the expansive room once again. Making her way over to my mother's bed, she swiftly removed the bloodied sheet, tossing it aside before hurriedly spreading a clean one on top. She gathered up the soiled sheet, bunched it tightly, and then hurled it onto the floor. With deliberate care, she used her sturdy right foot to scrub the floor, bringing a mirror-like shine to its surface. In just a few moments, I could see my own reflection clearly. She scanned the room one last time, ensuring everything was in perfect order, and then made her way toward the door, picking up the dirty sheet on her way.

"Yuh mother soon come," she said, her voice laced with fatigue. "Make sure yuh bathe and put on clean clothes before she come; yuh know how she stay."

"Yes, Aunty Norma," I replied, watching her walk toward the door, her movements heavy with tiredness.

"Aunty Norma!"

"Yes, me dear," she paused briefly to look at me with a contemplative expression.

"Yuh should a did lite him a fire, cause that a what him said him would a do," I said to her through subsiding hiccups, my emotions still raw.

"A that me should a did do," her voice sounded heavy with a deep sense of sorrow and regret. "A that me should a did do," she repeated slowly, then turned around and walked out the door, leaving me still in a state of shock.

I was numbed by the moment. That day, I didn't fully understand what had transpired, but I learned three crucial things. One; I was not alone as I had always used to think in my solitude. Two; I had to learn to be brave and strong, even when fear consumed me. And three; I had to learn the weight of keeping secrets, a burden that felt too heavy for my young shoulders.

When Janet finally came home from the market that bustling Saturday afternoon, sweat was pouring off her, but she looked so elated, almost radiant. She had bought three large bags of food, their contents a testament to her hard work.

While carefully putting them away, she suddenly threw a black plastic bag at me with a flick of her wrist. Inside were three brand new pairs of brightly colored panties, a shiny pair of shoes for school, and navy blue socks to match the shoes perfectly. She had never bought me so many new things before, but my fleeting happiness at receiving them had been abruptly stolen away by the heaviness of the day's events.

5. Chicken Killer

Deidre didn't have idiotism; she was, in fact, the smartest of all my mother's children—at least, that was what she loved to tell herself and us, her siblings, as we got older and began to question everything. Growing up, she never acted overly stupid or naive like Klam and I often did. I couldn't pinpoint if her apparent intelligence stemmed from a different genetic makeup or if it was simply the fact that she spent far more time with her father and brothers, where she was encouraged to truly express herself. It was fascinating to consider how this environment allowed her to think critically and grow mentally, ultimately resulting in her distinct personality. She was fortunate to have intelligent role models and positive influences precisely at the time when it was needed the most.

Her father was a man of the government, and she delighted in bragging about his extensive education and impressive earning potential. She, indeed, had certain advantages that the other children lacked.

Her father was acutely aware of the kind of woman he had for a daughter's mother, which led to some complicated feelings. He regretted ever getting involved with her, until he eventually discovered that she had given birth to a daughter—something he had always longed for. For many agonizing years, he had tried to gain custody of her from Janet, but she remained firmly unyielding and resolute. However, eventually, circumstances shifted, and he was finally granted the opportunity to see her. She even spent time staying with him occasionally. Yet, despite all of this, Janet stubbornly refused to fully acknowledge him as her true father.

Danny, my brothers' father, was a remarkably talented musician and a passionate singer whose voice could fill a room. He wasn't particularly school smart, but he possessed a sharp streetwise intuition that often proved to be more valuable in life. Growing up in Kingston, Jamaica, he understood that being street smart had a tendency of trumping book smarts in many situations, especially in the vibrant and often unpredictable streets of the city.

Danny took it upon himself to teach his boys that if they weren't exceptional in academics, they should at least be vigilant about what was happening around them in the streets and learn how to navigate through it all. He emphasized that no matter where in the world they found themselves, if their heads weren't firmly on their shoulders, they wouldn't survive for long. To them, Danny was not just a father; he was their steadfast guide and teacher, their cherished role model. His sons grew up filled with admiration, dreaming of emulating him and walking in his footsteps.

On the other hand, Janet consistently warned us with her voice laced with meanness, "Don't bother go fuck and breed. If you oonuu fuck and breed, don't even think about coming back in this house, because it's just not going to happen." Her words were clear and left no room for misunderstanding.

Klam fared better with my grandmother, who had her own way of managing things, but I truly felt completely alone during that time. That was until I made a surprising discovery that my aunty was keeping a watchful eye over me. The day she resolutely cut off Wayne's prick, I was a nervous wreck, anxiously awaiting the aftermath.

When Janet returned from the market, she seemed completely oblivious to anything unusual happening around her. I had already finished all my chores and found a hiding spot under the bed, keeping my head low. I didn't dare come out until she called my name. I stayed there, with my two fingers stuck in my mouth and one finger resting awkwardly up my nostril, silently watching her—just like I normally did when I felt uncertain and vulnerable.

She was genuinely happy, radiating joy as she danced and sang with enthusiasm while stirring the big pot of the most incredibly delicious pigeon peas soup I had ever tasted in my young life. The aroma wafting through the air made my stomach rumble in anticipation. By seven o'clock that evening, I was clean, with a belly full, tucked comfortably in my bed, pretending to do homework. She had kindly volunteered to do the dishes after our delightful dinner, and I kept watching her, sneakily and quietly, through the wide-open door, fascinated by her movements. By eight o'clock, I had completely stopped pretending to focus on my homework.

She was also in her bed, watching a captivating movie on the small eighteen-inch television set, lost in the flickering images. By nine-thirty, I had drifted into a deep sleep. The stressful ordeal of the day had left me utterly exhausted, and I slept right through the night without stirring a bit.

The next morning when I woke up, I discovered with embarrassment that the bed was soaked through and through. I had become what some might call a "pisser bed." I couldn't seem to stop pissing the bed, much to my chagrin. Janet had to keep replacing the old sponge we used as a makeshift mattress ever so often due to the uncomfortable infestation of bedbugs.

Sometimes, in my restless sleep, I would even piss on Klam and Deidre, which added to my mortification. When Janet got into one of her crazy moods and the bedbugs became overwhelmingly bothersome, she would throw out the entire old mattress, forcing us to sleep on the cold and hard floor instead.

She didn't even notice that the bed was wet, and that I had taken the bed sponge out to let it soak up the sun and dry, along with the damp sheets. Janet was simply too preoccupied with her thoughts. Wayne hadn't shown up yet, and she was deeply worried, wondering if everything was okay with him. She seemed completely oblivious to the fact that his clothes had gone missing, too. After two long weeks without a word from Wayne, Janet reluctantly resigned herself to the reality of being a single woman once more. Although she didn't revert to her old ways of seeking out casual relationships, she did, however, return to focusing on domestic work to fill the economical gap in her life.

I kept out of her way most of the time by staying hidden beneath her bed. It had become my secret hiding place, a retreat from the world. Another two weeks passed, and she finally secured a job as a street sweeper. This new employment brought in a steady and much-needed income to the household. Although she seemed safe to be around, I didn't fully trust the situation, so I continued to keep my distance.

When Janet left each morning for work, I would sneak over to Aunty Norma's house to learn new things. I had become inspired and aspired to emulate her strength and resilience. She taught me how to fold my fist into a strong punch, how to position my hands perfectly to deliver a precise bitch slap, and even gifted me a small cutlass to help me learn the chilling art of chopping up a body, which she kept stored safely in her house. She taught me how to chop up and kill chickens without hesitation or fear. For several months, I diligently practiced everything she had taught me. Typically, this would occur after school when I got home and completed my homework and all my household chores.

I used two hundred dollars from the money, Aunty Norma had generously gave me, to purchase a dozen small chickens. My intention was to raise them so I could hone my killing skills on them. When my mother first saw the little chickens, she assumed I was raising them as pets.

"Where yuh get the money from to buy chicken?" she asked, clearly surprised.

"Me buy them with the lunch money yuh give me," I replied excitedly, feeling a sense of pride in my venture.

I was almost nine now, just a couple of weeks away from that milestone birthday to be exact. With a newfound goal in my mind, I was determined to work diligently toward it. My aunt was also teaching me how to grow my own food. Already, I was planting things just the way I had seen her do it. A part of our backyard had transformed into a flourishing vegetable garden that I watered religiously, morning and night. It was filled with all my favorite vegetables. Janet didn't mind my efforts; in fact, it was benefitting both of us tremendously.

I waited patiently for the chickens to grow so that I could practice my killing skills on them, just as my aunt had taught me with her own methodical approach. I also chose to practice on Sundays, specifically, so that Janet could prepare a nice, warm chicken dinner for us. Every so often, I replaced the chickens with new ones, always ensuring to keep the supply coming. Chris graciously made me a large chicken coop, complete with plenty of yard space in the back of the house, allowing the chickens to run around freely and giving me room to play with them without raising any suspicions from my mother.

What I didn't realize was that Janet had started questioning the morality behind my personal killings of these pets, despite the fact that she had once forced me to kill a chicken herself. I still vividly remember that day; I couldn't bring myself to eat it afterward. She literally had to bitch slap me just to get me to swallow it down, and I remember crying as I did so. I had named that chicken Big Boy, and he had quickly become my friend, so when she forced my hand to take his life, I was deeply traumatized and shaken to my core.

I was only seven at the time, and I had no idea how to kill a chicken properly. After several failed attempts with the heavy machete I wielded, I eventually managed to do it, but not without getting chicken blood and feathers splattered all over me. While I used to enjoy eating chicken, all that changed in an instant, and I found myself unable to eat it after that traumatic experience. Yet, in her household, I had no choice; I had to eat whatever she placed in front of me, chicken or not.

Now she was wondering why on earth I was killing my pets? I didn't know she was watching me that particular Sunday morning, as I got up to carry out my chicken killing ritual. I had taken the cutlass, a sturdy yet sharp tool my aunt had given me, which I now kept conveniently hidden away by the side of the chicken coop for easy access. I had already meticulously planned which chicken I was going to kill that day.

As I approached the coop, I carefully selected the tallest and biggest chicken among the flock. Although I was very small in stature, I had learned to handle them with surprising dexterity. My aunt had taught me this skill, instilling in me the belief that in everything, size didn't matter as much as confidence and ability. I had to learn to work with it, or around it, to get the job done. However, I didn't lift it the way she had shown me; it felt far too heavy in my grasp. I stepped into the coop and gently ushered that particular chicken out, relying on the trust I had built with them over time. It wasn't difficult; they saw me as their protector, like a mother figure. I watched as the chicken sprinted into the yard, its movements instinctual and carefree, while I exited the coop, ensuring to shut the door securely behind me.

The large chicken stood still, watching me warily, as if it somehow sensed its time had come. With a sense of determination, I cautiously reached for the small cutlass I had hidden on the side of the coop, remaining vigilant about the very tall chicken. I made sure it wasn't contemplating a desperate attempt to fly off. I circled it slowly, just as my aunt had instructed. The chicken mirrored my movements, circling me like a fighter in a carefully choreographed spar. I was not afraid. Long ago, I had ceased to let fear interfere with my resolve. I remained focused, observing my prey in the same way it was observing me. Then, without hesitating, I pounced. In less than four seconds, the chicken's head lay on the ground while its body ran around in shock, flapping its wings wildly. I watched with satisfaction as the head had come off cleanly in one swift motion. I was getting better with each passing day.

"But kiss me bloodclaat!" I heard my mother exclaim in utter disbelief, her voice echoing with surprise.

I swung around, completely shocked that I had gotten caught in the act.

"Yuh turn chicken killa, now?" she asked in disbelief and shock, her tone a mix of accusation and humor.

My mother couldn't contain herself; she fell to the ground, shaking with uncontrollable laughter. She rolled around on the ground, laughing so hard that I seriously thought she might either die of laughter or, even worse, accidentally roll over my carefully tended vegetables. I stood there with the cutlass in my hand, dripping blood, observing her with a mix of concern and trepidation. I had learned long ago that laughing when she laughed could lead to unexpected consequences, so I remained silent, weary and alert, listening to the sound of flattering wings that was fading quietly behind me.

The backyard was my domain, a small paradise I had maintained just the way my aunt had diligently shown me. For now, it was still just the two of us in the large one room space, a strange tranquility that felt almost foreign had taken over. She hadn't returned to her abusive ways yet, but I could sense that it was only a matter of time. My mother had been such a bad mother over the years; I found it impossible to trust this quiet, nice, friendly version of Janet that she momentarily embodied. I simply didn't trust her. So I stood there, keenly watching her as she laughed herself silly, my heart pounding as I waited anxiously for the nasty words, or perhaps the big slaps to come, but neither materialized. Eventually, she managed to get to her feet, clumsily struggling with the extra pounds she had gained over the months while engaging in street work.

"Swofiyah," she said with a tone that was both commanding and casual. "You don't have to kill your chickens every single Sunday just for me. I buy some oxtail for our dinner today, so don't go killing any more of your chickens, not until I ask you to. Aright?"

"Yes, Janet," I mumbled somewhat reluctantly, feeling a wave of disappointment wash over me.

"She thinks I'm out here killing my chickens just for her. Now I can't even practice my swings properly. I really have to find a different solution," I thought to myself, a heavy sigh escaping my lips.

I wanted so desperately to hiss my shaking teeth in indignation. Yet, deep down, I knew I wasn't in the mood for her inevitable backhanded slap today. I watched her disappear into the house, my cheeks puffed up with air and my lips pushed out in frustration. I felt incredibly disappointed.

6. Things Will Never Be The Same

Over the months of rigorous training with my aunt, I had somehow also become known as the little terror at St. Michael's Primary School, which I attended alongside all my brothers and sisters.

Klam typically played an exuberant game of dandy shandy with her close-knit group of friends during our lively lunch breaks. Deidre, proudly flaunting her— princess status, had notably separated herself from the rest of us, choosing instead to elevate her social standing. She was sitting cross-legged with her back perfectly straight, fully embodying the role, her neat and tidily pressed uniform, with its razor-sharp pleats, elegantly spreading around her chubby frame. On her feet, she sported a shiny new pair of shoes and eggshell white clean socks. I made a point to pretend not to notice her friends desperately trying their best to emulate her every move. My three smaller brothers, meanwhile, were always bustling about with their boundless energy. Two of them were enrolled in the basic school located on the same premises, and they usually met up at the same spot for lunch.

They were always hungry after a long morning of classes and play. David was the oldest of the three boys, Mark was the second, and Pete was the youngest, the last of my mother's children.

Unfortunately, Pete wasn't fully potty trained yet, which sometimes led to uncomfortable situations. There were times when he would have accidents, resulting in him soiling his pants, and either Klam or I would be called upon to clean him up. Pete didn't particularly like it when they called for Klam. His reaction would often be to cry loudly and throw himself on the ground, which only created a bigger mess for us to deal with. This was partly because she would pinch him when she didn't want to take on the task herself. So, his teachers learned quickly not to summon her for help. I, on the other hand, didn't mind cleaning up after Pete. He was my little brother, whom I adored with all my heart, and out of all my brothers, I definitely loved him the most. During the time they were living with us, Pete was often left in my care, especially when Janet tried to conveniently pretend she didn't have any parenting responsibilities to juggle.

I had taken up the important responsibility of becoming their protector at school, a role that I embraced wholeheartedly. Sometimes, the boys would foolishly spend all of their lunch money before they even reached school, and by the time lunchtime rolled around, they would be left feeling very hungry and dissatisfied. To help them out, I would use some of the lunch money that Janet had generously given me, or I would prepare enough lunch for myself so I could share it with them. These acts of kindness were simply part of my assumed responsibilities, and as a result, the teacher would often call on me if there was ever any trouble, which thankfully was not very frequent.

My three brothers were exceptionally tall for their ages, a trait they inherited from their very tall father. David, in particular, liked to think of himself as tough and rebellious, believing he was a street fighter. However, whenever he found someone who matched his size and toughness, he would inevitably come running to me, tears streaming down his face, pleading for my help.

Nobody dared to trouble my family or my friends when I was around, and after a while, the other students at school began to understand that truth.

In addition to my other responsibilities, I had also taken to carrying my little cutlass with me to school each day, a precautionary measure that helped ensure my safety. St. Michael's Primary School was located in a very rough area of downtown Kingston, where danger often lurked around every corner. A girl had to learn how to take care of herself, and I was determined to defend not only myself but also those who looked up to me.

Once, I had tried to chop up a boy who lived right in my community. He was a year older than I was and had already developed a teenage body that was unmistakably thick and strong. He was known as the male bully of the Primary School, often terrorizing younger kids without mercy. To make matters worse, he also knew that I had a secret: I was the unfortunate child who wet my bed. The entire community had become aware of this embarrassing fact, leaving me feeling exposed and vulnerable.

Janet attempted to shame me into stopping this humiliating habit of wetting my bed on several occasions, she would forcefully drag me up and down the street, parading me with the ill-fated sponge, encased in the soaked-through fitted sheet, which rested awkwardly atop my head—the crown of shame. As she marched me up and down the community , she would chant with a mocking tone, "piss-a-bed a Jrong crow, yuh no shame a yuh self? Yuh piss up the bed all night long."

The commotion would summon curious neighbors to their doorsteps, while some of the other kids couldn't resist pointing and laughing, relishing in my misery.

The last time she subjected me to this public humiliation was three months after Wayne had mysteriously disappeared. Although she had stopped physically beating me, her cursing and verbal taunts had resumed unabated. Meanwhile, the bedbugs were also making a desperate comeback, infesting her bed and adding another layer of torment to my already miserable existence. She thought I was far too old to still be wetting the bed, and in her eyes, I desperately needed another scare to get my act together. This time, while she was energetically chanting up and down the bustling street, my aunt emerged from the house to see what all the commotion was about. It was well after seven in the morning, and I had that wet, bedbug-saturated sponge precariously balanced on my head, traipsing along with Janet right behind me, knocking loudly on an old, rattling paint pan while chanting fervently. She was truly making a pantomime of the whole ridiculous scene. Witnessing this, my aunt became very angry and indignant at Janet for what she perceived as mistreatment toward me.

"Hey bloodclaat gal!" she shouted, hurling curses at my mother with palpable outrage. "A what yuh a do to yuh pickney? Yuh bloodclaat mad, or something?"

My aunt's voice rang out, filled with concern for my well-being. She then turned to me and said with a firm but caring tone, "Swofiyah, go put that down and get yourself ready for school."

I hurriedly made my way back home, the soaked mattress still precariously perched on my head. Once I arrived at home, I placed it in its usual sunlit spot before dashing off to prepare for school. I quickly got ready and made my escape before Janet returned to the scene.

That particular day, I found myself running extremely late and decided not to bother with showering, which was usually customary. I hastily put on my school uniform, along with my shoes and socks, grabbed my bag, and raced all the way to school, still clad in my sodden underclothing, with no time to spare. The bully of the school, a notorious figure known for his disruptive antics, was unfortunately in my class. He walked into the classroom that morning with an air of arrogance and plopped himself down right in front of me, making it impossible for me to ignore him.

"Something smell renk," he said loudly, to none in particular, clearly trying to provoke a reaction from those around him.

That proclamation instantly captured my attention, and I felt my heart race. I could tolerate the embarrassment and humiliation from Janet, as painful as it was, but I'll be damned if I was going to stand there and take being belittled by anybody else.

"Yuh no smell something renk?" he asked the boy sitting next to him, his voice dripping with disdain.

"No mon, I don't smell anything," the boy responded nervously, avoiding eye contact.

The bully then turned his piercing glare on me and said, "Yuh piss up yuh bed and no wash you renking ass."

He should not have crossed that line with me. I already bore the brunt of that relentless shaming from my mother at home; I didn't need to endure it from some overconfident brute as well. Before I even realized what I was doing, I reached into my uniform and pulled out the cutlass I had been hiding all day, a weapon I had been sneaking to school for protection.

"Black ass, smell this," I shouted defiantly, swinging the sharp blade at him, hoping to chop off his head, just like I did with the chickens I was raising back at home.

The bully was incredibly fast. He managed to skip out of the way just in time to narrowly miss getting struck by the sharp edge of the cutlass, which would have sliced across his neck. In his frantic hurry to escape the imminent danger posed by the cutlass, he inadvertently disturbed the desk situated right in front of him, sending it toppling over in a chaotic mess. His quick thinking and rapid movements earned him an impressive scar on his upper arm, a lasting reminder of his near-miss.

I was absolutely furious that I hadn't been fast enough to catch him. In a fit of determination, I leaped onto my desk, disregarding whether the other students could smell my very soiled knickers. With my left hand confidently resting on my hip, I pointed my sharp little cutlass directly at the unsuspecting bully and firmly told him, "The next time yuh smell me, yuh better keep it to yuhself, or it will be the last time yuh smell anybody around here."

The bully was clearly taken aback by my sudden boldness. He didn't expect such a fierce response, and neither did the rest of the class. They all watched, wide-eyed and speechless, as I tucked the cutlass back into my clothing and returned to my seat, their mouths hanging open in astonishment.

After that rather unfortunate day, he never uttered another word to me. Nor did he ever reveal to his parents how he had acquired that noticeable scar. The teacher happened to be absent from class that morning, completely unaware of my moment of insanity, and the students—all too intrigued—never breathed a word about it afterward.

In that moment, the old bully was put down, and I stepped up to claim his mantle, becoming the new force to be reckoned with in the classroom.

~~~~~

Janet still hasn't learned about my favorite past time. I had recently begun to sell the excess tomatoes, vibrant peppers, and sweet corn from my flourishing vegetable garden. During certain fruit seasons, I would climb people's trees and pick as many of the ripe fruits as I could, selling them to the eager students at school during lunchtime to make extra money. I also took the time to make delicious tamarind balls and prepared stew tamarind to sell to the kids in my neighborhood or at school, becoming a regular young entrepreneur in my community.

The three thousand dollars my aunt had given me had now blossomed into three thousand eight hundred. That was quite a substantial amount of money for a little girl at that time, and I was proud of my efforts. I now had buyers for the chickens whose heads I was still chopping off. My chicken and egg business was thriving impressively, too, thanks to Aunty Norma, who was stealthily helping me with that venture.

All of these entrepreneurial activities I had to keep secret from my brothers and sisters. When they curiously asked me about the items I was selling, I told them that a teacher had given them to me to sell. They never inquired further about the name of the teacher, and I was never one to volunteer that information. They remained blissfully unaware of the chicken and vegetable farm I was secretly managing. They hardly ever came to the house anymore, which gave me even more freedom to pursue my hidden ventures.

Janet was always incredibly busy with sweeping the streets and maintaining cleanliness in our neighborhood. Sometimes, she would leave early in the morning, just as the sun was rising, and then return home late at night, well after everyone else had settled in for the evening. I was, essentially, on my own most of the time, learning to navigate the world around me without her constant presence. But I didn't mind it too much; I got to spend more quality time with my aunty and cousin, who were both instrumental in teaching me about becoming an independent, self-sufficient, and strong young girl who could hold her own in any situation.

My self-defense classes with my aunt became even more challenging and demanding, but I genuinely loved every minute of it, and I was surprisingly good at it too. As I trained, I was getting very light and swift on my feet, and I hardly ever fell down anymore, which was a significant improvement.

Sometimes, Chris and my aunt would mysteriously disappear for days on end, only to return with bruises all over their bodies. They never bothered to tell me how they obtained those bruises, leaving me to wonder in silence.

"You're too young to get into big people business," she would often tell me dismissively whenever I tried to inquire about it further. However, I couldn't shake the feeling that I knew how they got those bruises, especially after hearing the local News broadcast on the radio about the unfortunate events and murders that were taking place in our community. At such ominous times, she would gently remind me to, "Go do yuh homework and practice yuh spin, jump and chop," diverting my attention back to my training and studies.

Chris, my aunt, and a few others had inevitably become the steadfast protectors of our close-knit community. Because we lived freely, more people, or rather, a troubling group of undesirables, wanted to move in and disrupt our lives. When they did, their presence created absolute havoc, triggering the involvement of the army to restore order and peace.

The people in the community appreciated and cherished the way we were living, valuing our independence and unity. They didn't want government officials or outsiders getting involved in our day-to-day business or meddling with our lives. Thus, the undesirables had to go, and this painful process involved chopping up, shootings, and unregistered burials in unmarked graves, all of which weighed heavily on our collective conscience.

7. Who's Going To Love Me Now?

As Janet began to drift further into her role as an absentee mother, I found myself becoming more and more settled in the life that I was slowly growing to love and appreciate. My little mind often prayed fervently that things would continue down this path until I eventually grew up and moved out to carve my own way in the world.

At that point, I had over four dozen chickens now, some small and lively, some medium-sized, and a few incredibly big ones that strutted around with pride. I tried diligently not to kill the hens, as the precious eggs they produced were a significant income stream for me. Furthermore, I made sure there were plenty of roosters around as well, knowing their importance in the whole process.

My Aunt was teaching me, in a very covert manner, about the birds and the bees. The roosters' responsibility, of course, was to mate with the hens to ensure the continuation of egg production. Every Sunday, I had taken to practice the task of chopping off the heads of two roosters, carefully selling them to the highest bidder at the local market.

The chickens were organically grown, thriving on natural feed, which made them more expensive to raise, but worth every effort. My eggs were also a little pricier due to their specialized feeding, yet people didn't mind paying me a little bit more for the quality I offered. On average, my hens were producing over five dozen eggs each week, and at times even more, which filled me with pride.

My regular customers were well aware that should Janet happen to be home, no transactions would take place, as she was often the barrier to my entrepreneurial efforts. The ones who were my guardians, like my Aunt and my cousin, also recognized that I was training and exhibited great potential. They continually encouraged me to excel and study hard in school, emphasizing that education was the key to my success.

"I want yuh to be self-reliant," Aunty Norma had told me one day with sincere conviction. "Yuh not too young to learn how to make yuh own money and take care of yuh self. When me gone, yuh should already know how to be independent and stand on yuh own two feet. Yuh hear?"

"Where yuh going, Aunty Norma?" I had asked her, my curiosity piqued and a sense of foreboding settling in the pit of my stomach.

"Me not going to be here for too long," she had replied, her voice tinged with an unsettling finality, lacking any meaningful clarification. I had felt something tear at my heart, a deep sense of loss washing over me, and my breathing became increasingly labored. But Chris, in his typical fashion, had cut her off abruptly, as if the very thought of her not existing in our lives had never crossed his mind. The truth was undeniable; she was scaring the living daylights out of him—out of all of us—with her grim talk of her own demise.

It seemed she had been addressing this topic far too often lately, and it weighed heavily on our hearts. My aunt had four children, three girls and one boy, all of whom were now grown up and living their own lives. The three girls had been residing and working in England for quite some time now, distant from the home that once held them close. She had tried to send Chris away to join them, but he wouldn't hear of it, firmly rooted in his decision.

"Somebody 'ave to stay here and look after yuh," he had told her with unwavering conviction.

She didn't pressure him to leave; instead, her gaze had a wistful sadness that suggested she hardly ever spoke about her daughters, though I could tell she missed them deeply.

~~~~~~~

I knew it wouldn't last, although I fervently prayed it would. It was simply too good to be true.

After six long months of settling into a mirage lifestyle, the street work program unexpectedly shut down, and Janet unfortunately lost her job. Little did she know that she didn't have to work so incredibly hard, as I was making enough to support us both comfortably. However, I didn't trust her enough to divulge that crucial information. I feared she would have dominated my endeavor, taking all my hard-earned profits to fund her ganja smoking and Lotto buying habits. My aunt wasn't assisting me for that purpose. She understood I didn't have anyone reliable, so she wanted me to learn the essential skill of self-reliance.

I had finally stopped sucking my fingers and wetting the bed during the months I was embarking on this journey of learning to be independent and brave. Janet had kindly replaced the old sponge mattress on both beds, so the unpleasant scent of stale pee no longer permeated the small interior of our little one-room house. It was kept neat and tidy, being the only one there most of the time, despite the circumstances.

After losing her street cleaning job, Janet decided to stay home and sleep for an extended period. For almost a month, she remained there, surprisingly nice and calm. She noticed that the vegetable garden was flourishing abundantly, and the chickens in the coop were multiplying steadily, yet she said nothing. Since we lived rent-free, she didn't have to worry about paying any bills. This newfound freedom allowed her to stash away a little something for herself on the side, which was a small comfort in these uncertain times.

My money-making venture had come to a complete standstill after she unexpectedly lost her job —except, of course, for the lucrative fruit-picking opportunities. It was the glorious mango season, and mangoes were absolutely prolific around this time of year. I managed to make extra cash by climbing into people's mango trees, meticulously picking their ripe mangoes, and then selling them to my classmates during the lunch break and directly after school. However, with Janet being home all day, she was unknowingly undermining my other business efforts, and I often found myself wondering when she would finally secure another job. As her unemployment continued, she began smoking heavily, which was depleting her previously saved money stash at an alarming rate. Two months into her unemployment, she once again started revealing her monster-ism, which was quite disconcerting.

As her money stash hit rock bottom, she suddenly had what she thought was a brilliant idea: to throw some of her ganja seeds into my garden, where they could potentially flourish. Initially, I had no idea what the peculiar bushes were when they began to sprout up, so I decided to unearth one and take it to Aunty Norma for her wisdom and insight.

"A where you get this from?" she asked, incredulously, when I presented the plant to her.

"Nuff a them a growing in me garden and I don't know where them a come from," I told her very indignantly, puffing out my cheeks in defiance, with my little lips pushing out in frustration.

"That bloodclaat woman there yuh see mon," she whispered under her breath, glancing around to ensure no one was within earshot. "Alright, tell yuh what! When you go back over there, yuh going to pull out every one a them and throw them in the garbage. Yuh hear?"

"Yes, Aunty Norma, but a what kind a bush it is?" I insisted, my curiosity piqued by her fierce tone.

"A ganja," she replied, her voice barely above a whisper, afraid to say it out loud in case somebody was listening in. "I think I know a who plant them, but don't worry, just go pull out every one a them. Yuh hear?"

"Yes, Aunty Norma," I reiterated firmly, shaking my head at her insistence while trying to understand the weight of my task.

The fear I felt of my mother had never truly left me. It came back full force, yet I reminded myself that I was stronger now than before. I shouldn't be afraid.

It was a typical Monday morning, and I had stopped over there on my way to school. I promised to de-ganja my garden after school that day, not giving it a second thought at the moment. After a long day filled with lessons, I finally went home, determined to fulfill my promise as I pulled out all the ganja plants I could find, feeling a mix of anxiety and resolve.

Growing ganja in Jamaica, then, was considered a very serious crime within our society. In our little community, which was frequently monitored by the army and the Constabulary Force, it made it exceedingly unsafe to cultivate any kind of hallucinogenics, including marijuana. My mother understood that risk well. Aunty Norma understood that risk too. The entire community was acutely aware of the dangers. Yet, despite this knowledge, this woman actively tried to ruin me by stealthily planting ganja in my garden, where I had worked so hard.

I was filled with anger. For the very first time in my nearly ten years of life, I found the courage to be openly angry at her. So when she stormed into the backyard and discovered that I had uprooted her handiwork, I was on the ground before I could even comprehend what had hit me.

"Yuh likkle bloodclaat raas, a who tell yuh to pull them out? A my house this, not yours," she spat with such venomous rage, her words slicing through the air, while she ruthlessly pulled out the vegetables, the corns, and the green bananas that I had tenderly planted and were sustaining us.

"The next bloodclaat time yuh see them in there touch them and see," she threatened ominously.

This was the very first time I realized, with a jarring clarity, that my mother really didn't seem to possess much common sense. That she truly held no genuine love for me. That she was suffering from a very severe case of idiotism. She completely destroyed my garden, along with my new-found self-confidence and bravery. After she so thoroughly dismantled "the new me" and mercilessly abused my still very small and fragile body—I had thought was finally getting stronger—she coldly instructed me, "Clean dat up, dutty bloodclaat gal," and walked away, leaving me in excruciating pain, hardly able to move for several days. With the feeling of despair settling heavily upon me, overwhelming misery, and deep frustration, I was left to finish what she had started. In sheer, raw anger, I chopped down everything I had planted. I uprooted everything, bagged them up, and disposed of them in the garbage pile. That night, I went to bed utterly tired, deeply disappointed, bruised all over, and enveloped in despair.

~~~~~

Meanwhile, that fateful night, Wayne was meticulously plotting his sinister plans for Aunty Norma. Two nights later, he dispatched one of his men with the grim task of cutting her throat under the cover of darkness.

Chris was blissfully unaware of the chaos unfolding around him, as he sat in the cinema engrossed in a movie with his new girlfriend.

Janet had ventured out again, seeking to spread for money, seemingly more concerned with her own needs than that of her family.

The following day, I woke up feeling unusually off-kilter. My body was still stiff and sore from being pummelled the night before, but an unsettling feeling churned in my gut, hinting that something deeper was amiss. However, I was too young and naive to figure it all out.

My mother walked into the room, looking stranger than she typically did, her eyes red and swollen, as if she had been crying for hours.

"You Aunty Norma, dead," she stated flatly, devoid of any emotion, and then turned to go back outside to her favorite spot on the so-called veranda, where she often sought solace. I followed her out, watching her with disbelief, silently waiting for her to elaborate on the shocking news. She reached for the hefty ganja spliff she had tucked behind her ear, placed it to her lips, and ignited it with a flick of her lighter. Drawing in a deep breath, she exhaled a thick cloud of smoke that obscured her greasy face as she bent her head and began to sway her upper body to some imaginary music that only she could hear.

I watched her in complete shock, my heart racing as I waited for her to elaborate further and grappling with the unsettling thought that perhaps she was this wicked to have concocted something so deceitful.

Noticing that nothing more was forthcoming from her lips, I made the decision to leave her side. Before I fully realized what I was doing, I found myself running, sprinting as fast as my bruised and stiff legs would allow me, desperately trying to reach my aunt's house. I was incredibly fast when I'm not falling down; I arrived there in no time at all. As I approached her house, I was compelled to stop dead in my tracks. The entire community was gathered right in front of her yard. There was simply no clear path for me to walk through to gain entry. With an alternative, I turned in the other direction, only to find that side was also packed with even more of our community members. Driven by a sense of urgency, I forced myself through the throng anyway and was met with more concerned individuals, all of them murmuring amongst themselves.

In Aunty Norma's small backyard, the respected members of The Community Protectors were gathered. There were some kids my age as well as older ones, creating a blend of youthful energy and solemnity. Chris, my cousin, was sitting on the steps that led inside, an unlit cigarette in his hand, seemingly lost in thought and drifting in a daze—confused and overwhelmed by the gravity of the situation.

The Community Protector, a role that had once been held by my aunt, seemed poised to transition. Ever since she started sensing the shadow of her own demise looming over her, she had begun preparing Chris to take on his new responsibilities as the next head. They were all gathered there, silently waiting for his instructions, fully understanding and respecting his grief, knowing without a doubt that he would be a smart and just young leader when he finally found his voice amidst the chaos.

Danny, my brothers' father, had heard earlier that morning about the tragic events that had unfolded and was there to provide his unwavering support during this difficult time. He was very close to my aunt, and his presence brought a sense of comfort amidst the sorrow.

In the kitchen, someone was diligently cooking Aunty Norma's favorite dishes, using the fresh vegetables from her garden alongside whatever was already available in the house. This beloved custom we called nine-night would continue in full swing until the day of her burial, honoring her memory with every meal prepared and shared.

By the time afternoon rolled around, there was an array of liquor brought in—Appleton Rum, White Rum, Red Label Wine, and much more to toast her life. We were treating ourselves to Mannish Water, Curry Goat, Stew Oxtail, and a beautiful assortment of foods, fruits, and drinks. Aunty Norma was well known and deeply loved not just by our family, but throughout the entire community as well. The soulful sounds of Bob Marley songs were already blazing through the air, resonating with heartfelt nostalgia. Many people were crying, including me, as the harsh reality of what had happened slowly sunk in, it weighed heavily on my heart.

She was the only one I had who genuinely cared for and looked out for me. I kept asking myself, who was going to love me now? My despair deepened, and visions of a bleak future filled my mind, overshadowed by the threat of verbal and physical abuse creeping into my thoughts. Overwhelmed, I fell against the ground beneath her banana tree, where the broad leaves concealed my small body as if they instinctively understood I needed this time to grieve in solitude and peace. My little frame shook with pain and loss as memories of my aunty flooded my mind.

So consumed by my grief and loss, I didn't hear the soft approaching footsteps behind me. It was my cousin, Chris. He had seen me seek refuge in the comforting embrace of the banana bush and had come searching for me. He also understood the depths of what I was going through, sharing in my sorrow as we both grappled with the weight of our loss.

He picked me up in a way reminiscent of how my aunt had done just over a year ago. The gentleness of his embrace made my entire body sink deeper into a well of all-consuming grief.

"No body wasn't here to help her," I sobbed loudly, the words escaping me in a rush of emotion. "No body wasn't here to help her. How come no body never here to help her?" I screamed in desperation. "She dead all by herself." I sobbed so hard that my entire body trembled with the force of my heartache.

He, too, began to cry, and the intensity of his emotions made him shake so violently that he had to sit down beneath the shelter of the banana tree, still cradling me tightly in his arms. With my arms wrapped securely around his neck, he gently patted my back as I continued to cry and cry. Eventually, his soft touch, reminiscent of a soothing gesture for a baby, began to comfort us both, and gradually my tears began to subside. When he felt he had regained control over his emotions, he leaned in closer and whispered in my ear, "Swofiyah, listen good! Wayne going to come after yuh again, so keep yuh eyes them open and don't talk to no strangers on the road. No man, no woman yuh don't know, yuh hear?" He asked, pulling me away slightly to look me directly in the eyes, mirroring the way my aunt had done.

The way he mirrored his mother's actions triggered another wave of uncontrollable tears to wash over me, and I nodded my head, unable to form any words to respond. We stayed under the banana trees for what felt like another hour, wrapped in the sounds of reggae music, the chatter of people mingling nearby, the clattering noise of pots closing in the kitchen, and the melodic calls of birds communicating with each other.

In that moment, my life felt as if it had ended, leaving a void that seemed impossible to fill.

8. The Community Protectors Organization

I learned that Wayne was not alone in his sick, ritualistic practices of raping and burning young girls alive. The Community Protectors discovered a disturbing small group of Voodoo worshipers who not only practiced dark arts but also engaged in horrific human sacrifices. Wayne was at the head of this grotesque operation, leading this group situated in the shadowy corners of Dunkirk, Kingston Central. With the collaboration of the surrounding communities rallying together, an amber alert was sent out urgently for six individuals — four men, including Wayne, and two women. They were now classified as armed and dangerous, with their intentions clear and sinister.

My aunt was tirelessly ensuring the safety of all the young ones, such as myself, within our community. After Wayne's decapitation, the violence and killing had only escalated, marking the beginning of the uncomfortable and chilling discovery of this group's dark activities. Wayne couldn't engage in his twisted desires anymore, so it had to be someone else who continued the horrific acts.

Wayne thought he was off the hook, blissfully unaware that Chris had taken it upon himself to keep a watch on him. The day Chris kicked him out of the community, leaving him half dead and battered, something significant was gnawing at him. Wayne had far too much money on him for someone in his precarious situation. He knew that his mother had discreetly taken a roll before he came onto the scene; he had seen her hide it within the folds of her bosom. The other roll he found had him deep in thought. Wayne couldn't have possibly been the only one abducting those innocent girls. Physically, he was not capable of such actions; his skinny, frail body appeared too weak and fragile. Yet, despite his physical limitations, he had the money and the cunning means to achieve his sinister ends.

Wayne also had a chain with an intricate emblem on it tucked away securely in his back pocket alongside the money he had fortuitously found. He recognized that particular design, as it had been tattooed beneath the chin of a couple of guys he had encountered before. Something felt profoundly off about the entire situation. Not wanting to draw unnecessary attention from his mother, he hastily stuffed everything into his pocket, hoping to avoid any questions.

Chris had watched intently as another guy, roughly his age and completely unfamiliar to him, emerged from the shadows to assist the unconscious Wayne. He instinctively knew that no one in the tightly-knit community would have stepped forward to help

Wayne that day. The silent members of the Community Protectors were vigilantly observing, ensuring that everything unfolded as planned. He discreetly motioned with a slight nod of his head to two of his trained young men from the secretive group, signaling them to follow discreetly.

A couple of days later, Chris learned alarming news: I was the next ceremonial sacrifice chosen by their leaders. The plan had been for Wayne to come and get me, to dress me up, and then take me out of the community as if I were his own daughter. If he had only adhered strictly to the plan, it would have worked seamlessly. However, Wayne's reckless desire to see my "likkle pumpum" had caused him to lose precious time, leading to his capture. Now, driven by a thirst for revenge, he would stop at nothing to rectify his mistake.

When Chris finally confided in his mother about the situation, she had already suspected something ominous and was discreetly involving King, one of the revered elders, in her plans. Being a well-known figure in the community, she made a concerted effort to remain out of sight to avoid drawing unwanted attention to herself.

Very few people know of the existence of the Community Protectors Organization. Those who were aware were usually the ones intricately involved, as it operated as a highly secretive society. Although our community was often perceived as poor by outsiders who had never set foot within its borders, we had secretly begun to thrive and achieve considerable success in our own unique way.

The Community Protectors Organization(CPO) had put into place an innovative education system that allowed both the adults and the young ones who were eager to pursue continuing schooling the opportunity to do so. For the students whose parents often had to work extended hours and overtime, the CPO secretly provided a safe and nurturing place for them to comfortably stay and diligently complete their homework, with the committed assistance of several volunteer teachers who were finishing their master's degrees at the nearby university. These dedicated volunteers worked tirelessly to ensure that the students were not only helped academically but also provided with a nourishing dinner and a warm place to sleep until their parents, exhausted from their long shifts, returned home from work. It was a pioneering initiative, the first of its kind in Jamaica, and it was working so effectively that even older students were now welcomed into some of these facilities to further their education.

Additionally, there was a vibrant community center that offered engaging Bible studies and enriching Sunday school classes for the religiously inclined members of the community. This center had a nurse's station that functioned as a small clinic, along with a dentist's office to cater to the health needs of the residents. Moreover, the community center featured a large computer lab equipped with internet services that fortuitously fortified the community with vital knowledge, allowing them to become more technologically savvy. They were eagerly learning to rely on solar energy as a means to become more self-sufficient and independent, thereby reducing their reliance on government assistance. Through the vast resources of the internet, the community was increasingly learning to become more creative and resourceful in providing better services for the people, ensuring a brighter future for all.

With my aunt serving as the head, the Community Protectors Organization (CPO) was actively empowering the local community to collectively strive for improvement and growth as a unified group. Recently, the government had implemented an innovative new program that allowed parents to take a more hands-on approach in assisting with their children's educational development. While in many other areas, parents complained that they were too busy and simply did not have the time to engage, the Bower Bank Community and its dedicated CPO embraced this golden opportunity to get involved in their children's learning process. They stepped up by providing additional volunteering teachers who would help instruct students in essential critical thinking skills during the week, particularly after school hours. They also made thoughtful provisions to assist parents in developing effective strategies to support their children's cognitive thought processes. As part of this effort, a night course was offered to interested adults and parents, aiming to demonstrate just how crucial critical thinking skills were in making informed long-term decisions for their families and futures.

The CPO went around discreetly taking careful notes of what required repairs and fresh coats of paint, and then coordinated teams of men to tackle these repairs using money they had earned from their Community Development Funds. They also provided much-needed assistance to parents in the form of food to nourish their children and clothes for them to wear. For those whose educational abilities were above average, the CPO encouraged even more learning opportunities and provided the necessary support for them to thrive academically. They promoted subsistence farming and small-scale cottage industries, mirroring the valuable lessons my aunt was teaching me. Consequently, more community members began learning how to grow their own food and vegetables while also raising chickens, goats, and pigs. The excess produce and livestock were then either sold among the community members or taken to the local market, generating additional income for families.

In addition, there was a small yet well-maintained marketplace constructed just outside the walls of Bower Bank by the CPO. With the remnants of produce from the subsistence farming endeavors, residents were encouraged to sell their leftover goods in the vibrant little market, fostering a sense of community and economic resilience.

My aunt was a talented dressmaker known throughout the community for her exceptional skill. Not only did she create beautiful garments, but she also devoted her time to teaching numerous women and men in our community how to sew and craft their own clothing. Together, they collaborated to make an impressive variety of clothing items, which they then sold at the bustling market. In the evenings, those who possessed culinary skills were encouraged to showcase their talents in the kitchen. This was where

Chris truly excelled, as his expertise in baking brought joy to many.

Baked goods, ranging from fresh bread to delectable pastries, were sold in the marketplace day and night. People from all over visited the market to purchase these delicious items. The residents of our community were actively encouraged to reinvest their earnings back into the local economy. It was understood that the only way for individuals to build wealth was for the community as a whole to thrive and prosper. Working together in this way empowered each person, helping them to achieve greater success.

Recently, a small secret bank had been established by the community with invaluable support from the Community Protectors Organization (CPO). The residents were inspired to invest in themselves and their futures, utilizing the banking services that had been set up for their benefit. The community was becoming increasingly engaged and making significant progress under the careful guidance of the CPO. This initiative had begun even before I was aware of its existence and potential impact.

Through the dedicated encouragement of the CPO, a reading system linked to the library van was also launched, ensuring that every Saturday, it arrived in our community filled to the brim with quality books available for us to borrow. Children and adults alike were actively encouraged to expand their horizons and immerse themselves in literature. Education was not just valued; it was ardently promoted as a vital part of our collective growth.

~~~~~

Aunty Norma made the critically important decision to send her beloved daughters away to England in order to pursue their ambitious studies in the demanding field of medicine. Their heartfelt ambition was to become dedicated doctors without borders, a noble calling that would empower them to serve underserved communities in need, no matter where their invaluable skills were required around the globe. From an early age, Aunty Norma had keenly recognized that Chris possessed a remarkably strategic mind, and she took it upon herself to lovingly nurture that talent by partially homeschooling him, ensuring he received both academic guidance and enthusiastic encouragement.

She harbored grand dreams for the long-term betterment of the community. Aunty Norma impressed deeply upon her community that with the expansion of the cottage industries into something far greater, the wooden houses that once beautifully symbolized their rich heritage could eventually become a relic of the past. They were thoughtfully considering converting these beloved wooden houses into sturdy brick structures that would offer significantly enhanced protection against the destructive forces of hurricanes during the turbulent hurricane seasons that plagued their region. With an increasing number of dedicated community members willing to collaborate and work together as a cohesive, unified team, she envisioned this innovative housing project materializing sooner than anyone had previously anticipated. The Community Protectors Organization (CPO) was already taking proactive and strategic steps by sending several of the enthusiastic young adults, who had recently graduated from high school, to study interior design and architecture at Dunoon Community College. Additionally, the residents who owned local furniture shops were actively teaching interested youth the intricate art of expertly crafting beautiful and functional furniture pieces, further enriching the community's skills and resources.

It was with these innovative ideas firmly in mind that the dedicated members of the community rallied together in a concerted effort to protect their own from the negative influence of undesirables, individuals whose malicious goals were to instigate violence and elevate their own status in the process. In response to the troubling and disturbing music that not only sexualized young girls but also glorified violence, which celebrated the very people who instigated these heinous acts, the community took a courageous stand and subsequently decided to ban such music from being played in any public venues. The residents clearly understood the necessity and urgency of these measures and, united in their strong resolve, collectively agreed on this important decision for the overall welfare and safety of their cherished community.

Almost everything she did was intentionally leading towards the community becoming significantly more resourceful and self-sufficient. She was dedicated to helping them understand that it was indeed their collective responsibility to care for, protect, and nurture each other. This essential involvement included taking particular care of the vulnerable children in their midst, as well as reclaiming the protective power that rightfully belonged to the community—power that had unfortunately been ceded to the schools and the government regarding the safeguarding of children.

"—I'm not talking about the collective as a whole. I'm speaking specifically about the individual child. Certain groups seemed excessively focused on the collective welfare. We will, instead, concentrate on the needs of the individual by reclaiming the authority to ensure the safety and well-being of each and every child within our community. Centuries ago, our ancestors firmly believed that it took a united community, working together, to successfully raise a child. Unfortunately, that vital sense of collective responsibility has been taken away from us. As a disheartening result, abusers and sexual molesters now appear to have more rights regarding our children than the community does—an unacceptable reality.

The heartbreaking truth is that many unfortunate children had no one to stand up and protect them during their times of need. It's no wonder that so many individuals grew up struggling with some form of mental illness or even suicidal tendencies as a consequence of this neglect. Let's take back the power that rightfully belongs to us and safeguard our future for the wellbeing of the next generation. Let's protect the children, together."

The community was listening intently to their passionate leader, drawn in by her charisma and vision for a united future. United in purpose, they decided to reclaim the age-old concept of collective responsibility when it came to raising children. Realizing that relying solely on individual families was insufficient and often led to gaps in care, they collectively agreed it was in the best interest of both the children and the families to have everyone come together. This way, they could ensure that each child was not only cared for but also thrived in a nurturing and supportive environment, surrounded by the love and guidance of the entire community.

Bower Bank was on track to become one of the best-run communities in Jamaica and perhaps even the entire Caribbean. The warmth and camaraderie among the people in the community inspired a renewed sense of hope and possibility for betterment. They were willing to work together as one cohesive unit to achieve their collective goals. The realization dawned upon them that this collaborative effort was truly the only way to pull themselves out of the cycle of poverty that had long plagued them.

Yet, amidst this wave of optimism, only a handful of people, including my mother, were not on board with the community's vision. She didn't make friends with the neighbors, nor did she want her children to associate with the other families in the community. She deliberately chose not to attend the meetings, remaining blissfully ignorant of the transformative changes that were taking place around her. Although she could see the evident growth and positive changes occurring, she seemed to be indifferent to the prospect of improvement. As she sank further into her own mental instability, she turned to ganja, which ultimately became her only source of comfort and companionship during this turbulent time.

In the less than three remarkable years since the Community Protectors Organization (CPO) was established in Bower Bank, the local community was reaping substantial benefits, although most residents did not fully grasp the profound extent to which the group was dedicated to ensuring a safe, healthy, clean, crime-free, and progressive environment for all. The people collectively recognized that no politician had ever worked as tirelessly, or collaboratively, to generate innovative ideas that were now vividly manifesting before their eyes.

The residents were holding tightly to this newfound sense of hope and progress. This unwavering attachment was precisely why they found themselves in sheer shock at such a shocking event occurring to their most forward-thinking community leader. How had this unimaginable incident happened? Who could possibly want to harm a person whose boundless imagination and visionary foresight were so crucial in empowering the entire community? What steps were they going to take now that their dreams seemed to hang in the balance? The dreams they shared were indeed the dreams of Aunty Norma, cherished and adopted as their own.

Aunty Norma did not care to build personal wealth for herself, for she had long since learned that merely having wealth did not equate to happiness. She understood that possessing money did not automatically make all your problems simply disappear. Through her experiences living with her husband, she discovered that bad people with money often became even more monstrous in their behavior. Nevertheless, she also recognized that money, when in the hands of good and genuine individuals, could be a powerful tool for doing many wonderful deeds.

Less than ten years ago, after moving into the neighborhood with her four children and witnessing the pervasive poverty and deep sense of hopelessness, she made a firm decision: the only way for them to ascend out of this dire situation was to work together as one cohesive unit.

When she made the brave decision to run away from her rich, wife-beating, whore-mongering husband, she took with her not only the four precious children but also the money she had been quietly hoarding over the years of enduring a life filled with fear and abuse. She relocated to a modest area where she felt safe, knowing with all certainty that he would have never thought of searching for them there.

At first, the three girls felt a strong sense of retaliation; they longed for the comfortable and privileged lifestyles they had grown accustomed to. Yet, deep down, they loved their mother fiercely and wanted to see her truly happy in a way that their father's tyranny had never allowed. They had reached an age where they could see the darkness that lay within their father's soul and recognized the utter lack of respect he had consistently shown toward them. This awakening opened their eyes to the realization that life held much more than the narrow confines of their previous existence.

Under her loving guidance and with her open-mindedness, they learned to appreciate the beauty around them and developed a sincere compassion for others who did not share the same privileges they once had. Emerging from the tangled web of their father's corrupt influence, they became enlightened to the realities happening around them, which sparked a deep desire to help others, whole-heartedly and without reservation.

The sudden death of their beloved mother was an unimaginable shock to us all, leaving a deep void in our lives. We mourned her loss with all our hearts and souls. For the nine and a half-year-old version of me, she was more than a parent; she was my role model and the person I aspired to become when I grew up. She was the only anchor I had in a turbulent sea of life.

That fateful day beneath the banana tree, I knew instinctively that my life would change forever, and sadly, it would be for the worse.

9. The Funeral

My aunty's nine-night was undeniably the biggest and most elaborate gathering I'd ever seen. People from far and wide made the journey to Bower Bank to pay their respects and mourn her loss. Her daughters, my cousins whom I didn't know very well at all, hurriedly arrived on the first flight they could find, desperate to be there for the ceremony. They managed to arrive on the third night of the nine-night—a time when emotions were running high, and the air was thick with grief.

While we were enveloped in sorrow, my mother was smoking her neurons into premature adult apoptosis, which many people would label as early Alzheimer's.

Since I had been ignoring my chores by spending more time at her deceased sister's house, she had taken it upon herself to do the cleaning diligently. That was how she stumbled upon my hard-earned savings, which I had carefully stashed away between the uneven grooves of the concrete and the wooden floor, snugly tucked under my bed.

When she discovered the stash, she mistakenly thought the money belonged to the disappearing Wayne, an incessant source of turmoil in our lives. She ransacked the entire house, desperately searching for more caches of money that she believed might be hidden. The four-thousand two hundred and twelve dollars I had saved was a significant amount—one my mother had never held in her hands at any point in her life. To her, it felt like an unexpected blessing amidst the dark cloud of grief.

Janet chose to stay away from the nine-night ceremony entirely. She didn't like the people or the overwhelming emotions that crowded the space. However, she did attend the funeral, which drew an astonishing number of participants to the church to send off my beloved aunt. The small church was simply too packed to accommodate everyone—many were forced to stand outside in the street. My brothers and sisters were also present, along with my grandmother, countless aunts, uncles, and numerous cousins, all gathered to commemorate a life well-lived. We were all dressed in white, which was my aunt's favorite color, symbolizing purity amidst the sorrow. The church across the street from Bower Bank was the very place my aunty had regularly attended over the years, and it was there that the solemn service had taken place.

At the end of the funeral, Ms. Green, a dedicated community activist and a well-respected member of the Community Protectors Organization (CPO), pulled me aside and discreetly pressed a wad of cash into my hands. Earlier that day, I had sold her a dozen plump, well-fed chickens for dinner. The dinner was specifically for the 'after funeral departure' of the deceased, a new custom thoughtfully implemented by our close-knit community to honor our loved ones. Each chicken cost a steep sixty dollars, reflecting both the quality and the significance of the occasion. I hurriedly tucked the money into my little handbag, a cherished gift from one of my cousins, grateful for the unexpected assistance.

I had gone to the funeral service accompanied by my mother, who, unlike many others, didn't stay to dilly-dally and socialize after the service. As soon as it concluded, she left, dragging me along with her in a hurry.

"I don't want to carry no ghost in a me yard. Make the dead go bury them dead," she declared firmly, resolutely refusing to go to the gravesite for any lingering farewells.

In fact, I didn't even get the chance to see where the she was buried, which weighed heavily on my heart. My brothers and sisters were instructed to come straight to our one-room house after the funeral, reinforcing Janet's belief that she didn't want any 'ghost' walking behind us on our way home.

That day marked the first time in a very long while that we were all packed tightly together in the same space, sharing both grief and the solace of family.

My grandmother came for a visit after the burial, which was a significant occasion for our family. She stayed for a couple of hours, filling the house with a comforting presence. While she was there, my mother had to make a considerable effort to abstain from smoking. I guess having her mother in her house, visiting her after such a profound loss, was something that had never happened before, and it held immense importance. For her it was definitely worth it, despite the challenge.

Deidre had unfortunately become a "stuck-up little raas," someone who refused to eat anything served in the so-called "poor house." She really should have known better, especially since everyone in our family was well aware that Janet didn't play like that when it came to food. By the end of her visit, she had been compelled to chug down a large plate of delicious chicken and rice and peas, accompanied by a hefty cup of refreshing soursop juice. My brothers, however, were completely unfazed and ate with genuine enthusiasm and relish. They had grown to love Janet's cooking, and it was no secret that they were always hungry. After all, they were growing boys, they need their nourishment.

I felt very happy to have them all in the house that day. I missed them dreadfully. Even though I saw them at school every single day, it truly wasn't the same as having them here in the comforting and familiar surroundings of our home. I didn't feel quite so alone when they were around, filling the space with their laughter and energy.

At the end of the visit, my grandmother gently dragged Klam along with her back to Spanish Town, while Danny came to pick up my brothers, and Deidre's father arrived to collect her. Once they all departed, I was left alone again with my mother and her ever-present ganja cloud, which lingered in the air like a constant reminder of our complicated lives.

~~~~~

It was a week after Aunty Norma's funeral when I first discovered my money mysteriously missing. I had carefully hidden it between the narrow grove of the concrete flooring and the load-bearing wood that supported the rickety wooden wall. This particular area was conveniently tucked under my bed. I had chosen this spot specifically because I was absolutely certain that Janet, who had no real business being there, would never find it. After all, she had stopped cleaning the moment she discovered she didn't need to, anymore, which had been quite a relief for her

It was a late Friday afternoon, and I was alone yet again, as was often the case. School had ended early, right at midday, because of a scheduled teachers' meeting. I had decided to take this opportunity to clean today, so I wouldn't have to do too much work the following day. I stripped the beds of their linens and put the sheets into a mixture of soap and bleach water to soak, making sure not to mix the vibrant colors with the pristine whites. After that, I dragged the big, heavy wash pan out into the sunlight, allowing the powerful sun and the bleach to work their magic on the fabric. Once I was satisfied with the soaking process, I went back into the house and meticulously took out all the small items that were either on the floor or hiding beneath the table. I placed them outside on the so-called veranda. Some items I placed on the beds, including the three plastic containers Janet had tucked away underneath her bed filled with her freshly cleaned clothes, all perfectly folded. I also moved another two medium-sized containers containing sheets and pillowcases, which were also neatly folded and arranged, ensuring that everything was in order.

When I was absolutely certain that there was nothing more on the floor to obstruct my cleaning, I carefully grabbed the sweeping cloth and began the process of sweeping. I couldn't kneel due to the painful, watery sores on my knees from a fall I had taken a couple of days ago. Over time, I had become quite skilled at stooping and cleaning efficiently. I pushed Janet's bed out of the way to ensure that I could clean that area thoroughly without having to go under the bed itself. The front door was securely closed, which meant I didn't have to worry about the possibility of anyone unexpectedly coming in while I was occupied with my cleaning task.

As I moved my own bed to sweep that area as well, my eyes automatically flicked to my savings corner, the little spot where I kept my hard-earned money. I did a double take when I noticed that the familiar brown paper I typically used to wrap the money was missing. My heart sank as I dropped the sweeping cloth and hurried over to the spot to look down, feeling an unsettling sense of dread. There was absolutely nothing in that corner. I was shocked by the sudden absence of my savings.

"A who could a take it?" I asked myself in a hushed voice, as I began searching everywhere, my heart racing frantically. I pushed my small hand down into the groove to see if perhaps it had fallen down there, hoping to find it wedged between the floorboards and the concrete. I even ventured outside to look beneath the nonexistent cellar, checking to see if it had somehow slipped underneath. Logically, there was no way it could have ended up down there. The concrete and the load-bearing wooden wall had come right down to the ground without any gaps. Still, I couldn't help it; I went down on my belly anyway, not caring in the least that I was getting myself dirty in my desperate search.

I went back inside, trailing dirt all over the freshly swept floor, determined to make sure it wasn't hidden somewhere, unnoticeable to the naked eye. Then a thought crossed my mind, "Maybe I put it somewhere else." But deep down, I knew I hadn't placed it anywhere else. There was just one safe place in the entire house I could trust and that was the spot where I was certain Janet would never have thought to look. I started pondering this, with air stuffed in my cheeks and my lips pushed out in frustration. Suddenly, it hit me like a cold slap—I realized she had found it.

As wave after wave of despair washed over me, I began to cry, because I was utterly certain, without a doubt, that Janet had discovered my money. A sinking feeling settled in my stomach. She was far too happy about something lately. She was smoking heavily, indulging in her shopping spree far more than usual, and was always skipping around the house singing her heart out. And then there was her recent behavior, which became exceptionally nasty toward some of the neighbors. In my heart, I felt it—she had found my money. I fell hard on my butt in the house and started rolling around on the floor, kicking my legs and crying, filled with fury and helplessness.

Aunty Norma had specifically told me to remind her to take me to the secret bank to open an account, a promise that now seemed painfully far away. But now she was gone, taken from me far too soon, and Janet had cruelly stolen my money. The money my loving aunt had given me was not just cash; it was a cherished reminder of her love and support, the only thing I had left to hold onto in memory of her.

10. Kidnapping

I was crying so hard that I didn't even hear the distinctive sound of the aluminum fence that stood separating Janet's yard from the neighbors'. In my overwhelming world of misery and despair, I suddenly heard Wayne's voice urgently saying, "grab the likkle raas!"

In a panic, I started screaming at the top of my lungs for Chris, my only source of comfort, as I felt myself being picked up off the ground, forcefully. My thoughts of my missing money and my thieving mother had successfully vanished from my mind in that terrifying moment. I was now facing a more serious and immediate danger. The person whom I couldn't see at all lifted my small body as if it were nothing more than a mere chicken feather. In a frantic attempt to escape, I began wiggling my body furiously, twisting and turning with all my strength, hoping that he might suddenly lose control and drop me. But his grip was unnervingly tight, and he was moving incredibly fast.

"Help, Chris! Chris! Chris! Help!" I screamed at the top of my lungs like an aspiring soprano singer, desperately hoping someone would hear my cries. I was astonished to discover that I possessed such a high pitch within me, but I was utilizing it as if the very world were collapsing around me. And for me, in that moment, it truly felt like it was coming to an abrupt and terrifying end. With one final, desperate breath, I opened my mouth wide and screamed "Chriiiisss!" as loudly and powerfully as I possibly could, just as I felt a hand clamp tightly over my mouth, smothering my voice like a steel mask. I twisted and turned, my skinny legs flailing wildly like fragile tree limbs caught in a ferocious category five hurricane, seeking any chance to break free. But despite my frantic efforts, my kidnapper was incredibly strong and unwavering. He was sprinting forward with Crotchless Wayne hopping along ahead of us. I guessed Wayne was still trying to adjust to his shocking lack of a penis, or perhaps it was due to his recent knee injury that had left him more deformed.

I fought tirelessly beneath my kidnapper's firm hold, who by now had settled into a comfortable grip that felt impossibly restrictive. With his hand still covering my mouth to silence my desperate pleas, they dashed through Mikey's yard, carelessly trampling across Ms. Gladys' vegetable garden. It was clear they had no regard for her hard-earned crops; their singular focus was on escaping the scene before anyone could possibly notice what was happening.

When they finally arrived at Trevor's front yard, my eyes caught sight of a sleek white Honda Civic with heavily tinted glass, parked discreetly by the curb. Wayne quickly took something small out from his pocket and pressed down on it firmly, causing the car to emit a faint but unmistakable beeping noise. Crotchless Wayne, in a flurry of urgency, hopped towards the car and swung open the back door for his accomplice. Without hesitation, his accomplice aggressively shoved me into the back seat, all while maintaining a relentless, iron grip on my mouth, before sliding in next to me. Meanwhile, Wayne was already inside the car, starting up the engine with determination.

Once the door was closed, the accomplice forced me down onto the hard floor of the vehicle and wrapped a suffocating black sheet tightly around my body. Next, he cruelly draped a thick, heavy black blanket over me, securing his hold by placing his feet firmly on my back to restrain any movements I might attempt to make. The interior of the car was entirely black, rendering me virtually invisible; anyone looking into the vehicle would be none the wiser to my presence or plight.

Exhausted and numbed from my struggles and frantic screams, I found myself quietly mumbling

"Chris, Chris, Chris" deep in my throat, clinging to the faintest hope that, by some miracle, he would suddenly materialize out of thin air to rescue me from this nightmare. "Chris, Chris, Chris, Chris, Chris," became my mantra, but all I could feel was the oppressive weight of my kidnapper's feet pressing down on my small body, as the car moved at a steady pace along the roughly paved road.

They began to pick up speed as the vehicle exited the Bower Bank Community, making a sharp left turn onto Windward Road. I felt the car drive for what seemed like an eternity—about twenty minutes—before it finally pulled up somewhere and came to a complete stop.

"Bring her come in here," Crotchless Wayne ordered with a menacing tone. "Move you pussyclaat and hurry up no!" he snapped impatiently.

His accomplice, with surprising strength, yanked me out of the car without any effort, swiftly carrying me into the building. A loud door slammed shut behind us, and moments later, the black sheet covering me was ripped off, leaving me momentarily disoriented as I tried to adjust my eyesight. I soon realized I was inside a church of some sort. It wasn't any typical Catholic Church, nor a Kingdom Hall, and certainly not a Poko Church either. This place seemed to be a bizarre amalgamation of all of them, twisted into one unsettling atmosphere.

The interior of the church was adorned with numerous black, grotesque masks that loomed ominously over the walls. Countless ugly bamboo dolls filled every nook and cranny—dolls fashioned from coconuts and draped in brightly colored beads, along with some that were entirely naked, while others were adorned in eerily all-black outfits.

Jesas! Crotchless Wayne and him friend them love to play with dolly babies, I thought, feeling an unsettling chill run down my spine.

"But is how them dolly baby here look so ugly?" I blurted out without thinking, before instinctively pushing my two fingers into my mouth, a subconscious action driven by fear and confusion.

As I continued to suck on my fingers, my wide eyes darted around the room, taking in the horrifying sight of the many ugly dolls. It was then that I realized how close Crotchless Wayne had approached me. Abruptly, he grabbed me by the collar, yanking me towards him with a sinister grin.

"Listen likkle gal! Yuh a go make me the happiest man alive this evening, cause what I have plan for yuh, yuh a go wish yuh mother did kill yuh," he looked so menacing and undeniably scary, and yet, having grown up with a mother like Janet who could be truly terrifying, I knew that unless he was actually holding something dangerous in his hand to threaten me with, I wasn't going to let him see any sign of fear flickering in my eyes.

"A yuh kill me aunty?" I asked with wide eyes, my fingers still in my mouth.

Stunned by the unexpected question, Crotchless Wayne replied incredulously, "a what kind a bloodclaat pickney this? Before you think 'bout yuh self, yuh a concern yuhself 'bout yuh dead aunty. Yeah, a me kill her, and when me done with yuh later, me a go done her son too."

Listening to him talk, it felt like the room was closing in on me, and I couldn't do anything else but stare at him in terror. There was something disturbingly strange in his face that I had never seen before; it was as if madness was creeping into his very soul. I glanced over his shoulders and, to my utter amazement, realized that his accomplice was none other than Nevel, my mother's friend. He had been at our house just the previous night, drinking Red Stripe Beer and smoking ganja with Janet, sharing laughs, engaging in lively conversation, and playing a game of Ludi.

My fingers had fallen out of my mouth the moment Crotchless Wayne admitted to killing my aunt, but upon discovering that Nevel was mixed up in this horror, I felt the urge to jam them back in, sucking noisily as I stared at Nevel with focused, terrified eyes, trying to process the situation unfolding before me.

It wasn't the reaction Crotchless Wayne was expecting at all. In fact, it angered the shit out of him more than I could have imagined. With a sudden burst of aggression, he pushed me down to the floor with as much force as he could muster, barking a harsh command at Nevel, "Tie up the likkle raas and come. Sundown, we deal with her." With that, he turned his back on us and strode out, moving with a more pronounced hop that accentuated the way he dragged his wounded leg behind him, a remnant of the gunshot he had suffered.

I remained on the ground, still sucking my fingers, my gaze fixed on Nevel. He crouched down under one of the doll stands, rummaging until he pulled out a bloodstained rope that looked like it had seen far too many uses.

"Give me yuh hand them!" he ordered, his voice sharp with authority.

I continued to suck my fingers and stared at him, seemingly unfazed.

"Little shit, me say yuh must give me yuh hand them!" he insisted, his patience clearly wearing thin. He punctuated his demand by knocking me sharply on my forehead with the knuckles of his right pointy finger.

The sudden jolt of pain shot through my head like a bolt of lightning, and instinctively, my hand with the fingers I that had just been sucking, flew to the impacted spot. I rubbed it nervously, winced in pain, and blew air into my cheeks while pushing my lips out in a silent protest. When my compliance was still nowhere to be found, he grabbed both of my hands with an iron grip and roughly bound them together, in front of me with the bloodied rope. In one swift motion, he then discarded me onto the ground, pushing me into the corner as if I were nothing more than a filthy stack of laundry that needed to be tossed aside.

"We'll deal with yuh later," he threatened, a menacing undertone lacing his words that sent chills down my spine.

I was still able to suck my fingers, so I stuck them back in my mouth, deliberately ignoring the blood that had stained the coarse rope and silently watched him walk away into the shadows.

I didn't understand this eerie place, but a strange sensation washed over me, one that made me feel like I was not truly alone. Although the church stood empty and I couldn't discern the presence of any other person, an unsettling feeling crept over me. I felt the fine hairs on my arms rising as if a chill had rushed through the air. My heart began racing uncontrollably fast, and my already large eyes grew wider in an attempt to locate the inexplicable presence I sensed nearby. But there was no one visible to my frantic gaze.

As I continued to look around the small church, my eyes fell upon what appeared to be an altar situated in front of a magnificent stained glass window, its beauty obscured from the outside by rough brick and mortar. On the floor surrounding the altar lay an assortment of vibrant red pillows that seemed inviting. The flooring itself, crafted from shiny black ceramic tiles, gave the space an otherworldly aura. The altar was made of the same glossy tiles, now marred and dirtied with soot and ashes, hinting at some long-forgotten ritual.

Six feet away from the altar stood rows upon rows of black bamboo chairs, each one wrapped in luxurious red velvet cushions that looked incredibly comfortable. I found myself imagining how lovely it would be to have four of those chairs in Janet's cozy house, arranged around a beautiful bamboo table where we could gather and enjoy delicious dinners together.

Like the dolls scattered throughout the church, there were red candles everywhere. Rows and rows of shelves hung with red candles, their waxy forms glinting in the dim light.

"Crotchless Wayne and his friend dem sure do like their red candles." I commented to myself, still sucking my fingers as I continued to take in my unusual surroundings.

Suddenly, the room was abruptly filled with an overwhelming chorus of chattering voices, yet I couldn't see a single person, and I found myself utterly baffled by what was being said. I continued scanning my surroundings, noticing several windows on each of the walls. They were reinforced with iron burglar bars, solid and unyielding. I got up from my spot, still sucking on my fingers, and made my way over to one of the windows in the hope of catching a glimpse of the outside world. As I approached the window, I quickly realized that I was too short to see out clearly, so I reluctantly extracted my fingers from my mouth and decided to drag over a black bamboo chair, elegantly adorned with red velvet upholstery, to reach the window and get a better view.

Even after climbing up, I still couldn't see anything beyond the glass. To my dismay, I noticed several ugly dolls staring down at me menacingly from the windowsill. With my hands still tied up tightly, I took a chance and swept aside a few of them, their grotesque coconut brush heads tumbling down to the floor, shattering into pieces. The silence that descended after the sound of the shattering dolls was deafening and suffocating, heightening the tension in the room. Determined, I climbed up onto the windowsill, fear radiating from every pore of my being, urging me to act with a heightened sense of urgency.

The window was equipped with a latch, and as I dragged it down, I was taken aback when it unexpectedly opened. Eagerly, I squeezed my little head through the burglar bars to assess how far the drop to the ground was. To my relief, it wasn't very far down at all; Janet's roof was significantly higher, and I had once reveled in the thrill of jumping off it. I told myself this would be nothing. However, I had never actually attempted jumping off a roof with my hands tied up, but the gravity of my situation made it clear that this was indeed a life-or-death matter. Nevel had tied the rope around my wrist with an unwelcome level of security, and I had yet to learn how to free myself from a knot that was so tightly bound.

Since my head had unexpectedly gone through the tight space of the burglar bar, I felt a flicker of hope that my little body could easily follow suit, just as I had envisioned it. Suddenly, the eerie chattering started again, but this time it was much louder and more frantic. The hair on my body stood up in response to the unsettling noise, and my heart began to palpitate rapidly, sounding like a drum in my chest. I felt as though I might drop dead from the overwhelming sense of ominousness that surrounded me. The urgent need to hurry surged within me, fueling my frantic movements, and before I truly understood what was happening, I found myself outside, landing on the ground with surprising agility. I had somehow managed to land on my feet. I quickly stood up and scanned my surroundings. The premises were eerily surrounded by towering trees and protected by imposing high brick walls.

I didn't shout for help or call out to anyone. Something in my gut told me that it was best not to make a sound. I instinctively started to run, darting and skating behind the sturdy tree trunks for cover. The vast yard was densely populated with various fruit trees, all heavy with ripening fruit. Some of the branches hung perilously over the high brick walls, enticing yet dangerous. The sudden and sharp sound of dogs barking from nearby spurred me on, amplifying my desperate need to exit the premises as quickly as possible. It was impossible to sneak onto people's mango trees when you feared the chaos that barking dogs could cause. While dogs had never particularly scared me, I had learned long ago that their loud barking could attract unwanted attention.

Running was quite a challenge, especially with my hands tied up, but I struggled to maintain my speed. As the cacophony of barking dogs drew perilously close, I leaped up, instinctively locking my hands around a small, sturdy tree branch and pulling my body up with surprising ease. I had to be careful not to grip my hands so tightly that I couldn't release my upper body when needed. With some careful maneuvering, I found myself nestled in the tree, walking gingerly along the branches, my tied-up hands gripping the upper limbs for balance as I tried to keep my wits about me.

11. Escaping

The yard was so densely populated with an impressive variety of fruit trees, including several splendid mango trees thriving under the sun. I nimbly maneuvered my way from one tree to another, swinging effortlessly like a monkey from one sturdy branch to the next, all the while making sure that the thick rope did not get caught in the leafy branches overhead. That would have been quite the predicament, to see the rope ensnared on a mango tree, and considering the branch was far too thin, I'd end up hanging there like an oversized East Indian mango, much to the amusement of onlookers. So I was exercising great caution and speed simultaneously, ensuring my agility allowed me a safe passage.

As I glanced down at the ground below, my gaze fell upon two playful dogs circling the very first tree I had climbed. They seemed to be acting rather foolishly or perhaps just a bit confused, as they ran around the trunk of the tree in circles, resembling silly dogs chasing after their own tails.

"Bloodclaat mon! A where the little gal go?" I heard a man call out from a distance, his voice echoing slightly in the open space.

"She in a the church," someone quickly replied, as the conversation carried through the air.

"No! She not in there," the man insisted, clearly convinced.

"You look under the chair dem? She little, she probably under one a dem a hide," came the logical suggestion, implying that finding me would require a bit of searching.

My heart skipped a beat in a way that felt alarmingly intense. I stealthily made my way to the brick wall, carefully ensuring that the branches didn't shake or make any noise that could betray my presence. When I finally reached the weathered wall, I leaned over and looked down on the other side. Below was a busy road, chaotic and unforgiving, with no sidewalk in sight to offer any refuge.

"Check the bloodclaat back before Wayne come back," somebody shouted loudly, their voice echoing in the air.

The thought of getting hit by a car and dying in the process felt strangely more welcoming than the horrific alternatives of being raped and then burned alive. Gathering my courage, I swung myself onto the brick wall and looked down again, trying to assess my risky situation. The wall was significantly higher than the window, but I knew I had to try. I bent my knees, grabbed hold of the rough surface of the wall, and swung my body over with the grace of a gymnast. I didn't just jump down; I held on tightly to the wall, praying that a motorist would see me and stop before it was too late. As if in response to my silent plea, a few cars started blowing their horns furiously.

"Good, dem see me," I thought, relief washing over me. The traffic had come to an unexpected halt, and to my astonishment, people were getting out of their cars and rushing over to me with urgent concern. I was still gripping the wall tightly, my heart racing.

A woman looked up at me and exclaimed, "Jesas Christ, little gal! A mad you mad?"

In that moment, I blew air into my cheeks and pushed out my lips as a pair of big, strong hands reached up to lift me from my precarious position. Overwhelmed by the whirlwind of emotions, I started to cry, big, heavy drops of tears streaming down my cheeks in a flurry.

"A who tie yuh up so?" The man who lifted me asked, his voice filled with both concern and disbelief.

"Little pickney, a kidnap, dem kidnap yuh?" a concerned lady's voice inquired urgently.

"She alright?" another voice asked, filled with anxiety.

"Somebody call the police them?" a different voice suggested, clearly alarmed at the situation.

"A what a go on?" yet another bystander questioned, confused by the unfolding events.

"Little girl, you alright?" the man who was holding me asked once more, his tone softening.

"Yes, me awright," I managed to reply through my uncontrollable hiccups, trying my best to convey that I was okay.

"A what happened to you?" he pressed gently, seeking to understand the ordeal I had just endured.

"Him did a go come at sundown to rape me and burn up me body on the altar," I cried out loudly, my voice breaking through heavy sobs and relentless hiccups.

They saw the bloody rope that was cruelly tied around my trembling hands and began to take pictures, documenting the horror of the moment. Someone in the crowd had called the police, and soon, several individuals sent their grim photos to RJR News, eager to share the shocking news. A few men were climbing atop their cars, trying to peer over the high brick wall that separated them from the unfolding tragedy. Suddenly, more cars began to pull up, and people poured out, anxious to witness what was happening. An ambulance arrived, accompanied by several police vehicles with their lights flashing.

The paramedics swiftly emerged from the ambulance with a gurney and carefully lifted me onto it, their expressions a mixture of concern and urgency. The police officers approached me, their eyes focused on the rope still tightly bound around my wrist. They gently began to untie the rope while I lay on the gurney, feeling a mix of relief and pain as the pressure eased. I watched helplessly as one police officer placed the bloodied rope into a clear ziplock bag, a grim piece of evidence in a horrifying situation.

"How you feeling?" one of the paramedics asked with genuine concern, but by now I was crying uncontrollably, the weight of fear and trauma crashing down on me. I felt utterly lost and unable to respond.

"What is your name?" a female officer asked me in a gentle tone, her kindness evident as she looked into my tear-stained face.

"Me name, Swofiyah," I managed to answer, my voice trembling through uncontrollable hiccups and quiet sobs that escaped my throat.

"Swofiyah, are you feeling okay enough to talk?" the officer inquired with concern, her eyes searching mine for reassurance.

"Yeeeessss, maaammm," I drawled out, shaking my head slowly in a feeble effort to gather my thoughts.

"Can you tell me what exactly happened?"

"Me in the house a clean when me see that my mother thief me money, so me start to roll on the ground a cry, feeling angry and frustrated. Just then, me suddenly feel two big hands lift me up from the floor. Me couldn't see the face of the person that lift me up, but me could see Crotchless Wayne."

"Crotchless Wayne? Who exactly is Crotchless Wayne?" the female officer inquired, her expression shifting to one of genuine curiosity mixed with concern.

"He is me mother's boyfriend," I answered, struggling to gather my tangled thoughts through the tears that blurred my vision.

"Oh, I see," she said, diligently writing down every detail I was relaying, clearly intent on understanding my story. "Continue!"

"Them run through Mikey's yard a carry me, like I was just a little bungle of laundry, then them dashed through Gladys' yard and broke up her vegetable patch, causing her prized tomatoes and cucumbers to scatter everywhere. After that, them sprinted through Trevor's yard and jumped into a Honda Civic that was parked right up in front of Trevor yard," I sniffled, with tears streaming down my cheeks and mucus flowing from my nose into my mouth, making the situation all the more uncomfortable.

The paramedic, displaying kindness and empathy, took a napkin from his pocket and gently told me to blow my nose into it. I did as I was instructed, feeling a mix of embarrassment and relief as he wiped my nose and chin clean of the remnants of mucus that had betrayed me in my moment of distress.

"And then what happened next?" the policewoman asked, her tone kind and patient, reassuring me that I was safe and free to tell my story.

"And then them put a black sheet over me and put me down in the bottom of the car. Nevel put him foot them on me, so I couldn't move," I cried harder, this time, the painful memory of the heavy feet on my body surfacing in my mind, intensifying my distress.

"Then them drive off slow at first along the empty streets, and when them turn, them suddenly drive fast for what felt like twenty long minutes. Finally, them come to a stop right in front of the church. Wayne then tell Nevel to bring me inside. Then him shout again at Nevel with urgency, telling him to ""hurry up and bring the bloodclaat gal in.""

I was still crying, feeling overwhelmed as I relived the harrowing experience for the police officer, my heart racing with every word.

"When Nevel carry me inside the church, mi notice that the church full up a nuff ugly dolly staring at me. So mi said, "a how them dolly here look so ugly?" But Wayne quickly collar me and tell me that I make him the luckiest man in the world for what him have plan for me. It was in that moment that I see the man who carry me was Nevel."

"Nevel? Who is Nevel?" The police woman cut me off again to ask, her pen hovering over the notepad.

"Nevel is my mother friend who was over the yard last night playing Ludi and a drink beer," I answered, my voice trembling as I spoke.

"Okay, I see," she said, still writing rapidly, her focus unwavering.

"Continue," she instructed, her eyes intent on me as I tried to gather my thoughts.

"The way I was so shock, I instinctively started to suck on my fingers. But Wayne never liked that, so him lift me up with him strength and threw me roughly down on the ground, commanding Nevel to tie me up securely until sundown."

I continued passionately recounting my harrowing story to the police officer, while the other people around me listened intently, silently absorbing every word.

Nevel found a length of sturdy rope and then insisted that I stretch out my hands for him, but I stubbornly continued to suck on my fingers, so he knock me on my head with his finger." I pointed to the exact spot where Nevel had struck me on the forehead and rubbed it gently, grimacing at the painful memory.

"Then he smirked and said, 'little shit, I told you to give me your hand dem. But I refused, so he roughly grabbed my hands and bound them tightly with the rope, looking down at me with a warning."we'll deal with you later."'"

I cried even harder as I finished my traumatic story, the weight of it all crashing down on me.

"A what kind of bloodclaat man dem ya?" A woman shouted in disbelief, her voice breaking through the tense atmosphere.

"Them man ya must dead!" Another woman said aloud, with anger.

"Do you know why them kidnapped you, Swofiyah?" The officer asked.

"Yeeeesss maaammm," I said, crying louder.

"Why?" She asked, patiently.

"Aunty Norma said that Crotchless Wayne and his friends want to rape me and burn me on the altar."

"Where is your Aunty Norma now?" the police officer inquired, his voice steady but concerned.

That question opened the floodgates of tears, and I began to cry, uncontrollably and without restraint.

"She dead! Wayne cut her neck because she cut off his buddy," I managed to say, struggling to get the words out amidst my sobs.

"She cut off his what?" The police officer pressed further, her expression reflecting confusion as he tried to decipher my words through my tears and hiccups.

"Her, aunty cut off him cock," a woman interjected, stepping forward and clarifying my statement with a sense of urgency. I nodded my head in agreement, grateful for the support.

"Is that what happened?" The police officer asked again, seeking confirmation with a serious look, clearly trying to piece together the gravity of the situation.

"Yes ma'am," I said firmly and shook my head slightly. "Was there an altar in the church they took you to?"

"Yes," I replied. "And plenty of candles and nuff ugly dolly baby."

"Where is the church?" she asked, her voice steady and probing.

"It's over there suh," I said, pointing to the sturdy brick wall from which I had just come.

"Are you absolutely sure that's where the church is?" the officer inquired, her gaze locked onto mine with an intensity that felt almost unsettling.

"Yes, ma'am, I climbed up into the trees with my hands tied, and walked carefully along the tree limbs until I reached that very brick wall, where I tried to jump down," I stated with confidence, hoping to reassure her.

"Now, Swofiyah, this police lady is going to accompany you into the ambulance, are you okay with that?" she asked gently, her tone softening.

"Yeeeesss Maaaam," I said, struggling very hard to control myself and suppress the flood of emotions rising within me.

"Don't cry, we're going to make sure you're safe. Alright?" the kind paramedic reassured me gently.

"Yeeeesss, Maaaaam," I said again, desperately shaking my head in an attempt to convey my agreement, even as tears threatened to spill over.

The Paramedics expertly pushed the gurney into the ambulance and allowed the policewoman to hop in swiftly behind them. One of the paramedics expertly closed the door behind us, while the other turned to me and started taking my vital signs, checking my temperature, heart rate, and blood pressure with practiced ease. She then expertly stuck a needle into my arm, attaching a long, clear tubing that snaked its way up to an IV bag hanging above me.

I could hear the siren of the ambulance screaming loudly as it quickly sped through the streets, racing towards the Children Public Hospital, nestled in the bustling downtown of Kingston. I must have been incredibly tired and overwhelmed by everything, because the next thing I knew, I found myself in a hospital bed, the sterile environment all around me feeling both unfamiliar and oddly comforting.

12. Chris: At The Hospital

After my mother's untimely death, I found myself burdened with the solemn responsibility of protecting her memory and everything she stood for. It was a sacred promise I had sworn to Mama in the stillness of the night, just before she took her very last breath. I clearly remember coming home from the Rialto Theater, my spirits lifted from the entertainment, only to be shattered by the sight of my mother lying lifeless in a pool of her own blood. The shock of that heart-wrenching moment didn't hit me immediately; it felt almost as if a strange, detached presence had taken over my body, watching in horror at the grotesque scene before me. I stumbled over to her, believing she had already succumbed to the darkness, but to my astonishment, she opened her eyes and locked her gaze onto mine. With urgency, I bent down, desperately pulling out my phone and dialing the hospital, praying for help. Simultaneously, I called on one of the elders in our community as I grasped my mother's hand firmly, filled with hope that she might hold on just a little longer. Deep down, however, I couldn't shake the sinking feeling that she was already fading, as it appeared she had lost all of her life's blood.

"Swofiyah. Take care of Swofiyah, awright," she whispered, her voice barely audible but laced with a fierce intensity, as she looked deep into my eyes with her piercing stare. For a brief, hopeful moment, I believed she might defy the odds, but deep down, I realized she was merely waiting for my response, her last wish lingering in the air between us.

"Don't worry about her, you just focus on yourself. I will make sure she is okay," I had earnestly promised. There was a slight hint of a nod in response, and then she slowly closed her eyes. Deep down, I knew they weren't going to open again. I could feel the life gradually slipping away from her. But as I knelt there, holding her frail hands in mine, I held onto the fragile hope that she was simply resting peacefully.

I had no way of knowing how long I remained there, lost in the moment while holding onto her. A gentle tap on my shoulder suddenly brought me back to the harsh reality of her lifeless body beside me. It was King, one of the respected elders in our community. He was looking down at her in disbelief and profound shock.

"The ambulance is outside," he said gravely, breaking the heavy silence that hung in the air. Just then, two paramedics rushed in with a stretcher, followed closely by three police officers. My mother's modest little house was now filled with uniforms, a sight she would have never allowed under normal circumstances. The officers approached me and asked a series of questions, and although I managed to respond, King quickly took over the conversation. I felt a wave of relief wash over me because I suddenly found myself utterly unprepared to be questioned. All that haunted my mind was the nagging thought of how I had left her all by herself. Why had I abandoned her in her time of need?

She had started talking about her own demise the very night after she shockingly decapitated Wayne. The first time I heard her whisper those chilling words, it had frightened the living daylights out of me. I had desperately tried to ignore it, hoping it was just a fleeting thought that would eventually fade away. I simply thought she was just going through some dark period that would, in time, pass like a fleeting storm. I had reached out to my sisters with panicked messages, and their shocked responses mirrored my own feelings of disbelief. I was not at all expecting her to end up like this, in such a tragic and sudden way. We had so many important things to do—an endless list of plans yet to be realized. The community was deeply relying on her leadership and vision during these uncertain times. She was the balm they needed to heal the fractures and help people begin to trust one another once again. Because of her unyielding determination, progress had been made, and people had begun to foster a sense of hope. Now, I anxiously wondered, what were they going to do without her?

I breathed in deeply, trying hard to suppress the rising tide of panic within me and focus on anything but that grim reality. The truth of the matter was, I didn't want to think about the heavy new role that had been unexpectedly thrust upon me. I definitely wasn't ready to take over the leadership of the CPO. I didn't think I could handle it—not in the same way she had so gracefully managed it. How could I possibly undertake such an immense responsibility, especially when my family was currently being threatened? I had made a solemn promise with the intention of keeping it, but now I found myself at a crossroads. I wasn't ready to assume a leadership role when there was a monstrous threat roving around in the shadows. How could I? Not until I was absolutely sure that Swofiyah and the other members of the community were safe, would I even consider accepting this daunting new role. That meant I would have to take matters into my own hands and search for Wayne and his ruthless men myself, to ensure they would no longer pose a danger to us.

Mama's last breath was Swofiyah, and I had promised to ensure that she was truly okay. That solemn vow propelled me into the weighty decision I found myself grappling with. I understood that if she was to be alright, she would need to return to the carefree existence of a normal child. However, with a mother like hers, I feared she might never experience that sense of normalcy. I was acutely aware that her rigorous training was aiding her in coping with her challenging living situation, but I harbored deep concerns that this very situation could lead her down a perilous path. There had already been troubling complaints at school indicating that she had been threatening her classmates with her small cutlass. The training would have to be halted until I could devise a better plan for her well-being. I sighed again, desperately trying to push aside the haunting memories of her grief following Mama's death.

Mama had explicitly warned me against interfering with the way her mother was raising her. Any attempt to do so would only serve to infuriate her mother further and worsen an already precarious situation. I felt an overwhelming desire to rescue her from that toxic environment, but her erratic mother had looked at me with a piercing gaze and firmly stated "No" without offering any explanation.

In the aftermath of my mother's death, I had assigned a couple of the trainees to keep a watchful eye on Swofiyah. I couldn't bring myself to trust Wayne; he seemed far too interested in her well-being. He would not let her slip away easily. This was how I became acutely aware that he was lurking in the neighborhood the day they kidnapped her. I witnessed them forcibly placing her into the Honda Civic and quickly made the decision to follow them. I needed to uncover their location—their ominous voodoo lair. I tried to suppress any feelings of guilt for using her as bait, but to ensure her safety, we had no choice but to let her confront this dangerous situation head-on.

When he turned into what looked like an expansive church yard, I noticed that several security personnel were stationed at various points, and I instantly knew I was at the right place.

"Security at a church?" I snickered, shaking my head in disbelief. "What them raas think them is? Jesas?" I couldn't help but find humor in the unusual combination.

"Don't stop! Just drive past," I instructed King, the driver of the other vehicle, through the walkie-talkie, urgency in my voice. I didn't want the security team to realize that we had found their hidden location. I stopped at the very end of the road and watched the scene unfold before me.

Half an hour later, I spotted Wayne driving out in his familiar Honda Civic. I quickly sent the first car to discreetly follow him. Another twenty tense minutes passed, and then I saw Nevel walk out. I stepped out of my vehicle and strolled past the church yard, attempting to count the number of security guards they had patrolling the area. My mind raced with worry, but I tried to push the thought of Swofiyah's safety out of my head. I had to hold on to the hope that she was okay. She was incredibly smart, resourceful, and very strong.

I followed Nevel as he moved toward another yard situated on Briden Street. I walked past the yard and quickly glanced in, noticing he was greeting a few people, three men and a woman. One of them handed him a spliff, and I felt a mix of curiosity and dread as I took in the scene. As I walked past, I took out my phone and dialed Randy's number. He was a dedicated member of the group that was actively searching for the devil worshipers, and I knew I needed to keep him in the loop.

""Hey mon! I know exactly where they're staying. They have Swofiyah," I told him urgently, and then provided him with the two addresses I had memorized. The sooner this situation was resolved, the faster things could return to normal. I let Randy take the initiative to call the police, while I made my way back to the church in hopes of finding her safe and sound. As I approached my car, I was startled by the sound of police sirens approaching in the distance. I quickened my pace, driven by a rising anxiety that made me worry about her well-being. I wouldn't be able to forgive myself if anything were to happen to her. Once I hopped into my car, I drove swiftly over to the church and was shocked to see it swarming with police officers. The entire neighborhood seemed to have turned out in response to the commotion. I noticed that the police had apprehended over a dozen men and around five women, leading them in handcuffs toward a waiting Ford pickup.

"Did you see a little girl come out of the yard?" I asked, growing frantic as the situation unfolded.

"A little girl escaped from here, nearly killed herself jumping the wall. She's the one who made the police come," someone volunteered, their words sending a chill down my spine.

"That sounds exactly like Swofiyah," I thought anxiously to myself.

"So what happened to the little girl?" I demanded, my concern heightening.

"They took her to Kingston Public Hospital," the woman answered, her voice steady but serious.

I walked back to my car with determination and drove directly to the Public Hospital, located downtown. The hospital parking lot was surprisingly busy, a whirlwind of activity that reflected the urgency of the situation. I didn't hesitate until I was directly in front of the hospital entrance. I parked with a sense of urgency, not caring that I probably wasn't supposed to park there in that spot. I quickly made my way to the receptionist's counter and asked about the little girl who had just been brought in moments ago, desperately hoping for good news.

"What's her name?" the receptionist asked, her tone a mix of professionalism and curiosity.

"Swofiyah Campbell," I answered, keeping my composure.

"Who are you to her?" she inquired with a hint of skepticism.

"I'm her guardian, Chris Campbell," I replied firmly, meeting her gaze.

"Do you have any ID?" the woman asked, her expression neutral but attentive.

I reached into my pocket, retrieved my ID, and

handed it over to her without hesitation. She took it, glanced at the details, then shifted her gaze back to my face before returning it swiftly.

"Another man came and said he was her father. He had a noticeable limp, but no ID to confirm his claims, so I couldn't send him in. She's in room 420," the receptionist explained, and promptly turned to assist another customer waiting nearby.

With a sense of urgency, I hurried to the elevator, my mind racing as I pressed the button for the fourth floor. Upon arriving at room 420, I opened the door and stepped inside cautiously. She was sound asleep in the only bed available in the room, looking so small and frail, curled up with her tiny fingers in her mouth. I sat down on the small, uncomfortable sofa provided, my thoughts spiraling as I wondered if they had managed to catch the other rapist and those involved in the voodoo worship? My mind drifted to the church, Wayne, and the many security guards I had encountered, contemplating just how many influential individuals might be wrapped up in this dark web of complicity.

This situation was becoming increasingly complicated by the seconds, adding layers of distress that were hard to ignore. Wayne was certainly not dealing with this challenge alone; there were other bank rollers involved in this intricate web. The architectural design, with its striking beauty, and the robust infrastructure of the church indicated that considerable money had been invested into it. However, it was clear that this was not Wayne's church; he was likely just a foreman or something similar, not the mastermind behind it. I knew I needed to get some answers to unravel this mystery. I quickly sent King a text, informing him of my growing suspicions and instructing him to put someone on the case. He quickly texted back, cryptically informing me that he had lost track of Wayne.

I had not slept well since the tragic death; the burden of this mystery, coupled with the responsibility of keeping the members of the CPO informed, was taking a significant toll on my mental and emotional well-being. After what felt like an eternity, I finally laid back on the sofa, closed my eyes, and allowed myself to drift away, hoping for a moment of peace. I must have fallen asleep, because when I eventually woke up, I found Swofiyah sitting up in bed, staring at me with her fingers in her mouth.

"I guess you don't need to go to the bathroom since the bed has substituted for it," I said lightly, looking at her with a mix of amusement and concern.

She puffed up her cheeks and pushed out her little lips defiantly, showing her spirit.

"Wayne said a him kill Aunty Norma and when him done with me, him a go done yuh too," she told me matter-of-factly.

"Is that what him tell you?" I asked her, maintaining a calm demeanor despite the chilling words.

"Yes," she replied, nodding her head solemnly.

"Don't worry about it. Are you hungry?" I asked her, making a sincere effort not to let her see the simmering rage I was struggling to contain.

"Yes," she replied once more, nodding her head with a look of eagerness.

"What do you want to eat?" I followed up, trying to keep the conversation light.

"Burger King," she said, her eyes brightening with a hopeful glint.

Just then, the door was pushed open and a CNA walked in, carrying a tray filled with food.

"Oh, you're awake now," she stated with a smile. "You must be hungry; I brought you something delicious to eat."

13. Being Followed

S wofiyah looked at me with a profound sense of disappointment etched across her face. "It's okay, I was just going to take her for lunch. It okay if she leave now?"

"Absolutely, she's perfectly fine. We were simply waiting for a guardian to come and pick her up," she replied reassuringly.

Ignoring the wet patch on the sheet that had clearly caught her attention, she turned to Swofiyah and gently asked, "How are you feeling, my dear?"

"Me fine," Swofiyah replied, her tone slightly more upbeat.

"Are you ready to leave?" the CNA inquired, her voice filled with warmth.

"Yes, me ready," Swofiyah affirmed confidently.

""Wait, let me quickly change your wet clothes," the CNA said with a warm and reassuring smile that made Swofiyah feel at ease. She stepped out of the room momentarily, and returned a few minutes later, holding a lovely little dress and a fresh pair of undies, all brand new and ready for Swofiyah to wear.

"That's better," she said, after gently wiping down Swofiyah and dressing her in the cute new clothes that brought a sparkle to her eyes. She neatly put the crumpled wet clothes in a bag then handed it to Swofiyah with a cheerful demeanor.

"Thanks," Swofiyah said to the CNA, her voice shy but filled with gratitude.

""Come on, let's go," I urged my cousin, feeling the pressing urgency of the moment really beginning to weigh on me. King had just texted me, and I absolutely needed to see what was happening concerning him.

"Thanks," I expressed gratefully once again to the CNA before I made my way out of the room, holding onto my little cousin's small hand protectively as if to shield her from any potential harm.

As we walked down the long and somewhat sterile corridor, I did my utmost not to appear as if I was mentally cataloging every little detail around me. My eyes were instinctively scanning the area, always on the lookout for Wayne and his group of voodoo-worshiping friends, fully aware of the very real potential dangers that might be lurking nearby. To my relief, my car was still parked in the spot right in front of the hospital—they hadn't towed it away, much to my surprise. We finally got in, and I carefully strapped on her seatbelt while she idly sucked on her little fingers.

"What are you getting from those fingers now?" I asked her, playfully initiating our little game we often played whenever we were together.

"Burger King Whopper and Dr. Pepper," she declared confidently, her eyes sparkling with imagination.

"That's all?" You not getting any fries tuh?"

"Oh, me forget the fries," she replied with a sheepish grin, realization dawning on her.

"So me don't need to get you any of those things then? How about KFC instead?" I asked playfully, hoping to lighten the mood.

"No! Me want Burger King," she insisted, her lips forming a little pout that was hard to resist.

"Awright, Burger King it is," I said, chuckling softly, trying to mimic her enthusiasm.

I drove carefully to the Burger King located in Half Way Tree. It was only when I made the turn into the drive-thru that I suddenly realized we were being followed by someone.

As I placed the order, I pretended not to see Wayne's white Honda Civic lurking in the background. He passed by as if he intended to park, but I had a strong feeling that he was actually just waiting for me.

"Here, take this," I said to Swofiyah, handing her the bag containing her order that I had just collected from the window. I forced myself to take a cautious bite of a fry, trying desperately not to let the panic settle in.

If only I could get her home safe, I thought, my heart racing as I glanced in the rearview mirror.

I sent a quick text to King, letting him know exactly what was going on in our situation. Since we found ourselves in the bustling area of Half Way Tree, I made the decision to drive up Constant Spring Road, all with the aim of giving Wayne the slip. I truly did not understand the root of his obsession, but I knew I had to put a stop to it before things spiraled out of control and it became too late to remedy.

"Swofiyah, listen up," I said in a serious tone, trying to convey the gravity of the situation to her. "Me not going to train yuh anymore, and I really want you to stop bringing the cutlass to school. A don't want yuh to hurt anybody, or worse, get hurt yourself, or end up in serious trouble and in jail." I firmly concluded.

She chewed on her fries thoughtfully, her brow furrowing as she considered my words. Finally, she responded, "When I have me cutlass at school with me, nobody don't trouble me. And Klam, them tease her all the time, so me have to defend her. Them afraid a me and me cutlass, so me like to have it at school."

"I know that, but me asking you to stop bringing it with you altogether. It will honestly make me feel much better if a know you're not waving it around carelessly," I explained, hoping she would understand my concern.

"A not waving it around. A just take it out when a need to," she clarified, her defensiveness apparent.

"Okay, but I really want you to promise me that you won't take it to school, period. You know you can fight if it comes down to it; you don't need to carry the cutlass around for protection. Promise me you won't take it to school anymore," I urged, hoping to instill some sense of responsibility in her.

She looked at me thoughtfully for a moment, her head cocking slightly to the right, as if weighing her options, and after a brief pause, she finally nodded as if she had come to a firm decision.

"Awright, me not going to take it to school, but if me see them troubling me too much, me a go take it with me," she stated earnestly, trying to sound more grown up than her tender age suggested.

"Tell you what, if you see them troubling you too much, just come to me first. Okay?" I replied, looking at her intently as we came to a halt at the stoplight.

I scanned the surroundings and quickly realized that I had lost sight of Wayne. I didn't feel any better about it at all. My feelings of trepidation were steadily mounting, and I really didn't like it.

"Okay, then," she said importantly, as if she held some significant power in the conversation.

I couldn't help but laugh at her serious expression and held up my pinky finger, signaling for her to seal the deal. We performed our little ritual, sealing and stamping it with a firm grip, then she returned to happily munching on her fries.

I knew her mother hadn't seen this thoughtful, sensible, and mature side of her. This was the side of her that I truly wanted to nurture and support. While Mama wanted her to learn self-defense and self-sufficiency—concepts that were undoubtedly valuable —in my mind, those were all good intentions but potentially misguided. With a mother like hers, who often imposed unrealistic standards, she might only end up feeling discouraged and downhearted—an outcome that could prove dangerous. As a result, she would learn to transfer that kind of anger and frustration onto the children at school—something she had already begun to do. I wanted her to concentrate on her mental development, because I firmly believed that focusing on her emotional and intellectual growth was really what would help her thrive later in life.

"Crotchless Wayne and him friend them love ugly dolly babies," she volunteered with a playful tone.

"Why you say that?" I inquired, not taking my eyes off the road as I navigated through the bustling traffic. I was still intently looking out for Wayne.

"Cause, him have many, many, many ugly dolly babies in his church. Oh, and him like candle tuh, you know."

"Why you say that?" I asked, again, genuinely curious.

"Cause him have many, many, many candles in him church," she explained matter-of-factly.

"Maybe him duh," I agreed, still focused on the very heavy traffic around us.

"No maybe, him love them," she insisted, dragging on her straw with a determined air. "Him church have nuff ghost tuh," she shared casually.

"Really, how you know that?" I asked, a bit surprised by her confident claim.

"Cause, me hear them. Them make me heart jump and the hair them stand up on me arm and on me head," she explained with an animated gesture.

"Did anyone of them chase you?" I asked, trying to keep the conversation light and playful.

"No, but them make me fraid," she said emphatically, her eyes wide with the memory.

"Were you super fraid, medium fraid, or just a little fraid?" I asked her with genuine curiosity.

"Me did super, super, super fraid," she replied, punctuating her words with animated gestures of her hands that illustrated just how scared she had been.

"You were very brave," I complimented her sincerely. "And the police managed to catch all the bad mon them because of you and your quick thinking."

"Me never feel brave, though. All the time, a think I was just going to fall out of the trees them. But me never fall down, and me was happy bout that," she said, her expression turning thoughtful as she recalled the experience.

"You very good at climbing, so why you think you did a go fall out?" I asked her, feeling a bit puzzled by her response.

"Because me hand them did tie up. I never practice to climb trees with me hand them tie up," she explained matter-of-factly.

I was very surprised by this piece of information, but I didn't want her to feel panicked, so I kept the conversation light and upbeat. "Wow! You must be

Jacky Chan to climb the trees with you tie-up hand them," I grinned, trying to make her smile.

"No, I was Bruce Lee," she corrected me with a hint of pride in her voice.

I laughed heartily and gently rubbed her head, saying, "Awwright, Miss Bruce Lee, you truly are the bravest."

"Yes, me is very brave, but me can't help but remember the ghost them. Do you think them going to come in me bed tonight?" she asked, her voice trembling just a little, betraying her fright.

"No, the ghost them fraid a you, and they can't leave the church. That's where them live and where they belong," I replied confidently.

"How you know that?" she asked, looking at me with a mixture of doubt and curiosity, giving me that special side look that made the conversation feel even more significant.

"Mama told me that when I was your age," I shared, recalling my own youthful fears of the ghostly creatures lurking about.

"You did fraid a ghost too?" she replied, her face filled with surprise and disbelief.

"Of course! Everybody fraid of ghost when them little like you," I explained, trying to comfort her with the shared experience.

"Oh, okay. So when I grow big me not going to fraid a ghost anymore?" she asked, her eyes wide with hope and anticipation.

"Of course not, I promise you that," I reassured her, wanting her to feel safe.

"Awright then," she said with a relieved sigh, her tension easing as she embraced the comforting words.

I was still keeping a vigilant watch for Wayne as we passed the National Stadium, which is situated near Nannyville. It was in this very area that a few unfortunate girls had fallen victim to the same ruthless cult. I reached for my phone and called King for an update, but there was no response. I made an effort to push those troubling thoughts aside. Instead, I decided to drive down Deanary Road rather than taking the more familiar Mountain View Road. If anything, I figured there would be more turn-offs available down that route. I adhered strictly to the speed limit, even though my anxieties were mounting steadily with each passing moment.

Swofiyah was never a particularly talkative child, which I came to appreciate deeply. I looked over at her sitting there quietly in the passenger seat, clutching a bag of unfinished burger and fries that she had lost interest in. She was fighting to keep her eyes open, probably worried that if she fell asleep, she might accidentally urinate on the car seat. I was driving down Jackson Road when I caught sight of the little mishap occurring again ahead of us.

"This bumboclaat bwoy must really want to die," I thought to myself, my anger flaring up at the relentless hounding. "Awright, look how me a go put a stop to this madness."

I promptly took out my phone and attempted to call King once more. Still, there was no answer, which made my concern grow significantly. I was in the process of turning right onto Windward Road when, to my surprise, my phone rang.

"Hello," I snapped at King, my frustration evident in my tone. "How the ratid you don't pick up your phone, mon?"

"Sorry mon, I couldn't find it," he replied sheepishly, a genuine note of apology in his voice.

"Listen up, the bwoy Wayne is right behind me on Windward Road. Me's about to turn in, so get the youth them ready. A time we finish this once and for all," I instructed him firmly.

"Awright," he said, and before I knew it, he hung up, leaving me to gather my thoughts for what was to come.

I turned into Bower Bank and watched as Wayne sped by in his car, leaving a cloud of dust in his wake.

I looked around to see if King had sent out anyone to go after him, but saw nothing in the dim light of the evening.

That bloodclaat obsession a go kill him, I thought with a heavy heart, as I stopped my car in front of Janet's gate, feeling a sense of dread.

"Come Swofiyah," I called out, getting out of the vehicle and hoping she was alright. To my surprise, she started to cry, her tiny body shaking with each sob.

"What you crying for?" I asked, genuinely taken aback by her tears.

"Me never done cleaning the house, so she is going to beat me," she sobbed, her eyes brimming with fear.

"It awright, she not going to beat you," I told her reassuringly. But my words only seemed to make her cry even louder, filling the air with her distress.

"You just get kidnapped, manhandled, tied up, frightened by ghosts, jumped out a windows, climbed trees with your hands tied up, and jumped a high wall, bravely, but now you fraid?" I asked her, letting her see how ridiculous she was being in this moment of fright.

She was crying pitifully now, utterly unable to speak a coherent word of comfort or reason. So, I picked her up, cradling her comforting little body, and took her to her mother.

"A where the little raas did guh?" Janet asked in her usual angry tone. She was sitting on her veranda, casually smoking her ganja as if nothing had transpired.

"Wayne come in here and kidnap her. You know what him was going to do with her? Him and him posse a the one burning up the pickney them," I told her emphatically.

Janet looked at me as if she didn't believe a word I said.

"Him tie her up and left her in a the church for later, but she manage to escape and quickly call the police them."

I looked at Swofiyah and noticed that she was trying to calm herself, wiping her tear-streaked eyes with the back of her trembling hands, hiccuping softly in distress. I glanced back at Janet again and saw the unmistakable insanity lurking beneath the surface of her expression. She was clearly an unfit mother, but the sad reality was that no one would step in to do anything about it.

"Make her stay in the house and don't send her anywhere, not even to the corner store," I instructed her firmly, hoping that she would care enough for once to want to protect her own child.

"Guh inside," she ordered Swofiyah firmly, taking a long draw on her spliff, the smoke curling slowly into the air. I gently placed Swofiyah down, watching her as she slowly walked into the small, one-room house, hugging tightly onto her Burger King bag and her hospital bag, the weight of both evident.

"Look out for Wayne; him still a try to get to her," I told Janet, locking my gaze with hers, searching for understanding. She appeared completely unconcerned, her eyes drifting off as if my words held no weight.

14. King The Traitor

After I dropped off Swofiyah at her place, I drove directly to my house to pick up my hardwares. We had a carefully curated selection stored away in a secret compartment hidden beneath the wooden floor of our modest two-bedroom house. I needed to strap up and prepare for action because this situation had to reach a conclusion tonight, no matter what.

Once I parked the car securely, I entered through the gate and immediately spotted King sitting patiently on the steps, clearly waiting for my return.

"You have any news yet?" I inquired, hoping he had some helpful information.

"No, not yet," he replied, rising to his feet and stepping aside to allow me to enter the house.

Since the incident with my mother, I had become vigilant and had started locking the door every time. As I turned the key in the lock, always making sure to stay mindful of my surroundings, I asked him, "So who did yuh send?"

"I sent the four schoolies to them. Them not going to get noticed," he reassured me confidently, his voice steady and infused with a bravado that seemed almost performative, as if that would truly put my mind at ease.

The door opened and I went inside cautiously. King came in immediately behind me, deliberately closing the door with a faint click. I turned around almost instantly, because I knew without a doubt that he was going to try something reckless. King didn't have nearly enough time to pull the trigger as he had anticipated. I had the gun firmly in my hand before he was even fully aware of its presence.

"Old bloodclaat coward, yuh did a go shoot me in a me back?" I asked in disbelief, my voice tinged with a mix of anger and incredulity, using the gun butt to slap him sharply across the jaw bone. I heard it crack ominously, and watched as blood began to trickle down his face.

The very first sentence that came out of Mama's mouth the night she died was etched into my memory:

"Don't trust King." That was before she made me promise to look after Swofiyah, a promise I intended to uphold fiercely.

I was prepared for this confrontation.

"A who yuh a work for?" I demanded with intensity, as I kicked out his right knee cap with precision and watched him collapse to the wooden floor like a broken down tree, helpless and vulnerable.

"Chris, don't shoot me. A yuh father send me, him and Wayne a work together," he pleaded desperately, his voice filled with fear.

"Me father? How me father come in a this?" I asked, feeling utterly puzzled and bewildered by the revelation.

"A him send man to kill you mother. The obeah church belong to him. Wayne and some a we a work for him," he replied, his eyes darting nervously.

"Me father send man to kill me mother?" I reiterated, sitting heavily on a chair near the door, grappling with the shock of this devastating new information. It felt like a bolder was shove down my throat and was resting on my chest. I couldn't breathe

"How much a yuh from the CPO working for him?" I inquired, determination starting to brew within me as I resolved to find out why my father wanted my mother dead.

"Me, Marci and Betty," was his quick response, an answer laced with unspoken implications.

"Betty? But she and Mama a good friend," I exclaimed, disbelief thick in my voice.

King had no reply to that; instead, he looked at me as if he had already been forgiven for the treachery that lay between us. He never even saw the stainless steel folding knife that I kept concealed in my back pocket coming his way. In one swift motion, his neck was sliced open before he even realized what was happening. I watched in a mix of fascination and satisfaction as the blood sprayed out, and he instinctively placed his hands over his throat. He died swiftly, collapsing to the floor, his body hitting the shiny red wooden surface before I could even process the gravity of my actions.

"Have no compassion for traitors," that was the very first piece of wisdom mama imparted to me. "If them betray you once, them going to do it again."

With those words echoing in my mind, I called two of the four schoolies King had deceitfully claimed to have sent after Wayne, using the walkie-talkie. Two of them were keeping a close watch over at Janet's place, while the other two were stationed at Bower Bank's gate, maintaining a vigilant lookout with the others. They were all spread out, pretending to be time wasters, disguising their true intentions.

A few minutes later, they showed up at the door. One of them had the ever-determined Betty in tow. I had strategically left the door half opened, creating just enough of a gap for King's body to remain hidden behind it. Troy was the first to step through the threshold. Towering and imposing, he had to duck his head to fit through the doorframe. Nathan followed closely behind; he was also tall, but not quite as tall as Troy. Their presence seemed to fill the small, empty space. Betty was trailing behind them, her chatter echoing in the silence.

"Yuh find Wayne yet?" she asked, her voice rising rather loudly, cutting through the tension in the room.

"Keep yuh voice down, mon, yuh chat too loud," Troy warned her, his words delivered in a slow, deliberate drawl that seemed to hang in the air.

It was then that she noticed the lifeless form of King sprawled on the floor, an unsettling sight that sent a chill down her spine. I had warned the two schoolies to expect something like this; the tension had been brewing for far too long.

"But kiss me raas! What in the world a go on here?" she asked in disbelief, her mind racing as she momentarily forgot to lower her voice, letting her emotions take control.

"Keep yuh bumboclaat voice down!" Nathan barked in response, delivering a sharp slap across her left cheek, his frustration palpable. It was in that instant she truly realized she was in deep trouble, far deeper than she had anticipated.

"Chris, me never want to do it, but yuh know how yuh father stay? Him threat'n to kill me and me pickney them. I had to do it," she said, falling to her knees, tears streaming down her cheeks as she rubbed her trembling hands together in desperation. "Please Chris, me never want to do it, but me pickney them. A me alone them have. Them no have nobody else but me," she pleaded passionately, her voice cracking with emotion, the weight of her circumstances pressing heavily on her shoulders.

She was my mother's best friend, a woman who had been trusted implicitly by my mother throughout the years. I vividly remembered the two of them sitting under the wide expanse of banana trees, drinking Red Label Wine together, their laughter ringing through the air as they chatted and shared stories, becoming progressively inebriated in the broad daylight of a sun-kissed afternoon. Her betrayal of my mother weighed heavily on my heart, making the metaphorical boulder pressing against my chest feel even more crushing. The disappointment I felt was profound and consuming, filling me with a desperate rage. In that moment, I wanted very badly to cut her throat; the darker, killer side of me screamed for retribution, refusing to show her any semblance of mercy. But then I remembered that she had four children, three of whom were training diligently to become defenders of our community, and I hesitated. Before I could act on my overwhelming impulse,

Nathan stepped in once again, delivering another firm slap across the same cheek, the sound echoing in the charged atmosphere.

"Shut yuh bloodclaat. Yuh don't betray family," he shouted passionately. "We, a yuh family, and yuh betray Mama, yuh betray your entire family. Instead of talking to her and allowing us to figure out things together, you chose to betray us all. We, a yuh family. Yuh killed the one person who was guiding this family down the correct path."

The pain etched on his face opened up the painful wounds I was desperately trying to ignore in my own heart. I turned to watch as silent tears began to cascade down Betty's cheeks, each drop a testament to the guilt, shame, and heavy sensibility that finally began to settle in. In that moment, I realized I had never wanted to harm someone as fiercely as I wanted to cut her now. Yet, I couldn't forget about her four children; I needed to learn to start thinking more like a leader, making choices that would serve our community rather than indulging my darker instincts. I breathed a sigh, attempting to ground myself in the reality of the situation.

"Bredda, you want me to do it for you?" Troy surprised me with his unexpected question. He was never one to take the extreme step of eliminating mothers.

"No," I replied firmly, glancing over at her with a mix of concern and determination. "Me a go give her another chance."

"You," I directed at her, my voice steady. "Go home and tell yuh three pickney them who a train, exactly what you've done. And make sure the big one call me!"

Without hesitation, she got up and rushed towards the door, guilt and pain clearly etched across her features. Suddenly, she paused and turned back, her eyes wide with urgency. "Marci and yuh father a grine. A she set us up with him."

"Awright," I replied, acknowledging her words. With that, she disappeared around the corner, and I listened intently to the sound of her fading footsteps.

"What yuh want us to do now?" Troy asked in a quiet voice, an edge of apprehension in his tone.

"Just get rid a the body," I instructed decisively, pointing my chin toward the corpse lying still on the floor.

"I have a meeting with me father," I continued, my thoughts already racing ahead.

"Me a come with you," they both said in unison, their voices filled with determination.

"What, the two a oonuu suddenly turn one brain twin?" I asked, looking at them both with a mix of curiosity and disbelief.

"Let me call the twin them to come take care a this," Nathan said, his tone becoming serious yet laced with his usual humor. "You need protection. Well, not really, but you need back up," he corrected himself with a slight shrug. "We a yuh back up man them."

Nathan had this incredible ability to lighten any situation, no matter how tense it was, with his contagious hilarity. I was truly glad that he was here with me in this crazy moment.

"Awright, make sure the two a oonuu strap up tight. We don't know what a go take place," I warned, glancing around. "And hurry up and get the twin them to come take out this dead body out a me place." I added with evident disgust, directing my gaze at the lifeless corpse that lay there.

I was putting the final touches to my strappings when I suddenly heard the unmistakable sound of a wheelbarrow rolling, noisily, up the street, accompanied by the carefree laughter of youths enjoying their day. Minutes later, there came a knock on the door.

"Come in, it open," I called out from the other room, hoping it was the help we desperately needed.

"Bring the bag, them come no mon," James called out with a hint of urgency to his identical twin brother.

They were both twenty-three years old, with just a minute separating their births, yet the older one often carried himself with the demeanor of someone at least a decade older. Jake, the younger twin, entered the room with a roll of heavy-duty garbage bags in hand, his expression serious and focused.

The twin brothers were strikingly light-skinned and physically robust young men, proudly claiming the title of cleaners. Both sported long, sun-kissed, honey-blonde dreadlocks that cascaded down their backs.

At that moment, they were in the process of wrapping the body in the thick plastic bags when I walked into my mother's favorite room, a place she had lovingly decorated and filled with so many cherished memories. I took in the fluffy brown leather sofa set that looked as pristine as the day it was purchased, even after nearly a decade of steadfast use. The shiny mahogany brown cabinet gleamed, housing her collection of expensive plates and elegant dinner sets that had never been used for anything but special occasions. The seven-piece dining room set dominated one-third of the space, capable of accommodating up to ten guests when my mother was in one of her entertaining moods, making every gathering feel like a celebration. My gaze fell to the area rug underneath, which lent a sense of elegance to the dining area and, for a fleeting moment, I could almost see her sitting there, laughing joyfully with her friends, including dear Betty. The buffet, adorned with her homemade juice set, was lined with an impressive array of alcoholic beverages she had carefully crafted, some of which she had planned to teach us how to make so we could sell them later.

I couldn't stand to see the room anymore, the chaos and mess overwhelming me, but as I was about to walk out the door, leaving the two chuckling youths to their cleaning up, I happened to notice that some blood had gotten caught onto Mama's favorite leather love seat. It glistened ominously in the dim light, a stark reminder of the earlier incident and the trouble that had unfolded.

"Oye, you better make sure all a the blood gone by the time a come back," I ordered firmly, trying to assert some authority in the situation.

"A who tell you to cut him neck in a the house?" James back talked with sass, crossing his arms defiantly. "If Mama was here she would a slap you right in a your neck back."

"Come make me do it for her," his twin quickly offered with a mischievous grin. "Oh wait, let me go for the wheelbarrow make me show you how strong me is when a pop you one with it."

"No, mon, you too weak, you need to eat more fish to build some real strength, but you can give him a backhand if you want," James corrected, giving his twin a playful pat on the shoulder, faking an expression of regret. "Even if yuh was strong enough, him still wouldn't feel it, him tough like turbit. Just make him gwon, don't bother to hurt yuhself today."

I shook my head in exasperation, feeling overwhelmed by the situation. Just two minutes around them, and I was already forgetting that I had intended to shoot somebody out of frustration.

"Don't leave no ghost in a me house, and lock up when oonuu done," I firmly stated, shaking my head as I walked out, hoping they understood the seriousness of my warning.

"Me tell you say him fraid a duppy," I heard Jake whisper conspiratorially to his twin.

I couldn't help but chuckle softly as I left them to their amusing banter, shaking off the tension that had been building.

15. My Father And Marcy

I met the two schoolies standing in front of my gate, gazing up at me with expressions that radiated youth and confidence. A fleeting thought crossed my mind as I looked at them—I prayed fervently that I wasn't inadvertently leading them to their untimely endings.

"Oonuu ready?" I asked them, taking a few purposeful steps toward the car and pulling the door open wide.

"The question is, are yuh ready?" Nathan, the most confident of the duo, shot back with a cheeky grin.

"We'll see when we get there," I responded, attempting to keep my tone light yet serious. "And don't bother to go big up oonuu self. Just follow me lead. Me father don't play." I continued in a firm voice as I settled into the car. Nathan quickly slid into the front seat beside me, while Troy made himself comfortable, stretching out in the back.

Some of the younger watchers were sitting casually at the entrance of Bower Bank, pretending to be idlers in a way that only they could pull off. My eyes met those of the other two schoolies, and I gave them a slight nod of acknowledgment, a silent agreement to keep our interactions discreet. I didn't bother to look for their responses; I was focused on my own thoughts. It was looking like a typical normal Friday evening when I drove out, the kind that promised the weekend's freedom and distraction.

My father lived in Constant Spring, a place that felt like a distant memory now. I had not seen him in years, not since Mama made the difficult decision to leave him. I was almost seventeen at the time, and in my youth, I was ready to shoot him because of the pain his actions were inflicting upon her. It was the only reason she ultimately decided to leave. Had it not been for my near murderous intent towards my father, she probably would have continued living there— enduring the abuse in silent suffering.

My sisters had been at school that unfortunate day when he decided to drink heavily and lose all sense of right and wrong. His drinking had become an unbearable part of our daily lives, but he had taken things to a new level by beating Mama after she discovered the truth about his infidelities, shattering our once fragile family bond in the process.. She had threatened to take the children and leave him, declaring that she could no longer endure the torment. In response, he had coldly told her she could do it, but only under his dead body. That was when the abuse, both physical and emotional, escalated to terrifying levels. It became as if he was openly daring her to take the children and leave the oppressive environment he had created. But she never did, because deep down, she was keenly aware of what he was truly capable of. She was genuinely afraid for our safety and well-being.

As I got older, I began to see the toll that this relentless cycle of abuse was taking on her. I witnessed the way she was sinking deeper into mental destitution and physical deterioration due to the relentless pressures of her situation. Each day, I felt myself becoming angrier at the injustice of it all, day by day. Mama had lost her once vibrant zest for life, yet she continued to put up a brave front for us, trying to shield us from the reality of her suffering.

The day she finally made up her mind to leave was the day I returned home earlier than usual from school. To my horror, I found him beating the sense out of her, as I could hear the muffled sounds of the struggle through the door. I knew he was hitting her, but I had no idea of the extent of the violence she was enduring. She never said anything to us about what she was going through, and she usually covered the bruises so that we wouldn't notice them.

I opened the door just in time to witness the shocking scene of my father raising a chair high above his head, aiming it at her, while she desperately held up her hands in a futile attempt to protect herself. It was useless; she collapsed onto the floor, trembling and utterly defeated, and my heart shattered at the sight.

I had not felt such overwhelming rage as I did that fateful day. I marched into his office with purpose and took out the gun I knew he had carefully hidden in the depths of his desk. I cranked it up in the same manner I had observed him do countless times before, and then I turned and walked back into the living room with determination. I aimed the gun directly at him and pulled the trigger, striking him squarely in the left ankle. He lost his balance instantly and crumpled to his knees, the pain evident on his face. With a steady stride, I approached him, pressing the cold metal of the gun against his temple.

"Yuh want to hit her again? Go hit her again! Hit her again!" I dared him, jamming the tip of the gun into his right ear, my heart racing with adrenaline. The intense rage within me demanded to be satisfied, but shooting him in the foot merely intensified my fury; it simply was not enough. So, in a fit of uncontrollable anger, I shot him again, this time aiming for his left thigh. He cried out, a desperate wail that echoed like a wounded animal trapped in barbwire, pleading with me not to pull the trigger again. But my rage still needed satisfaction, it was burning hotter than before. I pressed the gun back to his head, fully prepared to pull the trigger when suddenly, Mama cried out with a piercing voice, "No Chris, a yuh father, don't kill him." Her words cut through the red haze, tugging at the edges of my fury.

I looked at the oversized, pathetic excuse of a father and lowered the gun slowly. I tucked it into the waist of my pants and walked decisively over to her.

She had lost so much weight over the years, all because she had been subjected to brutal beatings like some sort of slave. I gently wrapped my arms around her fragile form and slowly helped her to her feet, careful not to cause her any additional pain. As we began to exit the living room, I glanced back over my right shoulder at him. To my surprise, he looked sobered up and was now slumped on the leather sofa, desperately holding on to his bloody leg where the gunshot wounds inflicted pain and despair.

"Next time yuh drink and get drunk and act like a fool, me a go cut out you tongue," I threatened him, maintaining a calm demeanor that contrasted sharply with the turmoil I felt inside.

I took Mama to her room and made sure to help her get comfortably into bed. She took some painkillers that day and slowly drifted off to sleep, exhaustion finally claiming her. I found myself remembering the moments I spent checking up on her throughout the long, sleepless night, making sure she was still alive and recovering. That ominous evening marked the last time we would spend in that house. Since then, I had not seen nor heard from him again.

~~~~~~~

The schoolies in the car were surprisingly quiet for once, and I was genuinely happy about that unexpected peace. Just then, my cell phone rang sharply, breaking the silence, and I quickly picked it up to check who was calling. It was Damian, Betty's oldest son, sounding a bit anxious.

"Yes," I responded, trying to keep the conversation light.

"Thank you, she's really not going to do it again," he promised earnestly, his voice tinged with relief.

"Good, yuh make sure 'bout it," I instructed him firmly, and with that, I hung up the phone with a sense of accomplishment.

"A good youth that," Nathan said, nodding in agreement and confirming what I had already known in my heart.

"Bumboclaat bwoy, how yuh can eavesdrop so?" Troy drawled slowly with mischief, backhanding his friend lightly in the neck in playful reprimand.

"But yuh a go on like yuh never a raas listen tuh," Nathan defended himself, his tone light despite the accusation.

I knew they were both listening intently, because the receiver was on speaker mode. I left them to their playful bantering, while I tried to figure out where my father would be at this particular time of the day. Even though I haven't seen him in quite a long while, I knew he hadn't changed much in his ways. He was a man of strict routine and habit.

While the church was a surprise to me, I quickly remembered that it was Friday, a day he usually reserved exclusively for his lengthy six-hour resting period. Additionally, the church was far too hot for comfort, so I instinctively knew he wouldn't be there. He wasn't that foolish.

I drove straight past his house, pretending to be just another motorist on the road. The property looked remarkably the same—big, well-kept, and vibrantly green. However, the cars parked up in the driveway were entirely unfamiliar to me.

The two schoolies noticed my intense focus on the yard and quickly became quiet, sensing the shift in tension. At the end of the road, I finally stopped the Toyota and turned to them, ready to share the thoughts racing through my mind.

"The two a oonuu come out here so and walk pass dah yard there, me will meet oonuu, up the road. Be oonuu self, but no over do it too much. Me father turn obeah man now, and a don't know what him truly can do," I instructed firmly yet gently. "Don't bother to do anything foolish right now, me up the road a wait."

"Awright," they both said enthusiastically, as they exited the car.

I watched them walked and played together like two energetic puppies, but deep down I knew they were the best observers the CPO could ever have in this situation. I looked closely as they passed the yard, then I drove up the road and patiently waited for them.

As I observed, I could see them starting to chase each other, their footsteps echoing loudly on the cemented sidewalk. Nathan playfully attempted to kick Troy in his backside, laughter filling the air.

I wish I had thought to tell them to keep it quiet, because I wasn't entirely sure if Marci was there or not. She knew the boys very well and would surely be keeping a close eye on their antics.

They jumped in the car, still playing for anyone who was watching, then they quieted down as we drove off.

"Two shiny SUVs and a sleek Mercedes Benz parked neatly in the yard. All of them looked impressively new, as if they had just rolled off the showroom floor, sparkling under the late afternoon sun." Troy reported with a hint of admiration in his voice.

"Chris, is your father rich or something?" Nathan stated, though it sounded more like a question, as if he was searching for confirmation.

"Oonuu hungry?" I asked, feeling the need to find a purpose for parking somewhere besides the side of the road.

"Me think you never did a guh ask," Troy replied, his tone dripping with sarcasm. It was evident that it was his dinnertime, and he was restless. "Just go into the drive-thru at KFC," he instructed decisively.

I did as I was told, my mind wandering to thoughts of Swofiyah. I couldn't help but wonder how she was doing and if she was managing alright.

"A who a look after Swofiyah?" I asked them, genuinely concerned.

"Blacka," Nathan answered matter-of-factly.

"The twin dem a go assist when dem finish cleaning up," Troy volunteered, as if this offered a reassuring solution.

I let out a deep sigh while placing my order at the drive-thru. They each seemed to know exactly what they wanted, their choices rolling off their tongues effortlessly. After we finished articulating our selections, I drove up to the cashier and handed the money to the friendly female at the window. As we waited patiently for about two minutes to collect our food and drinks, an air of anticipation filled the car. I then maneuvered into the parking lot where we settled in our seats to enjoy our meal.

In that moment, I found myself debating whether to go back to my father's house to see who the unexpected visitors might be, when Nathan suddenly leaned over, whispering with a mouth full of food, "A no the gal Marci that?"

"Which part?" Troy inquired, turning around to peer through the back windshield.

I had parked facing the street, deliberately positioning myself with my back towards the KFC. There was truly no pressing need for me to turn my entire body. Instead, I glanced through the side-view mirror, mimicking what Nathan was doing. Taking my time, I slowly chewed on my chicken breast while watching my father, who was strolling hand in hand with Marci. They were laughing together like young people completely smitten with love.

"A yuh father that?" Nathan asked, chomping down on his chicken leg, his eyes glued to the side-view mirror as if trying to capture every detail.

"Yea," I replied absentmindedly, still focusing on the man who had sired me into this world.

"Him look good. Him loose a few pounds and all a that," I remarked, noting the changes in him.

"No, a the obeah that him a work, taking the energy a the pickney them and all," Troy corrected, his tone suggesting he had some insight into the situation.

"Sounds like you know a lot about that shit," Nathan said, finally ungluing his eyes from the sideview mirror to take the last bite of his crispy chicken leg. "Make me find out," he continued, turning his attention toward Troy and playfully pointing the remaining piece of chicken at him with a grin.

Before Nathan even realized what was happening, Troy had snatched the chicken leg right out of his hand. With his mouth hanging wide open in disbelief, Nathan watched as Troy confidently sank his teeth into the succulent meat.

"Hmm, it's finger lickin' good," he declared, doing an exaggerated imitation of the advertisement with a laugh.

His antics were so hilarious that we all burst into laughter, unable to contain ourselves.

"Yuh raas yuh, yuh deserve that," I said to Nathan, who was now reaching for a piece of chicken wing, trying to regain his dignity.

I continued to gaze at the two lovebirds until they eventually disappeared into the KFC building. We sat there for what felt like another hour, enjoying our food and taking in the beautiful scene around us.

Eventually, I decided it was time to head back home, reminding myself that tomorrow was indeed another day filled with new possibilities

16. Marci

I eased out of the car park and onto the bustling manicure street of Constant Spring, one of the most beautiful area in Kingston and St. Andrews. Constant Spring boasted beautiful infrastructures with aesthetically pleasing designed houses. The streets and surrounding buildings were enveloped in lusciously manicure lawns and gardens, creating a rather developed community, comparable to many communities in developed countries around the world.

I wanted to see if the three cars were still parked up in the yard as I had seen before. As I passed by, I noted that there was only the luxurious Mercedes left.

I was utterly exhausted, both mentally and physically. I needed to rethink a much safer course of action moving forward. I craved answers, yet I wasn't going to be stupid about it and put myself in further danger.

The two schoolies had been around me long enough to recognize my habits and patterns by now. We drove in a heavy silence until we finally reached the stadium.

"What's the instruction?" Nathan asked, curiously glancing over at the brightly lit stadium.

There was an exciting football match going on inside, and I could hear the distant cheers of the crowd. The car parks surrounding the stadium were packed to the brim with enthusiastic fans. I was supposed to be at that match tonight, enjoying the game, but we had far more important things to deal with at the moment. I sighed deeply, slowing down to let pedestrians cross the street safely.

It was after nine o'clock now. It was enough time for them to get some much-needed sleep before they would need to go on the second watch.

"You already know the drill. Keep a close eye out for Marci. I have a need to talk to her," I said, speaking quietly to my passengers.

Less than twenty minutes later, I turned onto the lively streets of Bower Bank Community. The atmosphere was blazing with vibrant reggae music, filling the air with a sense of rhythm and life. There was an unmistakable air of festiveness and soaring expectations that seemed to wrap around everyone present.

The marketplace beside the community was absolutely alive with activities. Mama's dream was still progressing beautifully, drawing in a crowd. Parked cars lined Windward Road, stretching from the bustling intersection of Dunoon Road all the way to Camperdown Road. The people had come out in droves to patronize the vibrant market.

At the entrance of Bower Bank, the area was packed with people enjoying the lively scene. Some were eating delicious jerk chicken and festival, wrapped up in shiny foil papers, while others formed long lines in front of sizzling jerk chicken grills, eagerly waiting to buy mouthwatering jerk chicken and pork.

The men and women standing proudly in front of their jerk chicken grills were energetically turning over their expertly portioned chickens while joyfully dancing to the infectious beat of the lively music filling the air. Plumes of the delicious, mouthwatering aroma of perfectly seasoned jerk chicken and savory pork smoke wafted from the many grills, rising in graceful spirals toward the heavens above.

As I nodded my head, taking a moment to observe our community striving to rise from the overwhelming sadness of Mama's recent passing, the weight of my responsibility felt even more palpable and significant than before.

It was during that reflective moment, as I slowed down to truly look at my surroundings and my community, that I came to understand I had no need to fear my responsibility. It was, in fact, all of our responsibility to ensure that our beloved community remained taken care of and be united. I realized I was not alone in this task; we were all in this together, united in purpose.

The uplifting music and laughter that greeted us served as a heartwarming assurance that my family was right here with me, and I truly wasn't alone in this journey. I nodded my head to myself, silently accepting my mother's heartfelt wishes. The burden I had been carrying around since her death began to finally lift, fading away like shadows before the dawn.

"Yes, these wonderful people were my extended family, and we are going to be alright," I thought, nodding my head to myself once more. "Yes, indeed, we are going to be just fine."

A genuine smile broke across my face, one that felt real for the first time in what seemed like ages, and I felt lighter and brighter.

"Yep," Nathan said, his tone filled with quiet confidence.

"Hmm, hmm," Troy echoed him, as if they both understood the unspoken thoughts swirling through my head.

I parked the Honda carefully across the street from the bustling jerk chicken stands, taking a moment to gather my thoughts. We got out and mingled with the lively family, exchanging smiles and laughter as the enticing aroma of food filled the air around us.

~~~~~~

The knock on my door came abruptly at five the next morning, piercing through the stillness of the early hour. The music had finally died down around four, leaving behind a suffocating and almost oppressive silence that felt both familiar and unsettling. It was a condition I had come to accept as routine since the bustling marketplace went into operation, transforming my once peaceful surroundings into a cacophony of sounds.

The night before, I had deliberately left the schoolies and the rest of my family just around eleven, with clear instructions for one of them to wake me the moment they spotted Marci. I was utterly exhausted, needing every moment of sleep I could grasp. After taking a moment to check in on Swofiyah and the watchers to ensure they were doing alright, I went straight to bed, giving in to the sweet embrace of peaceful slumber.

When I finally got up, I felt surprisingly rested, even lighter in spirit. I suppose coming to terms with one's lot in life could have that effect on a person. I was in the process of putting on a comfortable pair of khaki pants and a clean white T-shirt when the persistent knock came again, louder this time.

I was acutely aware that all the Community Protection Officers, including myself, were on high alert following recent events. I had specifically cautioned those few who were aware of the situation to keep everything discreet and under wraps. However, one could never be too cautious or too trusting, especially in times like these. I was uncertain of my father's true capabilities or how many people he had strategically placed here to work on his behalf.

I glanced into the mirror I had propped in the window, my makeshift camera allowing me a glimpse of the outside. There stood Troy at the door, looking increasingly impatient. Recognizing the urgency of the moment, I quickly slid on my sandals and opened the door to him, ready to face whatever awaited me.

"A wha a gwon?" I asked with curiosity.

"Marci is on her way here; she's coming with Nathan," he stated matter-of-factly. Marci had moved into the community nearly three years ago. She didn't have any family nearby, except for the boyfriend she had chosen to live with. He was a fisherman, a man who, ironically, they claimed, couldn't swim, and sadly, he tragically drowned at sea. After his untimely death, Marci became more reserved and kept to herself. She was a hard-working individual who would leave for her job in the late evening hours and return home just as dawn broke. She eventually became a vital member of the Community Protection Organization, due to her generous contributions to the Community Funds, something we all eagerly anticipated. We never truly questioned her motives, nor did we doubt her loyalty.

Although Marci wasn't particularly one for a lot of socializing, we understood her introverted nature and made every effort to include her in as many activities as possible. Some people believed she chose to work nights because she simply couldn't bear the thought of being alone during those quiet, dark hours. Yet, we never really questioned it.

The morning was getting lighter as the sun slowly rose above the horizon, illuminating Mama bananas and other vegetables that were thriving beautifully. I was keeping a close eye on them. Occasionally, whenever my schedule became too hectic, someone would kindly come over to sweep the yard and clean the toilet and shower stalls. I never questioned who it was, though I must admit I had my suspicions.

"Yuh drink tea yet?" I casually asked Troy, hoping to share a moment of camaraderie.

"No, not yet," he answered.

I made my way into the kitchen to place three neatly sealed packets of Double Cup coffee into the coffeepot, ensuring I added the adequate amount of water for boiling. I prepared four steaming cups, the rich aroma of coffee mingling in the air, a familiar scent that had been a cherished morning ritual of Mama's, and which now had seamlessly transformed into mine. I pulled out two sturdy stools from under the adjacent counter and handed one over to Troy. We both settled into our seats, enveloped in a thick silence, simply waiting for whatever might come next.

At that moment, both of us instinctively looked up as Marci turned the corner, followed closely by Nathan. The comforting sound of coffee boiling had me rushing back into the kitchen, causing me to miss the expression on Marci's face altogether. I hurriedly finished preparing the coffee and handed everyone a hot cup, making sure to include Marci as well. I led them inside the house, aware that it was still far too early for any sort of confrontation. We gathered around my mother's dining table, quietly sipping our coffee as the silence hung heavily in the air.

"So, you and me father a grine?" I asked conversationally, after my cup had reach halfway fill and my thought had been gathered.

I took another sip of the steaming coffee and watched intently as she choked slightly on her drink, struggling to recover her composure. She was around seven years older than I was, standing tall and dark, with striking brown eyes that seemed to hold a depth of emotions. We used to call them cat eyes because of their captivating allure. I had liked her from the very first moment we had met, but she had, unfortunately, pretended not to notice my interest at all. Now, with a heavy heart, I realized why that had been the case.

"The two a oonuu look good together," I continued, trying to ease the tension that hung in the air. "How him a do these days? A long time me no talk to him."

"Him a do awright," she answered, still sipping on her coffee, the steam rising around her, as if wrapping her in a protective veil.

"So how long yuh a work for him?" I asked, genuinely curious.

"Around eleven years now," she replied, her tone hinting at the weight of their shared history.

"A long time that," Nathan cut in, breaking into our conversation with a casual remark. "Yuh never know a him father?"

"Yea, I was there when him shoot him father in a him leg," she answered, her voice steady but low.

That surprised me greatly. "Really?" I asked, incredulous.

"Yea, yuh mother catch the two a we in a bed. Him stone drunk and me a try to sober him up. She tell him she want a divorce and him just loose it and start to beat her up. I was in his bathroom when yuh come. Me see when yuh shoot him in a him foot," she finished, shrugging her shoulders nonchalantly, still sipping from her drink as if it were just another day.

"With all a that, how come yuh end up here so? Cause yuh obviously know who them was," Troy said, calmer than he was earlier, trying to piece together the story.

"Yuh father send me. Yuh know how he is," she stated, shrugging again as if it were all perfectly normal.

"So what was your purpose here?" I asked her, putting down my empty cup, curiosity getting the better of me.

"It take yuh father many long years to recover fully, after yuh mother take all a yuh and just left him like that. Him learn a here so oonuu is, so him send me. I used Tony for assistance, but him eventually discover me true motive; yuh father send man and the rest a history," she finished with a hint of finality.

"No, a no history yet, what is your true purpose here?" Nathan asked, feeling not quite satisfied with her answer. "What exactly yuh doing here now?"

"Just watching and reporting everything back, that's all," she said, maintaining her calm demeanor.

"No, yuh forget to mention the recruiting part tuh," Troy clarified, his tone more serious.

"Your father purpose was to get rid a yuh mother entirely. Him want yuh back on his team, desperately. Him see yuh potential shining bright and him really want yuh to join him. But yuh mother would never allow that, so him instructed King to…," she finished with an air of inevitability.

"So this a your day job, then?" Nathan asked, intrigued by the revelation.

"Day job, night job, call it what yuh will. I am exactly what yuh father want me to be," she said firmly, locking her gaze with mine, her expression void of any regrets.

"Whole soul devotion eee? A what him a give yuh so?" Nathan asked, a mix of curiosity and disbelief in his voice.

I got up, carefully taking the coffee cups off the table, the warmth still lingering in my hands. I looked at Troy and nodded my head in silent communication, then said to Nathan with a sense of urgency, "Go call the twin them. We have important things to do."

Nathan got up without hesitation and left to go fetch the twins. I took the opportunity to head to the kitchen and put the coffee cups away, leaving Troy alone with Marci.

When I returned Marci had a punctured wound in her chest, her body slumping dangerously backwards in her chair. I looked at her, trying to hide my shock while contemplating all the years she spent pretending to be an introvert, shielding herself from forming any real attachments, when she was actually here to do a job—a job she had always excelled at. I searched for any hint of regret within myself as I examined her dead corpse, and found none.

"This one for Mama," I said softly, looking up at Troy, feeling the weight of our circumstances settle around us.

"No, this one for all of us," he replied with a resolute tone, emphasizing the collective loss we now shared.

~~~~~

The sun was bright and fully up, while the roosters had finally stopped their early morning crowing. The expansive morning blue sky clearly indicated that it was going to be an exceptionally hot and completely cloudless day. Already, music was blaring loudly throughout the bustling market, and people were eagerly preparing for business.

A wheelbarrow rolled noisily up the road, its sound mingling with the sound of the morning, signaling to the twins nearby.

"That raas wheelbarrow only make noise when it a go pick up dead body," Troy murmured under his breath, a hint of unease in his voice.

I didn't respond to him, as my thoughts were already drifting toward my father and Wayne. If I knew my father well, which I did, I was certain that his little army must have grown significantly by now. The few men that the police had picked up at the church couldn't possibly be the entire group. I was sure there were many more hidden away, but the question remained: where could they be?

As a teenager, I was acutely aware that he was involved in many illegal activities and operations. These were the kinds of things that Mama didn't want us to know about or even be exposed to. Yet, despite this dark undercurrent, he was already guiding me, teaching me how to be smart about making money and how to effectively run the family business.

This was the greatest fear that Mama harbored deep within her heart. She desperately did not want us to be entwined within that corrupt industry. Aside from the beatings, it was the only other reason she had for wanting us to escape from under his oppressive roof.

I loved him with all my heart, but I didn't want to become like him. He was a cold, emotionless, and evil presence in my life. The day I pulled the trigger and shot him was the day I faced the harsh truth and discovered the emotional similarities that existed between us. That profound realization is why I didn't voice any objections when she meticulously packed our belongings the following day and decisively left.

17. Dead Wayne

I left the cleaners and their noisy chattering behind me and went in search of Swofiyah. When I found her, she was alone, absorbed in the task of cleaning the house.

"Where is yuh mother?" I asked her, trying to engage her in conversation.

"She gone a market," she replied, her voice heavy with the same downcast tone that had become all too familiar.

"What wrong with you?" I inquired, noticing the sadness etched on her face.

"Me just a think bout me tiefing mother. She take all a me likkle money and a use it up, now me no have nothing," she confessed, her words echoing with the weight of someone much older, someone burdened by responsibilities far too great for her young shoulders.

"Well, you just have to figure out a way to make back all of that money and more. But you too young to be worrying yuhself bout that kind of thing right now. Just focus on your lessons in school and how to be a child. I know you a go through a lot, but one day all of this will be a distant memory," I counselled her gently, hoping to ease some of the heaviness in her heart.

"Okay," she said softly, her voice trembling as silent tears trickle down her face, leaving glistening trails on her flushed cheeks, which were puffed out in a way that made her look even more vulnerable.

"You eat breakfast yet?" I asked her gently, standing up and surveying the large room filled with memories, intentionally avoiding the heaviness of the moment.

"Yea, me make callaloo and bread, with tea," she replied, her tone surprisingly mature, almost like a grown-up, instead of reflecting the innocence of the little girl she truly was.

"Okay, just make sure you lock up the door when you are inside a clean, alright? You want me to bring you back some Burger King later?" I offered, fully aware of how much she adored it.

Her face instantly brightened up, and I couldn't help but chuckle. In that moment, she transformed back into the joyful child she was meant to be.

"Yes, and don't forget the fries and the docta peppa," she insisted eagerly, her excitement almost contagious.

"Awright, I won't forget," I assured her, chuckling softly as I turned to leave her.

I glanced around, noticing Betty's two oldest sons engaged in a game that resembled marbles, but the truth was, they were really keeping a watchful eye on everything. Today, they were the designated guardians of the house. The oldest boy had a sense of responsibility that reassured me, so I knew she was in safe hands for the moment. My focus, however, was on my father, a task that loomed over me as the only goal I had set for myself that day. With determination, I walked towards the car, spotting Nathan and Troy waiting for me. I didn't want to involve them in whatever confrontation lay ahead, as I was uncertain how things would unfold.

"Oonuu go get some rest," I instructed them gently as I approached the vehicle, wanting them to be well-prepared for whatever might come next.

"Don't worry, Fada Chris, we get enuff rest already," Nathan shot back, trying to lighten the mood with his cheeky response.

I should have been more forceful, but the truth was, I needed the reinforcements. I didn't say anything else. I opened the door and allowed them in the car. I check to see how much gas was in the tank as I got in. It was enough to take me to Constant Spring Road and back. I buckled up with one hand, and started the engine with the other hand, reversing. All of these I did without thinking. Driving had become automatic to me.

I was diligently memorizing every detail of my community as I turned, carefully looking for anything that seemed out of place or unusual. All the watchers were strategically stationed throughout the area. Some were sitting casually in front of their yards, selling vibrant baskets filled with fresh fruits. Others were animatedly playing marbles, while some seemed to be merely pretending to hang out, engaging in light conversation. They were all vigilantly looking out for any strange faces or any unusual activities that might disrupt the peace.

Bower Bank was exceptionally lively at that moment. More watchers were standing around, feigning to be time wasters, but their eyes were sharp and watchful. A few of the men from the community were already enjoying cold beers and smoking, adding to the atmosphere. The music was loud and lively, creating a vibrant backdrop as the community market teemed with people eagerly buying and selling an array of goods.

A community that recognizes the crucial need to work together in harmony to ensure mutual growth is a community that will undoubtedly strive and overcome, no matter what the circumstances may be. Bower Bank Community was a place that had only just begun to accept the transformative idea of togetherness and collaboration in oneness, with the aspiration to see that everyone can overcome the persistent poverty we couldn't seem to shake off. It was a young concept—a foreign thought to some members, yet one filled with potential for a brighter future.

Because of the newness of this challenging endeavor, combined with the lack of complete trust and confidence in one another, I wasn't entirely sure how things would ultimately turn out if—God forbid —something should ever happen to me in the future. It was with these unsettling thoughts in mind that I made the decision to turn right onto Windward Road, where everything began to unfold in slow motion, as if time itself was stretching. The top of Bower Bank was lined off with a multitude of cars, creating a daunting barrier. Windward Road presented a similar scene; I observed that vehicles were parked on both sides, effectively blocking the view of Holy Rosary Road, which was also densely packed with parked cars, enhancing the already tense atmosphere.

As I turned onto Windward Road, I noticed the large, imposing garbage truck idling on Holy Rosary Road, waiting patiently. It did not have its indicator lights on, which seemed a bit odd given the circumstances. I navigated my vehicle to the right on

Windward Road when, all of a sudden, the garbage truck's indicator flashed to life, signaling that the driver intended to make a left turn. At this intersection, there were no stoplights to regulate traffic, and since I was already well into the turn, I believed I had the right of way. Just as I approached the bus stop, which was less than a hundred feet away from the bustling community market, the garbage truck swiftly changed its course. It then picked up speed in a manner that immediately set off alarm bells in my head.

Nathan shouted, "What the bloodclaat wrong with this driver?"

I could feel the palpable danger we found ourselves in. The garbage truck appeared to be new, sporting sleek, tinted windows that obscured the driver's face from my view. Despite not being able to see the driver, a gut feeling washed over me, telling me that the situation was dire. With barely any space to maneuver due to the parked cars lining the street, I was forced to proceed at a cautious pace. However, the garbage truck seemed to have no such intentions. It executed the turn with alarming speed, and for a brief moment, I thought it might actually overturn. Its objective, as it became painfully clear, was to drive directly into my vehicle, a realization that struck me way too late. Before I could react appropriately, the truck collided straight into me with a shuddering impact.

"A what do this madma…" Troy shouted, but he was abruptly cut off in mid-sentence as the massive garbage truck collided forcefully with our car's side, head-on. The deafening cacophony of metal striking metal and glass shattering filled the air around us, an overwhelming sound that drowned out all other noises. The truck momentarily reversed, creating a brief moment of hope, before it sped back towards us with relentless determination. It didn't hesitate for even a second; it rammed right into us with such furious vengeance that I could only think of one person I knew who would harbor such intense hatred for us. The garbage truck forced my car violently into the parked vehicles surrounding us, while I desperately tried to slam on the gas in an effort to escape its merciless grip, but I was trapped—the other cars were effectively blocking my movement.

The enormous truck came to a stop before backing up yet again. I watched helplessly as it reversed, but I was rendered immobile by the situation. The car door, which I was frantically trying to open, remained stubbornly stuck, refusing to budge.

"Oonuu come out a the car!" I shouted at the two schoolies who were still inside, but panic had rendered my voice almost inaudible, as if the words were caught in my throat. "Nathan, come out a the car!" I cried out once more, and I could see Nathan struggling to open his side of the door, but with the parked cars surrounding us like a menacing barrier, escape was proving impossible.

"Troy, come out of the car!" I hollered, my voice carrying a sense of urgency. No answer came, just an unsettling silence that filled the air. I was trying to move, but I couldn't. A jagged piece of metal from the door jam was painfully lodged into my side, preventing any attempt at escape.

"Oye, Troy, come out of the car!" I shouted again, my desperation growing with each passing second. Still, no response emerged from the wreckage.

Nathan was desperately trying to force the door open, but despite his best efforts, he was met with stubborn resistance. I attempted to slam my foot down on the gas pedal in a frantic effort to get the vehicle to move, but it refused to budge. In front of me, I found myself stuck halfway between a mangled car and the cold, unforgiving street. Behind me, another car sealed me in, trapping me further. Nathan continued to struggle with the door, frustration etched on his face.

"Nathan, climb over the back seat and see if Troy is alright," I instructed him, hoping he would find a way to check on our friend.

I watched intently in the rearview mirror as he climbed into the back seat to check on Troy, who was lying there in distress. He placed the back of his hands gently against Troy's nose in an attempt to feel if he was still breathing, then he glanced at me through the rearview mirror and nodded his head in a way that suggested Troy was still with us. I released a deep breath, feeling a rush of relief.

"Okay now, try the back door," I instructed urgently as I noticed there was just enough space for the door to open. "Hurry up!" I added, my voice edged with desperation.

I was watching the driver's side of the garbage truck closely through my side mirror, and I saw the door swing open. To my shock, I saw Wayne emerging, clutching an M16 Automatic rifle firmly in his right hand.

"This will have to end today," I thought resolutely as my fingers reached for my small handgun, my heart racing in my chest.

People were now rushing toward us, and I heard distant screaming echoing in the chaos, but my singular focus remained on Wayne, the imminent threat before us.

The cowardly excuse of a man paused just out of my range, then began indiscriminately shooting up the car in a desperate attempt to intimidate us.

"Bloodclaat! Me no tell yuh to leave me son alone?" I distinctly heard my father shout with fierce determination as he began to blaze up Wayne with unyielding ferocity. Suddenly, a wave of exhaustion washed over me, and an icy chill seeped into my bones. I could feel my entire body trembling violently and uncontrollably, as if I were caught in a raging ice storm. I couldn't find a way to stop the shaking that enveloped me.

"Chris!" Nathan yelled, panic evident in his voice. "Chris!" He sounded like he was calling from an immense distance, each syllable stretching further away. I desperately wished I could have answered him, but all I could feel was my body floating away from reality. My last thought, fleeting yet profound, was of Swofiyah. "A who a guh look after her now?" Then, without warning, everything faded into an impenetrable blackness.

18. Nathan

Never having a mother of my own, I had taken Norma for my own the very moment she had moved into Bower Bank, when I was just six years old. I was an unkempt scrawny little boy with an absentee father who seemed to care little for my wellbeing. I ate only when there was food available, and resorted to stealing when I was desperately hungry. One fateful day, I found myself in her kitchen, secretly stealing the leftover food she had reserved for breakfast the following morning, when she unexpectedly caught me in the act.

"Yuh likkle raas, a yuh a the rat that taking me food?" she exclaimed, her voice a mix of surprise and indignation. Instead of giving me a harsh beating like the other adults would have done, she took pity on me and sat me down on the wobbly stool in the corner of the kitchen. After warming up some of the food, she kindly dished out a generous portion for me, showing an unexpected kindness.

"Weh yuh name?" she asked, her tone softening as she began to realize I was just a hungry child in need of compassion.

"Nathan," I had answered shyly, my voice barely above a whisper, while eating as if it were my first meal of the week, ravenous with hunger.

"Where is yuh mother, Nathan?"

"She dead." Even though I still didn't fully understand what death meant in its entirety, I instinctively knew it meant she would never come back home to me. It had been over a year now without her warmth and presence.

"So a who a take care a yuh?"

"Me fada, but me no see 'im." I was eating so fast, chop-chop, my mouth devouring the food like a pig at a trough. She didn't say anything in that moment, simply looking at me with an expression that suggested she was deep in thought.

"When yuh need something to eat, just come ask me for it."

It was at that moment I had completely fallen in love with her. She was the mother I had never truly known or experienced in my life. Chris became the older brother I had always longed for, someone to look up to and share my thoughts with. I loved them with every ounce of passion and affection I had within me. I began to call her Mama, just like the other kids did, and I made myself readily available for whenever she needed something to be done—which honestly, wasn't much at all. I took it upon myself to regularly sweep her yard whenever she wasn't around, and I made sure to empty the garbage whenever the garbage truck came rumbling down our street. She kept me clean, ensuring I was well-fed, and always saw to it that I went to school without fail. In school, I poured my heart and soul into my studies—just for her. I wanted to make her proud and didn't want to disappoint her, so I studied diligently, pushing myself to become the head of my class, yearning for her approval.

When I had discovered there was a secret organization, it was on the very day she had told me about it that everything changed for me. In her gentle yet intrigued tone, she wanted to know if I was interested in becoming a part of something bigger than myself. I still remembered that day so vividly, as if it had happened just yesterday.

"Nathan, how old yuh is now?"

"Twelve, Mama."

"Yuh ole enuff to start training."

"Me a train to play football at school, Mama."

"Not that kind a training me a talk. I'm talking about the kind of training that's meant to protect the community. You like the community, Nathan?" She had asked me this while looking deeply into my eyes as if she was searching for something within my very soul.

"Mama, anywhere yuh and Chris is me love." I had told her seriously, holding her gaze with sincerity and conviction.

"Awright, yuh start training tomorrow."

And that was it. I had officially become a part of the secret organization, marking my first ever serious commitment to something larger than myself. Football, on the other hand, was my second love. I trained relentlessly, pushing myself to be the best player I could possibly be, and I genuinely loved every minute of it. Along the way, I discovered a few unexpected friends who shared the same passion, and their camaraderie truly gladdened my heart in ways I hadn't anticipated.

However, when Mama died, I was struck by the harsh reality of what death truly meant. It felt as though I died alongside her that fateful day, even though I had to keep it together for the sake of Chris. We both knew we had to remain strong to ensure the organization continued to thrive despite the turmoil surrounding us.

I'd like to think that Chris relied on me to stay strong during such a tumultuous time. So, I made the conscious choice to remain resilient, drawing my strength from a love that I felt for my brother.

~~~~~~

The moment I saw Crotchless Wayne emerging from the garbage truck while wielding the M16 Automatic, a chilling feeling washed over me, and I instinctively knew it was the end for us. After he backed up the truck with haste, I was frantically trying to open the door, my heart racing as all I could think about was getting Chris out safely. But the raasclaat door obstinately refuse to budge, and just as panic began to set in, I contemplated rushing to the back door to get it open. Suddenly, he yelled at me, demanding I check on Troy.

As quickly as I could muster the strength, I hurried over to Troy and felt a wave of relief wash over me when I delicately placed the back of my hand to his nose and sensed the reassuring rhythm of his breath. I nodded to Chris through the rearview mirror, silently indicating that Troy was still clinging to life. With urgency, I moved to open the back door. It creaked ajar, but there was only a narrow space available to squeeze through. I forced my way out, adrenaline pumping, and then dragged Troy out after me, determined to ensure his safety.

Outside the car, I heard the deafening sound of Wayne's M16 Automatic gunfire, relentless and blazing. Troy was on the ground, still unconscious and completely unaware of the chaos unfolding around him. I stood there, paralyzed and frozen with shock, as I observed Chris valiantly taking every shot Wayne unleashed in his direction. Then, almost instinctively, my brain kicked into automatic mode. I swiftly reached for the handguns that I had tucked securely into my back pants and began firing at Wayne. My aim, unfortunately, was thrown off and I couldn't achieve a proper hit; he was standing just outside of my effective range. Desperate for a better shot, I crawled on my belly, trying to get into a position where I could take aim at him more effectively. As I repositioned, I saw Chris' father emerging from behind the brand new garbage truck, aiming his own M16 Automatic directly at Wayne.

"Bloodclaat, me no tell yuh to leave me son alone?" he shouted, firing his weapon with fierce determination at Wayne. It was as if Wayne was paralyzed with fear, unable to retaliate against his obeah-working boss. He took every bullet aimed at him until he finally fell to the ground in the middle of Windward Road. His body shook violently for a moment before it ultimately lay still.

From my vantage point, I had a clear view of Chris' father, so I took aim, knowing that I only had this one chance. I understood the gravity of the moment and knew I had to make it count. Just as I pulled the trigger, he unexpectedly turned and looked me directly in the eyes. My heart raced as I watched the bullet travel straight between his eyes, witnessing him crumble to the ground, dropping the M16 Automatic from his grasp.

"That's for bloodclaat Mama," I said aloud, my voice barely above a whisper, but filled with an overwhelming mix of satisfaction and resolve.

I got to my feet and ran desperately to Chris. So did the others around me, who were frantically dodging bullets and watching with wide eyes as chaos unfolded. The market, once vibrant and bustling, was completely forgotten in the moment, as the sellers spilled out into the street in a panic-stricken frenzy.

I frantically tried to open Chris' side of the door, but the damn thing wouldn't budge, no matter how hard I pushed. Tears streamed down my face, though I was unaware of them at the time. I put every ounce of strength I could muster into it, hoping against hope to get it to open, but nothing happened—not even the tiniest squeak or creak to signal progress.

Suddenly, somebody appeared at my side, and together we both tried our best to force the stubborn door open. With effort, it eventually budged a little, just enough to give us a glimmer of hope.

Mark, Chris' mechanic, rushed over with a battery-powered metal saw in his hands, and without hesitation, he began cutting into the door with precision.

I knew, deep down, that we were late. I understood all too well that we would never have gotten to him in time, but still, I clung to a faint hope that he would be inside there somewhere—just a little longer. But when we finally pulled out his lifeless body, all that remained was just an empty, unfeeling corpse.

The profound emptiness that washed over me was unlike anything I had ever experienced in my life. At that moment, I felt as if I had nothing left to live for. He had been the one keeping me going, the one offering me hope, right after Mama's passing. Overwhelmed by a surge of rage and despair, I wanted to shoot something, anything, to release the pent-up fury inside me. I pulled out my gun and moved over to the two lifeless bodies on the ground, feeling an almost primal need to fire at them again and again. It was then, through the haze of my anger, that I caught sight of the Army squad approaching. Before I could react further, a sharp, stinging pain pierced my chest, and I found myself hitting the ground, the weight of my despair crashing down with me.

19. The Return Of My Sisters

The death of Chris was an overwhelming burden that I found hard to bear. I spiraled deeply into myself, withdrawing from the world around me. I was already a naturally silent person, so my mother, perhaps oblivious to my emotional devastation, didn't seem to notice the pain I was enduring. Or maybe she did see it but simply chose to ignore it. She continued to spend my money freely, unaware of its true source. In her mind, she still believed that the money belonged to Crotchless Wayne, and that thought gave her a sense of comfort.

As time passed, I stopped purchasing chickens and slaughtering them for practice. The few that remained had slowly dwindled down to a mere twenty-four. I tended to their needs, feeding them daily, but ultimately left them to their own devices; it was a small solace amidst my grief. In an effort to escape the heaviness that surrounded me, I began going to church early on Sunday mornings and found myself staying until the late evenings. If Janet ever desired a chicken to cook, she would have to go out and kill it herself, as I no longer felt the drive to do so.

My once beautiful garden, once vibrant and full of life, was now reduced to dry, cracked ground with the occasional stubborn weed pushing through its barren surface. When it rains, small families of see-through, mushroom-like fungi would suddenly shoot up from the earth, and I would delight in playing with them, imagining they were tiny, exquisite houses for little fairies who would come out to dance beneath the moonlight. However, when the sun emerged from behind the clouds and dried the ground, all traces of the see-through mushroom-like fungi would vanish almost magically, leaving my already disheartened garden feeling even sadder and more desolated than before.

I stopped the habit of climbing people's mango trees and picking their ripe, juicy mangoes to sell and make a small profit. Someone, who happened to know my mother quite well, whispered to her that I was stealing their mangoes off their trees. Upon hearing this, she came home in a furious rage and gave me a beating so severe that it resulted in a broken left hand, painful baton stick slashes across my back, and swollen cheeks from the vicious slaps she administered, leaving me both physically hurt and emotionally devastated.

I stopped picking tamarind for the purpose of stewing and creating delicious tamarind balls to sell to both my schoolmates and the community children.

Even though I was diligently keeping my promises to Chris, the other students were still fearful of me. I no longer carried my trusty cutlass with me to school, and I had significantly toned down on the fighting that used to define my reputation. I found myself only getting into trouble due to the actions of my brothers and sister, which complicated my efforts to maintain a more peaceful existence.

~~~~~~

Some students had started bullying Klam mercilessly. They cruelly called her stupid and ugly, words that cut deeply and left their mark. Klam, feeling the weight of their cruelty, stopped playing dandy-shandy during lunchtime and instead chose to hide herself away, avoiding the harsh stares and laughter from the other children. She had unfortunately become the outcast, forced into isolation because of their relentless bullying.

One day, I left the classroom under the pretense of needing to use the bathroom when I happened upon a shocking scene. I discovered a group of five girls, their faces twisted with malice, beating Klam up behind the girls' bathroom, completely oblivious to the injustice of their actions. Fueled by anger and a desire to protect her, I picked up a sturdy piece of tree limb that was carelessly lying around and pointed it threateningly in their direction.

They had heard the rumors about the boy I had confronted in class with my little cutlass, so they knew I was not one to back down or shy away from using the tree limb if necessary.

"A who for sister oonuu a beat up so?" I challenged them, my voice strong and unwavering, as I pointed the tree limb at them while placing my left hand defiantly on my hip.

I was fully prepared to start hitting back, but just as they sensed my readiness, they took off running away in a hurry. Frustrated, I threw the tree limb behind the pipe stand and quickly rushed over to my crying sister. She was diligently wiping away the tears that were streaming down her face, and I gently helped her by using my hands to wipe them away.

"Don't cry, Klam," I said softly, though the tears continued to fall more profusely down her cheeks as if they were uncontrollable. "If them trouble you again, just come and call me," I assured her, trying very hard to resist the urge to retrieve the tree limb and go chasing after those little wretches.

She nodded her head in response, gradually calming down as I spoke. Just then, the loud lunch bell rang, and she made the decision to stay with me for the remainder of the lunch period. We made our way to our usual spot, patiently waiting for my brothers to show up. I knew that Deidre wouldn't be joining us; she didn't want to be seen with us under any circumstances.

After the unfortunate incident with Klam, it seemed that more students began to show a genuine interest in befriending her. From that moment on, I took it upon myself to keep a watchful eye on her after realizing how poorly the other kids had really been treating her.

~~~~~

Two months later, my class was fortunate enough to receive the exciting opportunity to play netball. The dedicated physical education teacher made the decision to start a netball team, much to our delight. As a direct result of this decision, our physical education classes transformed into a series of enthusiastic netball tryouts. I was thrilled to be considered skilled enough to begin practicing alongside thirteen other talented girls. There were seven girls selected for the junior team and seven for the senior team, making the competition quite spirited.

We trained diligently every day after school, pouring our energy into each session. The constant practice under the harsh sun not only honed my skills but also made my body stronger and more resilient. The painful sores on my skin were finally beginning to heal, thanks to the sweating and the rigorous exercises I was experiencing. However, I noticed they were, unfortunately, leaving behind dark scars all over my body. With the relentless running, jumping in the sun, my skin gradually took on a hue that matched the color of those scars. I began to feel less conscious about their presence, and I also stopped worrying excessively about the new scars that would inevitably appear on my skin.

In this newfound routine, I discovered a much-needed escape from the chaos of home life. Often, I would return home late after training sessions, bracing myself for a possible beating, but to my surprise, when I stepped through the door, Janet would be gone. This unexpected reprieve allowed me to hurriedly bathe, tackle my homework with focus, and find something to eat from the kitchen before she arrived home.

Most of the times, however, it wouldn't really matter; she would wander out and stay gone until well after one into the late night. When she finally returned home, she would stumble through the door drunk and reeking of ganja, which had unfortunately become her ever-present and permanent eau de perfume.

Things changed dramatically in the community, as well. Aunty Norma and her son had long served as the steadfast pillars of the Community Protector Organization, providing guidance and support. After their untimely deaths, the vital ideas and values that the community had once adopted with enthusiasm and pride sadly died with them.

Soon, the CPO disintegrated into a mere shell of its former self. The people, feeling lost and disheartened, withdrew their money from the secret bank that had once been a lifeline. The once dedicated volunteer teachers stopped coming to help the children, while the nurses and dentists decided it was best to move their clinics to more stable areas. Even the essential computers from the community computer lab and the precious solar panels were stolen, further compounding the devastation. The community reverted to stealing electricity in the desperate to keep their homes illuminated.

The high school graduates who had dreams of attending college for interior design and architecture found themselves forced to drop out of school due to a dire lack of funding. It quickly became unsafe for the children to go to the protective shelters where they could once rely on doing their homework while enjoying a nutritious meal. They were left vulnerable and without support.

The Sunday school teachers were still coming, and that was truly a blessing for the children who looked forward to their guidance and support. The library van continued to arrive like clockwork, every Saturday morning at eleven o'clock sharp, bringing with it a world of imagination and adventure. I was still eagerly borrowing books, losing myself in their pages. I had become an addict to reading, and it quickly became my biggest escape from the harshness of reality.

Bower Bank was no longer the thriving community with excellent potential that it once promised to be. Instead, it reverted back to being just another poor, struggling community that depended heavily on the government for its very survival. The market that was initially built for the benefit of the community had now been taken over by anyone who had something to sell, and it was disheartening to see mainly outsiders stepping in to dominate what was once ours.

I no longer had to worry anymore about the numerous dangers presented to me by the infamous Crotchless Wayne and his sinister obeah working posse. The individuals who were fully aware that he was ruthlessly after my demise were secretly hunted down and eliminated by Troy, alongside a few other remnants of the once-feared CPO. Although it was no longer the tight-knit community that my beloved aunt had envisioned and dreamed of, it still managed to remain protected from the outsiders whose sole desire was to do us significant harm.

Unfortunately, my bed-wetting had returned with a vengeance. It didn't matter how hard I tried to stop pissing the bed; the moment my head hit that pillow, I was consistently wetting the sheets. Each morning, I had to put the damp sheets and soggy bedding outside to dry before leaving for school, hoping they would be ready by the time I returned. Sometimes, I would come home to find the sheets tragically wet and the sponge soaked. The rain had fallen heavily, and Janet wasn't home to take them in for me. When that unfortunate situation happened, I would reluctantly sleep on the floor, using whatever sheets I was allowed to use, which were typically the spare ones. I couldn't dare to use the sheets she used for her own bed, as that was not an option.

~~~~~~

Life continued, unfolding in its relentless manner. Finally, the money that Janet had stolen was entirely gone, evaporating like mist in the morning sun. The chickens I had been raising for chopping practices were all finished. Janet had used them for our Sunday dinners. Sometimes, she would even exchange one or two chickens for a role of ganja, ensuring that she never went without her vices. The empty chicken coop now stood as the only stark reminder of what was once there, echoing the silence that had replaced the bustling sounds of life.

With Christmas rapidly approaching, the atmosphere grew tenser. Janet had gone back to her routine of cleaning and washing to make ends meet. With the garden no longer flourishing and the chickens all gone, I found myself devoid of any contributions towards our meager food supply, which consequently led to more frequent and harsher beatings from her.

Then, Deidre decided to grace us with her presence three Sundays before Christmas, brightening an otherwise dreary existence. I was nearly eleven, and Deidre was just shy of ten. At that moment, Janet didn't have a single cent to her name. We were surviving on a monotonous diet of cornmeal porridge and plain white bread, which somehow, didn't bother me at all; I had grown quite fond of the comfort they provided. Janet, however, had grown accustomed to many luxuries that we were no longer able to afford. So, when Deidre came home for her short visit that day and began bragging about her spacious room, the numerous beautiful outfits that her stepmother had lovingly sewn for her, and the pretty dresses that filled her closet, something finally dawned on Janet. It struck her that not having Deidre under her roof meant less money in her pocket.

She looked over at Deidre with a sharp gaze and said, "Hey little bloodclaat gal, you need to pack up your pretty little frock them and bring your bumboclaat right back here because, yuh a turn in a bragging little wretch, so come back home!" My mother's voice left no room for nonsense, and Deidre, overwhelmed, started to cry.

"But me don't want to come back here so, Janet," she protested, her voice trembling, as big rolls of teardrops began falling down her reddened cheeks like a rainstorm.

"A what the bloodclaat!" My mother shouted in disbelief. "Yuh think yuh too good for here suh? You know what? Set you likkle bloodclaat down there suh," she ordered, angrily pointing to the floor beside her bed with a fierce determination. "Don't move!"

My mother was completely livid as she stormed out the door, her frustration palpable in the air.

I watched my crying sister intently, noticing the way the tears streamed down her cheeks like tiny rivers. Her hair was carefully combed into two sections, with big fluffy tufts that bounced with every movement. The pink dress she was wearing was designed just like a doll's dress, radiating a sense of sweetness and innocence. It featured adorable puffy sleeves and rounded white collars that framed her neck, complemented by a delicate white sash tied around her waist. The length of the dress hung straight down to her knees, but it flared out gracefully at the hem, giving her a charming appearance. Her feet were clad in a pair of ankle-length white socks, which seemed to glow against the backdrop of her skin. The shiny white baby doll pumps she wore, however, were left at the door, as if they were not meant to be worn while she was inside the house. She looked absolutely brand new, as if she had just stepped out of a fairytale.

Deidre had always had the biggest body of the three girls, standing out with her robust figure, but her time spent with her new family had contributed to her gaining even more height. She was noticeably chubbier and her skin appeared lighter , adding to the transformation that was unfolding before our eyes.

She was sitting down on the floor, beside my mother's bed, her face flushed a deep red from crying, looking utterly devastated. It was as though the world around her was crumbling, coming to an end. My heart ached for her, knowing what she would now be compelled to give up. A nice big room filled with all the amenities a young girl could possibly want—lots of pretty clothes, stylish shoes, and an array of delicious food that my mother could never even dream of preparing for us. But most importantly, she would be leaving behind the positive influence of an intelligent father and her wholesome brothers, who could have guided her toward a brighter future, only to return to a mother who was incapable of imparting anything valuable or uplifting. A mother who struggled with a debilitating form of idiocy and a frightening level of mental illness. A mother who seemed only able to feed us abusive language as her misguided version of positive reinforcement. She was coming back to share a bug-infested bed that reeked of old pee, with me there to unintentionally add to her misery. I looked at her again and felt an overwhelming wave of pity wash over me.

An hour and a half later, Janet finally returned, carrying a travel bag brimming with some of Deidre's clothing and personal items. I was engrossed in one of the three Nancy Drew books I had borrowed from the library van, completely absorbed in the mystery. Suddenly, Deidre began crying, even louder and more desperately when she spotted her travel bag. In a swift and shocking motion, Janet gave her a bitch slap right across the face. It silenced her immediately, as if flipping a switch. Those bitch slaps, unfortunately, I knew all too well. I had quite a few loose teeth to prove it, remnants of my own encounters. Deidre, however, had never experienced such treatment before. A devilish part of me felt a twinge of satisfaction seeing her endure what I had been going through for the past many months.

Janet dropped the heavy travel bag next to the door and quickly left without a second thought. I hesitated for a moment, then went to pick it up intending to take it to her, but she suddenly got up immediately and aggressively pushed me away from her bag. Her swift action sent an unsettling feeling crawling up my spine, and before I realized what I was doing, I was giving her another sharp bitch slap across the other cheek. It was not nearly as effective as Janet's stinging slap had been, but it shocked the hell out of her just the same. However, she didn't remain in shock for long. She retaliated by chucking me with her heavy hands, sending me sprawling violently against the wooden wall of our cramped one-room house.

The moment the killer instinct surged through me, all I could think about was how desperately I wanted to grab my cutlass and chop her up into pieces, like I used to do with chicken. It took every ounce of willpower to remind myself that she was my sister, trapped in the same oppressive situation as I was, even if she convinced herself otherwise. So, instead, I opted for a more restrained approach; I dragged my short, unpolished fingernails across her cheek and neck, envisioning them as tiny, lethal cutlasses. I observed with a twisted fascination as her skin peeled away, becoming even more inflamed and red.

Her fury was palpable. It was as if she had been waiting for a punching bag on which to unleash her pent-up rage. She looked like she was gearing up for a boxing match, too, as she primed her fist—the very technique my aunt had taught me—before landing a punch squarely in my stomach. It was a monumental challenge to suppress my training instincts and resist the urge to retaliate in kind. In that moment, I genuinely felt the desire to end her. With a swift motion, I seized her by the neck, applying just enough pressure while executing a calculated kick to one of her shins. My goal wasn't to cause any lasting injury, but merely to disrupt her balance—which worked perfectly. I still held her by the neck as she tumbled down onto her knees before me, finally surrendering when she realized that I was in control and she had lost.

"The next time yuh hit me, me a go chop off yuh fingers them," I threatened her, my voice steady and calm.

I let go of her neck, picked up my well-loved Nancy Drew book, which had carelessly fallen to the ground, and made my way to the back of the house, heading toward the chicken coop that had now become my favorite hanging out space. "If she thinks she can come back here and use me for her punching bag, me and her are going to have serious problems." I was seething with anger, but after a moment of intense focus, I managed to calm myself down, with much effort and determination.

I had meticulously cleaned out the interior of the coop, scrubbing it thoroughly with a mixture of bleach and water, then polished the surfaces with clear glaze polish, making everything gleam brilliantly as I shined it with the coarse coconut brush. Chris had constructed the roof so securely that I didn't have to worry about any leakage when the rain started pouring down. I had found a small piece of sponge from beneath the bed that Janet had accidentally put there and subsequently forgotten about over time. With great care, I bought a piece of colorful cloth to cover over it and protect it. Inside, some of my cherished books, along with the small dolls that were lovingly given to me by my aunt, were arranged comfortably, creating a cozy sanctuary in my special space.

I was still a small body, even though I was steadily growing. I was able to fit comfortably within the cozy confines of the chicken coop, with just enough space left over to accommodate my sisters—if they so desired to join me in my little sanctuary. I laid on the soft sponge bedding and continued reading my Nancy Drew book, completely absorbed in the intriguing mysteries unfolding on the page.

20. Merry Christmas

Janet had recently learned that her sister Jacky, had a grown daughter who was currently residing with their mother. This daughter, Freda, my cousin, happened to be one of the oldest among the multitude of cousins I had. Unfortunately, Freda had taken it upon herself to bully Klam, often resorting to physical confrontations where she would beat up on Klam whenever the opportunity arose. Recognizing the distress Klam was facing, Janet made the decision that it was time for her to return home for her own well-being.

Two weeks prior to Christmas, the atmosphere in the big one-room house was tense, with four females living under one roof. It was reminiscent of a scenario involving a big monster with three helpless little girls —well, more accurately, two genuinely helpless little girls, and one mischievous little wretch who thrived on chaos.

It was an absolute disaster. Deidre, being the undeniably privileged child in her newly adopted family, had learned how to skillfully manipulate those around her, effortlessly spinning them around her little finger during her time spent in their midst. She accomplished this with the lies she had meticulously learned to weave masterfully. As a direct result of her cunning ways, she became quite the close friend to my mother, which made everything even more complicated. The stronger their bond grew, the more hateful and resentful Janet became towards me. Deidre skillfully learned our little secrets, modified them to suit her purposes, and then relayed them to Janet in a manner that only served to enhance her own reputation. Janet didn't even bother to take a moment to reflect critically on what Deidre was telling her about us; she simply accepted every word as absolute truth and acted swiftly upon them. Before I could even comprehend what Deidre was orchestrating, I had inadvertently confided in her about my father's wife. I shared with her that I genuinely liked her, and that I thought she was truly pretty. Deidre then twisted my words and took them to Janet. Because of this alteration, when Janet later attacked me with the falsified information, I found myself completely bewildered. She became enraged, convinced that I was merely playing dumb and dismissing her anger.

"Likkle dutty gal, if you think your father is all that wonderful, then why don't you guh live with him and his nasty, turn color gal!" she had said with a sneer, delivering a heavy, unforgiving kick that landed right in my stomach.

Shocked and utterly confused, I crumpled to the ground, the wind knocked out of me. The painful fall had stolen my breath away, but when I saw her coming back with a menacing look, ready to inflict even more damage, I scrambled to my feet as quickly as I could and sprinted away in fear.

One week before Christmas, we still had to paint our small, one-room house, change the curtains to the new, vibrant ones she had bought, hang up colorful Christmas decorations, and put fresh, clean sheets on the beds to get ready for the holiday.

Every Christmas was strikingly the same. The house had to be spic and span by the twenty-fifth of December. I usually hated this time of the year the most, because it was invariably the moment my mother chose to showcase her unwavering belief that she had God residing within her. It was also the time when we had to endure her loud, almost overwhelming excitement as we all worked tirelessly to get the place beautifully readied for the Christmas holiday. If things weren't meticulously done the way she envisioned, the monster within her would come out in full force, demanding perfection. After the house was cleaned, then the Christmas cake had to be painstakingly baked to her high standards. By the time she finally decided that it was time for us to go to bed, it would be dawn the next morning. Everything would be perfectly in place for Christmas, and we would be so utterly exhausted that we would have no use for ourselves. Although she would graciously allow us to sleep through the morning, our breakfast would be saved and served for lunch instead.

On Christmas Day, Janet usually took charge of the cooking, a responsibility she embraced wholeheartedly. She didn't mind it at all, finding joy in creating a festive atmosphere. My father would generously give her money, and Deidre's father would also contribute financially. This influx of cash allowed her to indulge in her favorite purchases, like ganja and Lotto tickets. Afterward, she would send all three of us off to church in the afternoon, Klam and I both dressed in clothing she would obtain from the people for whom she did laundry, and Deidre in new dress made by her father's wife. After the service, we would return home to a delightful Christmas dinner featuring savory oxtail and fragrant rice and peas cooked down in creamy coconut milk, accompanied by sorrel mixed with wine for our festive drink. Each of us would be treated to a generous slice of rich Christmas cake for dessert. As the clock struck six o'clock, she would delight us with ice cream and jello.

Christmas Day usually turned out to be a wonderfully good day for us, filled with warmth. Janet would remain sweet and motherly until the second day of January, then everything would gradually revert to normalcy.

Taking down the Christmas decorations was yet another exhausting ordeal that brought out the monster in her, a vivid reminder of exactly why I despised Christmas and New Year holidays more than any other time of the year. If, by chance, the paint on the wooden wall got chipped during the process of taking down the decorations, the unfortunate soul responsible for it would surely feel her big, swift slap and hear a collection of choice bad words that flew from her lips.

Altogether, during both the enthusiastic putting up of the Christmas decorations and the subsequent, dreaded taking them down, the entire neighborhood had no choice but to hear her fervently chanting Bible scriptures while simultaneously hurling scathing insults at them, all in the same breath.

With the slight positivity in energy quickly fading away, the monster would return in full force, leaving us utterly confused as she seamlessly switched from being a terrifying monster mother to a seemingly nurturing good mother, only to revert back to her monstrous persona once again.

Living alone with Janet for the past two years had taught me not to trust the switch, because it was not genuine . I've learned to accept it when she transformed into this unpredictable version of herself. My sisters, however, had to re-adjust themselves to this kind of tumultuous behavior, so they were even more confused than I was. I just watched her carefully from a distance, and stayed out of her way to avoid provoking her further.

~~~~~~

In the house, I had two precious niches that provided me with a sense of solitude and refuge. One was tucked safely away beneath my mother's bed, a space of comfort and secrecy, while the other was located in the chicken-less chicken coop. However, with the unexpected return of my sisters, I found myself reluctantly forced to share these cherished spots with them. This shift meant that I had no alone time anymore, a luxury I had come to deeply cherish in my life. Having this solitary time allowed me to not only stay out of Janet's way but also provided me with the necessary moments to think through my feelings, complete my homework, or escape into the fantastical worlds of novels borrowed from the library van, which transported me to places far away from our household chaos.

Because we had started to engage in relentless fighting among ourselves, having my sisters back in the house was no longer a situation I welcomed. Gone were the simpler days when it was just me contending with Janet and her whims. Now, I was faced with the constant bickering and relentless arguments that seemed to erupt at every turn. We were all beginning to release the anger that we couldn't express towards our true tormentor, and with Deidre unleashing her hefty punches, a deep-seated rage—a rage I had no idea where it was even coming from—would erupt within me. All I could think about was how I wanted to chop her up and stuff her in a plastic bag, especially when she lied and twisted the truth, claiming that we had started the fight first and that it was I who bloodied her up while I was merely defending myself against her senseless attacks.

I had to make the difficult decision to get rid of the cutlass, and I found myself praying more fervently than ever before. I was now frequently visiting the churches, seeking solace just to get away from the murderous thoughts that were relentlessly plaguing my mind.

This was also my attempt to escape the harsh words and the beatings that Janet was now dishing out on Klam and me with increasing frequency. In this turbulent time, I was constantly reminding myself that there was a God watching over us, and that this difficult situation would not last forever. I just had to bear it with patience. I needed to be strong, no matter how challenging it became.

21. Leo The Fisherman

It was a couple of months after my eleventh birthday that Janet brought Leo to our small one-room house. Leo claimed, with a certain pride, to be a Rastafarian. He had long dreadlocks that clanged together and point to the sky in wild defiance, creating an almost striking appearance. His strong, straight teeth lined up perfectly behind a pair of lips that were almost always smirking, as if he held a secret. There was something enigmatic about his eyes that made me want to run away, though I struggled to understand why I felt that way. Perhaps I was simply too young to fully comprehend the instinct telling me to flee. Maybe, just maybe, it was because of the trauma I had experienced with Crotchless Wayne and my mother's other male friends that left me weary and distrustful of him. Leo was a fisherman by trade, with sunburned dark skin that told tales of long days spent under the hot sun, and he appeared to be a few years younger than my mother. He was, in fact, a little better looking than Crotchless Wayne, which captured my mother's attention. Janet was giggly and radiated happiness upon realizing that Leo seemed genuinely taken with us.

Deidre boldly approached him that first day and wrapped her chubby arms around him in a big hug, a gesture of innocence. Klam, the ever-forgiving one, followed suit, happily giving him a hug as well. Leo appeared genuinely pleased with the display of affection from the two girls. I, however, just stood there, with my fingers mindlessly in my mouth and one stuck up my nose, staring at him in silence.

"Swofiyah, come give him a hug tuh," Janet encouraged, her voice bright and inviting. I hesitated and did not obey her request. I just remained there, watching them interact with curiosity and confusion. Eventually, he smiled at me with a warmth that was meant to be reassuring and said, "It awright, she will hug me when she ready."

That day, a cheerful and delighted Janet spent her afternoon creating a hefty and sumptuous dinner of curry soursop fish, accompanied by a variety of boiled dumplings, boiled green bananas, hearty yam, and sweet potatoes. To complement the meal, she also prepared refreshing soursop juice that added a vibrant touch to the dining experience. While she busied herself with the cooking, Deidre and Klam found amusement in investigating and playfully tugging at Leo's distinctive dreadlocks. Initially, it was a source of laughter and entertainment for them, until Janet gently prompted them to go do their homework instead.

Janet had moved the stove outdoors to enjoy Leo's company while cooking. In return, he entertained her by rolling ganja spliffs, which they smoked together, enveloping themselves in a haze of laughter and ganja bliss. After dinner, they settled comfortably on the veranda for a while, sharing stories as they continued to smoke more ganja clouds, deepening their connection in the warm evening air.

That evening, Janet left with Leo and did not return until the early hours of the next morning. She had gone fishing with him and astonishingly returned with a cart-load of fresh fish that she was now pushing around while selling to eager customers. During the first week of Leo being introduced to us, my mother began to leave us alone in the house at night to go fishing. In the mornings, whatever fish that did not get sold at the seaside, she would diligently pushed around in a cart, marketing their fresh catch.

She had truly found something that she loved to immerse herself in, but there was, unfortunately, a particular downside to her newfound passion. Leo took on the role of weighing the fish, which meant he always knew exactly how much money he was supposed to receive from their sales. Consequently, Janet couldn't keep anything on the side for herself, as she relied solely on what he provided her, in addition to a small amount for her food expenses.

By the second week of Leo coming to stay at the house, they had developed a routine that felt almost like a ritual. Janet would accompany him fishing at night, then dutifully push the big, heavy cart the following morning, selling their hard-earned fish to customers. In the evenings, she made sure to have his meal thoroughly prepared and waiting for him when he returned.

Leo had unwittingly found himself a fool in this arrangement, while Janet began to realize that she was doing the bulk of the work. While he peacefully slept in the mornings, she tirelessly walked around the neighborhood, selling their catch. Sometimes, when their fishing efforts were remarkably fruitful, the relentless hot sun would mercilessly pelt her as she labored to push the heavy cart, hoping to sell off all the fish before they had a chance to spoil.

She became increasingly angry when she had to endure walking under the relentless, blazing sun; however, instead of talking to Leo and working together to come to a better arrangement, she instead took out her frustration on Klam and me, using us as her chosen outlet for stress management. When she cooked dinner, she divided the meal so that half of the pot was designated for Leo, while the remaining half was shared among the four of us.

Leo was not nearly as generous as Crotchless Wayne, but the reality of selling fish in the sweltering sun after a sleepless night spent on the water catching fish felt far more appealing to her than the exhausting tasks of washing clothes and cleaning houses.

Eventually, she realized that selling from the road was much more costly than simply having customers come to the seaside to buy the fish directly. As a result, she began adding her own little markup on the fish to compensate for what Leo wasn't providing her. This clever suggestion came from Deidre.

They both decided to designate Friday nights and Saturday nights as their time to relax and unwind, which meant they could afford to sleep in on those days when they weren't out fishing. After two months of Leo sleeping over, he began waking up early every morning to head to the seaside, where he still devoted some of his time. He would busily mend his fishing nets and patch up his leaking boat.

On one particular morning, Leo got up earlier than usual, deciding to skip breakfast altogether. Janet had already risen and was preparing a hearty meal of boiled banana, yam, callaloo, fried plantains, and rich cocoa tea. She shared a large plastic container filled with this delicious meal for Leo, and poured half of the cocoa tea into a large recycled Horlicks glass bottle, handing it to me to take down to Rae Town seaside for him.

"Hurry up and come back," she instructed me with urgency.

Unfortunately, I didn't get the opportunity to enjoy my own breakfast in the process. The seaside was quite a distance away, and while I genuinely enjoyed going down there, it would have been nice to have had the chance to eat my meal first.

It was after eight in the morning, and I was feeling quite hungry. I decided to cut through Bellevue Mental Hospital, which was conveniently located on one side of Bower Bank Community. It was undoubtedly the quickest route to my destination.

When I had no food available to eat, I often didn't think much about it at all. Sucking my fingers helped distract me from the hunger pangs that sometimes nagged at me. But with the irresistible smell of the callaloo and fried plantains mingling with the rich aroma of the cocoa tea wafting through the air, it was a constant reminder that I hadn't had anything substantial to eat since yesterday. The food I was carrying was a huge temptation that tugged at my willpower. It was all I could focus on since my hunger only continued to mount with each passing moment.

Halfway to the seaside, I couldn't take the unbearable hunger any longer; I decided to help myself to some of the breakfast my mother had packed up for her man. I stopped behind a sturdy tree, set my heavy bag down on the ground with a sigh of relief, and opened it up eagerly. I helped myself to a boiled banana, a generous piece of yam, two delicious slices of the fried plantains, and a scoop of the fragrant callaloo. I opened the Horlicks bottle, which took much more effort than I anticipated, and poured some of the hot cocoa tea into my mouth. Hmm! That hot cocoa tea, sweetened with rich condensed milk, was absolutely amazing. I really had to force myself to stop drinking so that it wouldn't look suspiciously short to him. I made sure to fix the food properly in the container with my fingers, and I wiped the mouth of the bottle with the hem of my shirt to ensure everything appeared as untouched as possible. Once I was confident that everything looked pristine, I discreetly wiped my mouth with my shoulder and continued on my way toward the seaside.

The seaside was, as always, remarkably beautiful. The blue sea, shimmering with diamond sparkles, appeared calm and serene under the golden glow of the early morning sun. There were several small boats lining the shore, and a few yachts were docked out on the vast expanse of the sea. Additionally, there were quite a few small fishing boats with their engines lifted out of the water, also anchored out at sea, making for a picturesque scene.

Looking far out across the shimmering water, I could see the distant land that housed Norman Manley Airport, surrounded by its many lush, green trees. On the other side, to the East, stood the imposing Worrika Hill. It was tall, majestically beautiful and vibrantly green, standing there like a vigilant guardian, watching over the vast expanse of water.

A very gentle breeze was blowing through the air. It had no effect on the calmness of the water, which reflected the serene sky above. An area of the picturesque seaside reserved for swimming was bustling with the joyful presence of adults and children, already enjoying the splendor of God's creation, laughing and having fun in the sun.

The calming sight of the seaside felt like a breathtakingly beautiful picture that I couldn't tear my eyes away from. The rows and rows of fishermen's quads, connected seamlessly to each other, created one long building adorned with multiple doors, adding intricate beauty to the scene.

I really loved this special place. Sometimes, I would walk this way from school, just to revel in the stunning beauty of it all.

I followed my mother's instructions carefully. As I reached the familiar rows of fishermen's quads, I came to Leo's section, which was located on the other side. Making my way over there, I was filled with unease, worried that he would discover that I had ventured into his food stash and tell Janet. I decided to put on a facade of innocence. As I got nearer, my nerves heightened, and my heart began beating uncontrollably in my chest.

I didn't have to ask for any directions, as Leo was sitting comfortably in the midst of nets, spread out across the warm sand, expertly knitting.

"Morning," I greeted him. "Janet said I must bring this for yuh."

He seemed quite happy to see me. He beamed widely, revealing straight rows of teeth that were not as white as one might expect.

"Go put it down in the house," he instructed me firmly, a command I had no choice but to obey.

"Which part it is?" I asked, a hint of curiosity in my voice.

"Just go around that building, and you'll see the green and white door; that's where I am," he explained, subtly pointing his chin in the direction he wanted me to go.

My little arms had grown weary from carrying his food, and all I truly wanted to do was set it down and tell him to take it there himself. However, I decided to follow his instructions, pushing myself to find his little quad. As I pushed open the door and stepped inside, I was unaware that he was following closely behind me. The moment I entered, he came in right after me.

The room was very small, almost cramped, and it featured a single bed that took up half of the entire space. A small wooden table accompanied by a lone chair filled up about a third of the remaining area. Next to the table, a two-burner kerosene stove stood proudly, with a tea kettle perched on top, while a big pile of fishing net lay bundled up in the corner, stark against the otherwise simple decor. There were no windows to let in light, only a standard-sized wooden door that seemed to loom over the space. The walls were constructed from a mix of bricks and cement, but the roof above was made from wooden planks and sheets of zinc, creating an unusual contrast.

"Put the food on the table," he ordered, his finger pointing decisively at it. I approached the table and carefully placed the food down, but just as I turned to leave, I found he had closed the door behind me.

"So, when yuh a go give me my kiss?" he asked, his tone suddenly shifting to something more unsettling.

"What you say?" I replied, feeling a wave of confusion wash over me.

"Yuh sister them give me a kiss; only you left to give me a kiss," he stated, his expression unnervingly intense as he looked at me, stirring feelings of discomfort from deep within.

I thought that if they had given him a kiss, it must have been on the cheek. I was envisioning a quick peck on the cheek, something innocent and fleeting. The quicker I pecked him, the faster I could make my escape from this awkward situation. I was already crafting a mental plan, vowing to never get caught like this again in the future.

But I couldn't believe it when he suddenly grabbed me with surprising force, held my head in place, and then stuck his tongue in my mouth, starting to kiss me as if I were an adult. He was dragging his hand down my chest with the tiny buds of my own burgeoning body just shooting out. When he was finally done with his unwanted advances, I wiped off my mouth with the back of my hand, feeling sick and violated.

"Why yuh wipe it off for?" he asked quietly, pulling me close again, forcing his nasty tongue back down my throat once more.

In that moment, I felt like I was about to vomit from the overwhelming sense of violation. When he eventually released me the second time, I seized the opportunity to make my escape before he could grab me again. Once I found myself outside in the fresh air, I took the hem of my shirt and started wiping off my mouth with it, desperately trying to rid myself of his touch. When that didn't seem to work, I resorted to throwing some gritty sand into my mouth, which only made matters worse and caused me to violently vomit.

All the food I had stolen from him, along with the hot cocoa tea I greedily consumed, came shooting out of me in a horrific mess. I used my foot to kick sand over the vomit, spitting out the vile residue. But even when I thought I had gotten rid of him from my tongue, my lips, and my entire body, my feelings of disgust remained. I hurried to the sea, dipping my hands into the saltwater, hoping to rinse my face off and wash out my mouth. Unfortunately, it didn't help at all; I still felt completely violated.

I walked into the area of the sea where both children and adults were swimming, despite being fully clothed. With urgency, I grabbed the sand and began scrubbing down my face, my lips, my tongue, and my chest—everywhere that his mouth and hands had roamed, I desperately tried to scrub away the memory with saltwater and sand. When I finally realized that I was not achieving the desired cleansing effect, I came out of the water, puffed air into my cheeks in frustration, pushed out my lips, and began heading home. My eyes were red from the sting of saltwater and tears, a visible testament to the turmoil brewing inside me.

"Leo kiss me!" I urgently told Janet, as I stepped up onto the so-called veranda and immediately saw her sitting casually there, smoking her ganja spliff while exuding a relaxed demeanor. She was shaking her head and shoulders rhythmically to the soothing sounds of Bob Marley's Redemption Song, seemingly lost in the moment.

"A no nothing that," she stated, looking directly at me with a piercing gaze.

"Him push him tongue inna me mouth and put him hand down me chest," I told her, my cheeks puffed up and filled with air, my lips pushed out in a childish pout.

"Come here, little gal!" Janet commanded, her voice unmistakably authoritative.

I knew her tone all too well, yet I didn't try to protect myself from her reaction. The trauma of just having been mouth-raped was still very fresh in my mind, lingering like a heavy cloud. I walked toward her slowly, with my cheeks still inflated and my mouth protruding comically.

She swiftly grabbed my ears—the kind of grip that was both demanding and assertive—and dragged me closer to her.

"Me did tell yuh to go swim?" she asked me, maintaining an eerie calmness that was unsettling.

I looked at her anxiously with trembling hands and quivering lips, trying to formulate a response.

"Answer me, dutty gal!" She barked, her voice cutting through the air like a whip.

I jumped in surprise, nerves frayed and fright coursing through me.

"No, but me did want to get him nasty mouth and hands off me, so me go inna the seawater to wash off myself," I told her, my voice wavering as I started to cry, tears spilling down my cheeks. I was shaking like a leaf caught in a fierce wind.

She suddenly jabbed her big fist into my small belly, a spiteful gesture that made me gasp, and said, "Next time me send yuh somewhere, don't stop, come back straight here. Go change yuh wet-up clothes and make sure you eat your breakfast."

She finally let go of my ear and watched me as I slowly walked into the house, hunched over in pain and holding my belly tightly. I felt sick to my stomach, and once again, I vomited. Good thing there was nothing left in me to vomit out, as my body had already emptied itself. I did not spot Klam nor Deidre as I hastily changed my clothes, using the wet clothing to wipe up the little spittle that had escaped and landed on the floor. After that, I took the green plastic bowl from off the table where she had my breakfast shared out, and I slowly walked toward the chicken coop, tears streaming down my face. I had one hand wrapped protectively around my belly while the other clutched the food I knew I wasn't going to be able to eat. I kept it in the chicken coop with me, anxiously waiting for Klam to arrive so I could hand it to her.

That day, I curled up in a tight ball in the coop and fell asleep, hoping for relief. When I finally woke up, I still felt sick. And for days, the nausea refused to leave my body. However, I had long learned to keep my sickness to myself, masking the turmoil within.

22. The Searching

It was shortly after that I began to experience persistent suicidal ideation. I found myself thinking of various ways in which I could end my life, and these dark thoughts became my mental escape from the overwhelming pain I felt. I truly believed I didn't want to live anymore. It was clear to me that no child should ever have to endure such troubling and painful situations.

The very first time such a disturbing thought had ever entered my impressionable young mind was at the tender age of twelve, shortly after I had started experiencing my menstrual cycles. My breasts had begun to bud around the age of eleven, and it was then that Leo started looking at them with the creepiest and most unsettling look I had ever seen on another person's face. Yet, I was already actively trying to avoid him ever since that troubling seaside incident that still haunted me.

Janet, my mother, had noticed the disturbing way Leo was looking at my budding breasts. In a fit of rage, she had viciously grabbed the painful young buds and squeezed them so hard that I genuinely thought I was going to pass out from the sheer agony of it all. Then, with a nasty tone in her voice, while still squeezing and pulling on them, she said, "Yuh a grow breast now? Yuh soon start see blood. If you ever go fuck and breed, don't bother come back in here."

"Me not going to fuck and breed, Janet," I could barely manage to get the words out, choked by the excruciating pain she was inflicting on me.

Meanwhile, Leo was lying on his back on her bed in the cramped one-room space we all shared, passively observing the entire painful scene unfold. His hands were casually placed behind his head and his ankles crossed, as he took pleasure in smirking at my discomfort. It felt like he was completely and effortlessly settled into our lives, with the intent of taking more than he ever should.

That very day, I resolved to start tying down my budding breasts and wearing oversized clothing to keep them hidden from view. It was a milestone in my life, as I had already begun to develop a deep-seated hatred for them.

My first period came twenty-one days after my twelfth birthday. It frightened the living daylights out of me when I realized what was happening. In a panic, I hid the bloody panties behind the communal water closet that we had started using recently. I was scared senseless to tell Janet that my first period had finally arrived. For several days, I stuffed toilet papers into my panties to catch the blood, hoping no one would notice. Luckily for me, my first couple of periods were just light drippings with no painful cramps or discomfort. I had thanked God countless times for that small mercy.

It was in the eighth month of having my period that Janet looked at me curiously and asked, "A how you look so? A fuck yuh a fuck?"

It was the end of summer, a time of transition. I had graduated from St. Michaels Primary School, and was eagerly getting ready to start Vauxhall Secondary School.

Jesus! I couldn't wait for school to start and everything that came with it. She had taken to looking into our vaginas to see if we were having sex. She called it "searching."

The "searching" had started a couple of months before that summer arrived. I had awakened one morning to the alarming sensation of Leo attempting to force his finger up my vagina. I screamed in sheer terror, believing a mouse was trying to invade my body.

It was the first time he had tried to go that far and molest me. Klam had complained to Janet that he had touched her inappropriately, and then, in a fit of rage,

Janet beat the living daylights out of her. Klam ended up in the hospital due to the severity of the beating.

That first night he tried to feel me up, he panicked and fled, retreating to pretend to be asleep when he heard me scream.

I was in shock after finding him over me, trying to stuff his finger inside my vagina. The experience left me unable to sleep for what felt like an eternity. The next morning, I confided in Janet about the incident. He flatly denied it, and, in an outrageous twist of fate, Janet boxed me down flat on the ground.

I should have learned from Klam's terrifying experience. But Janet was my mother; I was naïve enough to believe she would want to protect me. Yet, in that moment, I didn't learn the lesson I desperately needed to grasp.

The next time he tried forcing his finger up me, I was on my period. It was the last straw that ignited the suicidal thoughts that began raging through my troubled mind. I was so utterly ashamed of myself that I found it impossible to sleep at all that night. The next morning, weighed down by a heavy heart, I got up and took the courageous step of telling Janet, once again, that I felt Leo sticking his finger up into my private area, my cho-cho. I understood, deep down, that it wasn't the wisest decision to make, especially considering her harsh reaction the first time I spoke out, and the way she had treated Klam after she confided in her about what Leo had done to her— again. But I held onto a glimmer of hope, a maybe, that Janet would finally have a heart and show some semblance of concern for her own children, just a little. I was far too young to fully grasp that Klam and I would never truly be considered special to her in any way.

She had called Leo, just as she had done the first time I told her about the feeling up. And once again, he denied it right to my face, just like he had on that previous occasion.

"Yuh feel up Swofiyah last night?" she had asked him, as though he was actually going to admit to his wrongdoing.

"A what yuh a talk bout, Janet?" he asked, feigning a look of confusion and puzzlement.

"Swofiyah say yuh feel her up last night," Janet insisted, looking him directly in the eyes with a mix of anger and disbelief.

"But Janet, yuh is a light sleeper. If me did get up off a the bed, yuh would a know. A fuck the gal want. Search her to see if she a fuck," he ordered my mother with a tone of authority that made my skin crawl.

Janet then turned her gaze to me and delivered a hefty slap, jarring my head and loosening a few more of my already damaged teeth on the right side of my face.

"Take off you draws," she ordered with a chilling command, right there in front of Leo, completely disregarding my dignity. "Make me see if a fuck yuh want."

In that moment, my nightmare became even more frightening than I thought possible. Janet followed through with another brutal punch in the face, causing even more pain and further loosening my front teeth, all the while demanding that I take off my underwear, and acting as if I were the one engaging in sickening acts with her man.

She didn't know that I was having my periods. I had kept this significant fact from her all this time, and I supposed Leo must have seen it on the finger he attempted to push up inside of me. In hindsight, I should have drawn attention to this potentially embarrassing situation. But it had never crossed my mind that I needed to. I was far too scared to even think about anything but the immediate horror I was experiencing.

I slowly took off my panties with trembling hands. The bloodied tissue fell out, it was incredibly hard to miss. My overwhelming sense of shame was bewildering and suffocating, and I truly wished with all my heart that I could just drop dead right there on the spot. My mother was inflicting this kind of emotional pain on me was unbearable. The hate I felt for her had taken on a different, more intense form.

I desperately started paying attention to the sounds around me, trying to escape the nightmarish reality unfolding in front of me. I could hear Klam crying silently in the corner, a muted expression of her confusion and fear, while Deidra, my younger sister, was almost enjoying the twisted show.

"Yuh a see yuh blood!" Janet exclaimed with a sneer. "A fuck yuh guh fuck make yuh blood come?" She asked nastily, the words dripping with contempt.

At that shocking moment, the madness she tried so hard to hide came bursting to the surface, but Leo, oblivious to everything else, didn't see it. He was far too focused on the grotesque moment we were all trapped in.

"Lie down on the bed," was Janet's cold order.

Reluctantly, I laid down on my back on the bed, keeping my legs tightly closed. Klam and Deidra, still in the corner of the room, were now watching with a morbid fascination that made my skin crawl. Janet, hovering over my exposed and bloodied punaney, had

Leo right there beside her, watching the unfolding horror. At that moment, I wished that Aunty Norma, or Chris, was still alive to take care of him the way they had taken care of Wayne.

"Open yuh bloodclaat leg, dutty gal, make me see if a fuck yuh a fuck," she ordered with a cruel edge to her voice.

With trembling resistance, I opened my legs, exposing my bloody vagina, all to satisfy her unyielding demand. Without any protection, I could feel the warm blood running down the crevice of my bottom. In my twelve-year-old mind, the deep-seated hate I felt for my mother and her nasty man had taken root so profoundly within my hypothalamus that it left me completely shocked, it was bewildering.

I felt Janet's big, heavy hands on my vulva, parting them with a hard, invasive force. What was she looking for? I truly didn't know. She was not a doctor, nor did she possess any tools that could detect innocence. My eyes remained fixed on Leo, who displayed rapt attention to her hands as they explored my vagina, opening me for both of them to observe without any regard. In that moment, they looked like two uneducated scientists, searching desperately for stars amongst the dust scattered across the ground. I was overwhelmed by surprise at how much I could truly hate someone in that instant, especially Janet's man. Had it not been for him, she would never have thought it appropriate to engage in such a despicable act.

When she finally seemed satisfied that I did not appear to be fucking in any way, she said, with dripping disdain, "Get up, dutty gal, and go wash yuh nasty pussy."

As I slowly got up, I felt the warm blood running down my legs, while my mind was consumed with thoughts of grabbing the knife and slitting my wrist with it, or perhaps slicing through the delicate skin of my neck. I was desperate to alleviate the pain that was suffocating me and the chaotic thoughts that swirled endlessly in my mind. The rage that was taking hold of my consciousness was so overwhelming it made me start to tremble uncontrollably. I had no idea what I should do next. I quickly took clean clothes, fresh underwear, and more tissue to deal with the blood loss, then I escaped to the communal bathroom shared by thirteen, or so people.

The unsettling sensation of her hands lingering on my private parts haunted me, and I was unable to escape the painful thoughts or the great anger that consumed my head. When I finally stepped into the grimy bathroom with its peeling green walls, I hurriedly locked the door behind me and draped my clean clothes over the top of the door, the only safe place to put them. I was extremely cautious, trying hard not to let the tissue slip from my grasp and fall onto the wet, filthy floor that surely hadn't been cleaned in ages. I swiftly removed my dirty clothes, wrapping up the bloody tissue that I had been clenching in my hand, and carefully tucked it into my shirt pocket with the intention of disposing of it in the trash when I eventually returned to the house later.

As I turned on the faucet, the sound of running water seemed to amplify everything around me, and the tears I had been desperately trying to suppress came rushing forth uncontrollably. My small body began to shake violently from the sheer emotional agony I was experiencing. In a moment of despair, I started to hit my head repeatedly against the grimy wall of the bathroom, seeking a way to alleviate the overwhelming pain coursing through my head. The harder I struck my head against the unforgiving surface, the more that physical pain began to eclipse the emotional turmoil and the simmering rage I felt inside. It provided a strange sense of relief. The intense headache that replaced my emotional suffering was blinding, but it offered a temporary escape from the chaotic thoughts and rage swirling in my mind, at least for a brief moment. After my shower, feeling slightly more composed, I braced myself to step back into the world and face my tormentors once again.

23. Running Away

The very first time I attempted to escape, was a couple months after the first searching. I had recently found a friend who had moved to the bottom of our small community, and we ended up being in the same class together. Her name was Maxine, and she had a spark about her that drew me in. Maxine had noticed the bruises on my legs and knew what had happened. It was no secret in the community. They all heard us screaming on a daily basis, but no one tried to help.

She mentioned how her own mother would never inflict such pain upon her. "In fact, my mother would never do that to us," she had said with a fierce sense of conviction. "If I were you, I would just run away."

It was the first time I had ever entertained the thought of running away from my life. The reality was stark: I didn't have anyone to run away to. So, one night after I had abruptly woken up to Leo's unwanted touches, I tried to wake Janet up for help, but her slumber proved too deep. The next morning, filled with a sense of hopelessness, I tried to explain everything to her, but instead, she reacted with violence when he accused me of lying. After they eventually left that morning, I mustered all my courage, packed a few essentials, and ventured down to Maxine's yard to hide away from my nightmare. I had pleaded with her not to mention my presence to her mother, as her mother was one of the rare individuals my own mother had deemed a friend. I didn't want them to find out about my attempts to escape my reality.

As night fell, Maxine kindly made a small bed for me underneath her bed. Yet, the shame of peeing on the makeshift bed on the floor clung to me, I tried not to sleep; as soon as I fell asleep, I urinated on the floor, I couldn't control it. When Maxine's mother came to investigate and discovered the water mark streaming from beneath the bed that night, confusion filled her face. She looked under the bed and saw me hiding there.

"But see here, likkle gal, you did deh here so? You mother a search for you up and down. As soon as morning come, you a go back to yuh yard," she threatened with an edge of concern mixed with authority.

Panic washed over me, and I couldn't sleep for the rest of that night. Restless and fearful, I didn't want to return home, but I literally had no one else to turn to. The thought of the bloody beatings made me feel utterly hopeless, urging me toward a dark thought: the morning after, I took a knife from the kitchen, my hands trembling, and tried to slit my wrist with it, seeking a way out of the pain that felt unbearable.

Maxine saw what I was desperately trying to do and instinctively called her mother for help. Her mother quickly rushed outside and managed to grab the knife from my hands before I could do any irreversible harm to myself. She didn't follow through with what she had promised me the night before. Instead, she let me stay at her house for another night, contemplating the possibility of allowing me to live there permanently with them. However, that plan took a turn when Janet unexpectedly decided to pay a visit to the house and discovered me there.

In a sudden rage, she grabbed a rusty piece of iron pipe that had been carelessly thrown about in the yard and began to beat me mercilessly with it. The blows rained down all over my body, and blood was streaming from wounds that seemed to appear everywhere. Maxine was crying in distress, feeling helpless at the sight of the violence. Her mother attempted to wrestle the iron pipe from Janet, but the confrontation only escalated as Janet turned her aggression towards Maxine's mother and began striking her as well.

While Janet was momentarily preoccupied with attacking her newfound friend, I saw a brief chance to escape, but she had a firm grip on me, holding me tightly, preventing my escape. The neighbors, alerted by the loud commotion, started to come over, their curiosity piqued. They were well aware of the volatile nature of Janet, so they rushed to protect Maxine's mother from further harm. However, it was already too late. Maxine's mother was left with a few missing teeth and her brown skin bore several painful welts from the relentless blows of the iron pipe Janet had wielded.

Once the neighbors successfully managed to pull Maxine's mother away from Janet's grip, Janet's fury turned back at me, and she resumed beating me all over once again, with no sign of mercy.

That fateful morning, my shirt was unceremoniously wrapped around my neck, and my little buds were exposed for all to see as she dragged me, by the shirt—choking me in the process—up the narrow street of Bower Bank. The neighbors were observing the scene unfold, their eyes wide with concern, but not a single one of them dared to speak out or intervene. Once we got inside the house, she fiercely demanded that I take off my clothes without hesitation. Klam stood nearby, looking at me with tears streaking down her cheeks in silent sympathy, while Deidre simply glanced up from her homework, offering nothing but a slight shrug before returning her attention to her studies. I was firmly ordered to stand in the corner completely naked, my body bloodied and swollen in a state of humiliation.

There I remained in that dismal corner of the house all day long, with nothing to eat to ease my hunger, and the swellings on my skin continued to increase in size, each one a painful reminder of my situation. The blood that was running down from my head showed no signs of stopping, and I felt dizzy, teetering on the edge of fainting, but I knew that giving in to that feeling would be a grave mistake.

A couple of times, Deidre passed me on her way to the kitchen and muttered, "Yuh idiat, yuh should a did know better," her tone dripping with disdain, as if I were the one to blame for this torment. Deep down, I realized I should have known better all along. The next time I made the decision to run away, it would be to a place far away, somewhere where I could truly escape this reality.

24. Swimming Lesson

I did not pass the Common Entrance Exam, which was essential for attending what we all referred to as a good high school. My name simply didn't appear in the papers, unlike so many of my peers. Despite being assured that many students had passed without their names being published, I was utterly devastated by the news. I had put in countless hours of hard work studying for the Common Entrance Exams, believing that if I succeeded, my father would finally take a little more interest and put in a greater effort to support our family. He always knew that Klam faced a learning disability and had disowned her without hesitation. Nonetheless, I had hoped that he would behave differently toward me, that he would show more compassion compared to how he treated Klam. Not passing the exam only reinforced the idea that I was merely my mother's daughter, nothing more.

Mrs. Stuart, the only teacher from my primary school who had ever displayed even the slightest bit of genuine interest in my progress, constantly encouraged me to study diligently and do my best. She would always call on me whenever I raised my hand in class, pushing me to participate and share my thoughts. Thanks to her encouragement and support, I was confident that I wasn't as dumb as some of the people in my household insisted I was. She even urged Janet to go to the Education Board to find out why my name had been omitted from the list. Unfortunately, Janet didn't really care about such matters and seemed indifferent to my disappointment.

I felt let down by her lack of concern, but what did I expect? Vauxhall Secondary School was, without a doubt, the last school anyone wanted to attend.

Over time, I had come to accept the idea of attending Vauxhall, as I really didn't have any other choice in the matter. Eventually, I discovered that most of my former primary school netball team members would also be attending Vauxhall, which made me feel a bit better about the situation.

My first couple of weeks at Vauxhall were filled with a mix of nervousness and excitement as I tried out for the netball team alongside my old friends. We all enjoyed the opportunity to represent our new school, joining forces with players from other schools. These new players were tall and fast, which made the competition even more thrilling. We were all very excited about the prospects and challenges that awaited us.

The very first term when the two teams were officially established, we trained much harder than we ever did during our years in primary school. This intense training was beneficial for me, as it made me feel much better about my abilities and dedication. I took every opportunity to engage in activities that would keep me out of the house and busy.

Vauxhall Secondary School operated with two shifts: the morning shift and the evening shift. During my initial term at the school, I was assigned to the morning shift. After classes concluded for the day, we would have netball training sessions. Our netball coach was the remarkable Ms. Desun, a petite teacher whose gentle demeanor made her quite approachable. She saw fit to bestow upon me the title of 'Captain' of the Vauxhall Secondary School Netball Team. She must have recognized some potential in me that I, at the time, did not even see within myself.

Her kind and gentle nature was undoubtedly the primary reason why I felt so comfortable around her. Unlike many other teachers, she didn't shout, nor was she overly strict; I assumed that her approach was why I liked her so much. Had she been strict, she surely would have reminded me of my mother, and as a result, I likely would have found little enjoyment in playing netball. Ms. Desun held a deep respect for all her players, and because of this, we all admired and appreciated her greatly.

Klam was also a student at Vauxhall, having started her studies the year prior to mine. Due to her learning disability, she had been placed in the lowest grade upon her admittance, which made it challenging for her to engage fully in standard school activities. In fact, I had never seen Klam participate in any form of dance or performance, which was quite unusual.

Klam was enrolled in the lowest class of the eighth grade, and fortunately, we shared the same shift. Despite her struggles with the traditional learning methods, the Home Economics Department at Vauxhall discovered a hidden gem in her talents. They quickly recognized that she had a fantastic ability to connect with the children in their daycare section, and her proficiency at cleaning was impressive, so they promptly offered her a job to utilize her skills.

It became clear to us that Klam was quite frugal when it came to money and spending practices. She had a remarkable talent for earning and saving, and whatever income she generated, she ensured that she saved thoroughly. Nobody, including me, had a clue where she discreetly kept her money, and she was incredibly clever not to reveal her saving strategies to anyone around her.

When Janet made the surprising discovery that she was actually earning money while working at the daycare, she felt a strong desire for Klam to bring home some of that money too. However, Klam was firm in her insistence that she wasn't receiving any payment for her work; despite Klam's claims, Janet suspected that she was lying, but she had no evidence so she let it drop.

Klam's demanding job often kept her at school until as late as eight in the evening, waiting for the last parent of a child to pick them up. Given that Vauxhall was conveniently located just a quick ten-minute walk away from Bower Bank, Janet never took the time to question Klam about her frequent lateness.

~~~~~~~

It was Klam who told me that Ms. Desun had a sister who was in the same class as her. I was genuinely shocked by this revelation. I had never before met another person who shared the same learning disability as Klam, but to discover that this individual was actually connected to my netball teacher piqued my curiosity even further. I wanted to see if this sister bore any signs of abuse like Klam and I did. I felt a strong urge to understand if there were other children out there who were experiencing the same kinds of beatings that Klam and I received regularly. Moreover, I became increasingly interested in whether there were other children who were being forced by their parents to spread their legs, to determine if they were engaging in sexual activity. This burgeoning curiosity about the experiences of others compelled me to begin observing the children around me more closely. It was that very curiosity that ultimately led me to visit Klam's classroom during the second period one day.

Her class was tucked away in a distant corner of the building, situated right next to the noisy seventh-grade section. The atmosphere inside was lively and filled with commotion. When I entered the room, I initially expected to see the children making fun of Klam, just as the kids at St. Michaels Primary School had done in the past. To my surprise, however, I found them happily playing with her, and she was laughing joyfully. They were all energetically chasing each other around the classroom. Klam was the loudest of them all, her laughter ringing clear. I had never witnessed her so abundantly happy before. I stood there quietly, absorbing the scene and watching her enjoy herself. I was overwhelmed with happiness seeing her like this, to the point that tears began to flow down my cheeks, without me even realizing it. In that moment, I completely forgot the reason for my visit and remained there, transfixed by my sister's joy. Just as I was about to turn to leave, some of her classmates chased her towards the door, and that was the precise moment when she finally spotted me.

"Wait!" She came to a sudden halt, shouting at her friends and putting her hands up in a gesture of surrender as if to invite them to pause.

She approached me with quick steps, looking into my eyes with a depth I had never noticed before—eyes that held both wisdom and genuine concern. How had I managed to overlook the intelligence in them until now? I realized that just because she had struggled to learn in what others regarded as the typical manner, it didn't mean that she lacked intelligence. Rather, it allowed her mind to perceive things from perspectives that I had not recognized or appreciated until that very day.

"Swofiyah! Yuh awright?" She called out, as she kind of ran toward me, her tone filled with concern and care.

"Yea, me awright, a just want to see me teacher's sister, but yuh look so happy having fun with yuh friend them, so a didn't want to trouble yuh." I told her, feeling very sorry for myself and quite inadequate in that moment. I really wanted to feel a sense of happiness, too. Why couldn't I feel the joy that seemed so easily accessible to everyone around me? I wanted so desperately to forget everything the way

Klam was able to, and simply be happy without the burdens of my thoughts. But how could I achieve happiness when just that very morning, my monster mother had beaten the shit out of me once again, and then searched me roughly in front of her man who had so brazenly made me feel uncomfortable, all because I dared to voice that he had touched me inappropriately, again

I wished I had that strange glitch in my brain, the one Klam had, that allowed her to easily forget the traumatic experiences that had been forced upon her. That glitch that enabled her to be forgiving, regardless of the malice in the world around us. But I didn't possess that coveted ability to let go of the painful memories or to feel any sense of forgiveness for the constant wrongs done against me. I endured those assaults, both physical and emotional, over and over again, and then I was left to grapple with the horrible memories, desperately searching for something good and positive to replace them with, if only I could find it.

Even now, whenever I found myself alone in distressing circumstances, where I couldn't seem to find a way out or figure out a solution, all those past memories would come crashing down like an avalanche, pushing me deeper into my own distress and mental agony. All these haunting memories I had to contend with, couldn't escape and would have to live with for the rest of my life. I wish there was a way I could extract them from my mind entirely, to erase them from my thoughts and not have to see them again.

I tried to contain myself, putting on a brave face as Klam pulled me eagerly towards her classroom to introduce me to her classmates.

"Everybody, this a me sista," she exclaimed with a wide smile, and they all gathered around us, warmly welcoming me and saying "hi."

A shy girl, daintily gliding over to Klam, gently put her arms around her neck. She was very pretty, with beautiful sideburns and very thick, long permed hair that framed her delicate face. She had the most amazing long lashes I had ever seen on a dark-skinned girl, and they fluttered like butterfly wings when she blinked. She waved at me shyly, and in that moment, I knew this was Ms. Desun's sister. She didn't look anything like the picture I had previously imagined in my mind. Instead, she had beautiful unmarked skin and very gentle, kind eyes that seemed to radiate warmth and acceptance.

Again, the sadness I was feeling was rearing to show its ugly head once more. Maybe if those other children had looked the way Klam and I felt, with our constant scars and slashes etched across our skin, it would have told me that enduring such abuse was a normal occurrence, and my mother was simply acting in the way that a mother was expected to behave. But as I looked closely at these children, I felt a deep conviction in my heart that they were not being treated in the same harsh manner as my sister and I were being treated. Their parents might have disciplined them, but they were not subjecting them to the severe beatings that we were painfully enduring. Nor were they experiencing the horrifying molestation and invasive searches that marked our existence.

I was overwhelmed by a profound sense of sadness for both my sister and myself. I couldn't help the feelings welling up inside me, so I hurriedly told them, "hi" and "bye" before swiftly retreating back to my class, brushing the tears away from my eyes, while trying very hard to contain the raw emotions that threatened to spill over.

~~~~~

January arrived, and with it came the exciting beginning of our netball season. I quickly learned that most of our matches would be played at the renowned National Stadium. The truth is, I had never had the opportunity to visit the National Stadium before this season. As a result, I felt a rush of excitement at the prospect of exploring a new environment and embracing the thrilling experience that awaited me.

At the Stadium, the netball court and the basketball court were conveniently located in the same area, situated near the vibrant swimming section. In contrast, the expansive football stadium, complete with its track and field facilities, was positioned in a separate area that was surrounded by tall walls and even higher light posts, with their bright lights seemingly reaching high into the sky. The enormous enclosed National Arena stood across from the netball court, sectioned off by endless, towering wire-meshed fencing. To my young eyes, everything appeared so grand and impressive, though I would soon become accustomed to frequent visits and the sights there. I grew to genuinely love the exhilarating atmosphere of the National Stadium.

Most of our matches were scheduled on the weekends, and I would often be excused from classes on Fridays if we had early matches to play, but for the most part, the competitions took place in the middle of the afternoon and would frequently end quite late in the evening. On Saturdays, we would arrive at the National Stadium bright and early, sometimes as early as nine-thirty in the morning, giving us half an hour to warm-up before the competitions finally began at ten.

During my first season, I vividly remember training diligently and pushing ourselves to the limits, which fostered a remarkable confidence in ourselves and our collective abilities as a team. It was this unshakeable confidence that ultimately propelled our school to become the proud Secondary School Netball Champion of East Kingston. Therefore, every weekend, starting from Friday and extending through Saturday, we practically lived at the National Stadium as we engaged in a series of thrilling netball matches. The name Vauxhall had transformed into a formidable presence in the realm of netball sports, and I felt an immense sense of pride to have been part of such an illustrious journey.

Once the netball season concluded, with our triumph in winning the Kingston Central Secondary School Championship, I found myself uncertain about how to fill my time. Therefore, I would continue my routine of walking to the stadium on weekends, where I enjoyed watching other sports. It was during this time that I discovered the opportunity to join the swim team at the National Stadium. I realized that I had a strong desire to learn how to swim, which opened up new avenues for my athletic endeavors.

The swim section was a completely different world compared to the netball court I was used to. There, in that serene environment, the four expansive pools of vibrant blue water had the most profound and uplifting effect on me. It quieted my racing thoughts and calmed my restless soul, creating a peaceful oasis that I cherished deeply. It truly was the best decision I had ever made on that fateful day when I resolved to sign up for swimming lessons. In fact, it became the best thing I had ever done for myself, really—an essential choice that changed my life. It also taught me something invaluable about myself—the soothing and calming effects the water had on me felt like a form of therapy, a nurturing respite from the chaos of everyday life.

Not having money didn't mean anything to me; it didn't deter my spirit. I joined the team wholeheartedly and eagerly learned to swim. Best of all, I found myself mingling with high-class kids, observing their interactions with each other, and living vicariously through their experiences. I watched the way their parents treated their children, with love and care, and I longed for that same warmth in my own life. As I stood there as the darkest-skinned child in the pool, learning the art of swimming, I felt no shame. I didn't care that my exposed legs displayed a constant stripe of black, blue, and purple from the physical abuse I suffered, nor did I mind the curious eyes that glanced at my exposed bruises when I wore my swimsuit. I also noticed that none of the lighter-skinned children engaged in conversation with me, but it was okay. Just being in this enriching environment allowed me to visualize a different way of life, offering me a much-needed escape from my reality.

I loved to swim—it filled me with joy. I was good at it, and I learned very quickly. I was first taught how to float effortlessly on the surface of the water, then gradually how to move my feet like fins of a fish, and finally how to rotate my arms in and out of the water. They called this technique freestyle, and when I managed to master the euphoric sensation of freestyle, I was introduced to the elegance of backstroke, then the challenge of the butterfly stroke. Diving, I was told, was the most difficult for many aspiring swimmers, but I was captivated by the idea. I was already a jumper by nature. I used to practice my jumps by climbing onto Janet's rooftop and launching myself off. The exhilarating rush I felt while suspended in that space of emptiness prompted me to keep going, relishing every daring leap. Until one day, someone saw me and screamed that I was going to hurt myself, snapping me back to reality.

I wanted to learn how to dive more than anything else in the world. I had a strong feeling that it was a skill I was destined to excel at. Finally, the long-awaited time arrived for my diving lessons, and it filled me with excitement and anticipation. Just as I was about to participate in my very first lesson, I received the troubling news that my bills had not been paid. This lapse had been ongoing for three months, and I felt as if I had been making great progress. Unfortunately, that unfortunate day came when I was abruptly kicked out and told that I could not return until I settled my outstanding bills.

In Jamaica, life seemed to revolve around financial obligations, and I couldn't help but feel a tinge of disappointment that I had not had the opportunity to undergo proper training for diving. However, given all the other lessons I had managed to acquire, such as survival swimming, the sense of disappointment didn't linger for too long. I recognized that I still had other engaging pursuits like school, dancing, and drama to occupy my time and spirit.

25. Our connection

When Deidre turned twelve, she began to display a level of maturity, both mentally and physically, that was considerably more developed than that of Klam and me. The way she carried herself and interacted with others often led people to mistakenly believe she was the eldest of the three of us. She also took great pleasure in thinking that she was the smartest among us all. This notion was certainly reinforced by the fact that in every single class she entered, she consistently achieved the highest grades available. In comparison, I was always hovering around the second-best grades, while Klam, who struggled silently with a learning disability known as dyslexia—a fact that nobody seemed to be aware of—always found herself languishing in the lowest grades. It was just one more thing that Klam and I had reluctantly accepted: we weren't considered smart enough to excel like Deidre.

For all her pretentious claims of being the brightest, Deidre's name was nowhere to be found in the Newspapers the following year. That particular year marked the moment when I took the Common Entrance Exams, and we were frankly informed that with so many students passing, there simply weren't enough spaces available to accommodate us all. In contrast, during the year that Deidre sat her Common Entrance Exams, not nearly as many children passed.

Eventually, she received an acceptance letter for Vauxhall Secondary School. Like me, she felt a wave of disappointment wash over her. She certainly did not want to attend Vauxhall Secondary School, but, unlike Klam and me, she had the advantage of a father who possessed both the influence and the financial means to secure her admission into a different school. Naturally, she attempted to persuade us that she had indeed passed the exams with flying colors; her name just happened to be missing from the Newspapers. She boasted that her father visited the Education Board personally to get everything sorted out. Deep down, we all knew she was a great liar, and that her father did not perform any such machinations on her behalf. If he had, she certainly would have found herself enrolled in a proper high school instead of ending up at Holy Cross Secondary School, where we all knew her academic journey would continue.

~~~~~

Klam had turned fourteen years old, I was thirteen, and Deidre was twelve. Klam had started having her period shortly after she turned twelve, while Deidre's period had arrived just a couple of months before she reached her twelfth birthday. The very first time I had ever seen a Stayfree Sanitary Napkin was when Deidre brought one to me and asked, with a hint of nervousness, if I could show her how to use it properly. I was taken aback and momentarily stunned, but I knew I had to keep my cool and act composed.

"Where yuh get this?" I inquired, genuinely curious.

"Me stepmother bought me nuff a them. Them in a me room, but I didn't want to ask her how to use them," she replied quietly, glancing around as if to ensure no one else was listening.

"I see," I said slowly, trying my best to imagine how I could make sense of such a situation and figure out how to use it. As I took the pad from Deidre, I noticed there was a one-inch width paper running down the length of one side of it, which piqued my interest. The other side was soft to the touch and surprisingly smelled of baby powder, adding an unexpected comfort to the moment. All three of us were bundled up together in the communal shower stall, an intimate that we were all used to. They were watching me with curiosity, their wide eyes focused intently on what I would do next. This was indeed the first time Deidre had ever asked me about something like this, and I felt a strange weight of responsibility. I didn't want to look foolish or unknowledgeable, so I carefully took the paper off and realized there were three strips of adhesive on it.

"Where is the panty?" I asked her, needing the next piece of the puzzle. She handed me a crisp pair of white underwear, and I deftly placed the pad inside it, ensuring the adhesive side was firmly on the undergarment.

"Awright, put it on now, but no bother make the pad drop out," I warned her, my mind racing as I imagined the pad careening onto the wet bathroom floor.

Klam instinctively held onto Deidre to prevent her from losing her balance as she attempted to put the panties on, trying to be careful in this delicate moment. When she finally drew the panties up, we all leaned in to look down and see how it fitted. It was a little bulky, but in comparison to the tissue I had been using, it looked a lot more comfortable and practical for her needs.

"How it feel?" Klam asked her with a hint of curiosity in her voice. She also had never used a sanitary napkin before, which added an extra layer of vulnerability to the moment.

"I don't know," she responded, shrugging her shoulders slightly and turning down her mouth at both corners in a way that suggested uncertainty as well.

"It look comfortable, yuh will get used to it," I assured her, feeling older and wiser for a change, even if just for a fleeting moment.

That was the first time all three of us had ever really connected as sisters, truly sharing a bond in our private struggles. Deidre was no longer trying to be better than us, and Klam was not thought of any longer as just someone with a learning disorder. The fact that Janet never really took the time to explain to us about the finer points of body maturity and womanhood had unexpectedly drawn us closer together in our shared confusion.

We had begun to start becoming aware of our bodies in a new way, now that they were changing, prompting us to think the same thought—Janet was simply not fit, nor intelligent enough, to educate us on such sensitive matters. This realization pushed us to start learning from each other instead, creating a safe space for our discussions.

We were developing physically, mentally, and sexually, yet we dared not approach our mother for the essential girl talk we desperately needed. The only things she ever emphasized with any certainty were, "oonuu a grow breast and a see blood, if oonuu go fuck and breed don't bother come back in a me house." Her bluntness left little room for understanding or support.

Deidre's body was developing faster than both Klam's and mine, and I was left wondering if it had anything to do with the fact that we didn't all shared the same parents. It seemed that Klam and I inherited the smaller stature from our father, further compounding our insecurities. No wonder Janet couldn't stand the sight of us; every time she looked at us, she was reminded of the choices she made and the idiot she was.

Deidre, Klam, and I had started to take a bold step into the world of experimenting with each other's bodies, a curious endeavor to learn about ourselves and discover new depths of intimacy. We were beginning to get along quite well and were learning plenty from one another along the way. In our conversations, we found ourselves discussing boys, and Deidre was sharing vivid stories about how it felt to have a boy touching her here and there. We pondered what might happen if someone touched this or that, and she described what it felt like to walk, hand in hand, with a boy by her side.

It was my third summer off from Vauxhall, and during this time, Deidre was enthusiastically teaching us the nuances of French kissing, a technique that reminded me of the moment Leo had kissed me passionately at his ranch by the seaside. The memory of that encounter left me feeling unsettled and a bit nauseous. Just then, while Deidre was engaged in demonstrating how to French kiss to Klam, Janet unexpectedly walked into the small one-room house and caught us in the act. In a fit of rage, she unleashed a violent beating on all three of us, leaving us trembling in fear.

"A Swofiyah, Janet. A Swofiyah!" Deidre shouted, her voice shaking with fright as she pointed at me. "A she first start feeling us up."

"A lie she a tell," I screamed in disbelief, feeling the heat of Janet's anger intensify as she directed her fury at me.

"A she make we do it!" Klam quickly backed up Deidre, aware that by defending her, she could lessen the blows aimed at herself.

"Yuh bloodclaat lesbian," Janet exclaimed, her voice dripping with venom as she turned her disdainful gaze on me.

By the time she finished beating me that day, convinced that I was corrupting my sisters and turning them into lesbians, I could hardly walk. My entire body was a canvas of bruises and swelling, painful reminders of her wrath. She sent me to bed hungry, and from that day onward, I was branded as the lesbian, a label that would follow me like a shadow.

~~~~~~

It was no different when we had gotten caught stealing groceries at Lee's Supermarket, which conveniently located right in front of Dunoon Road, just off the busy Windward Road. Janet and Leo had planned to go fishing late into the night, leaving us with absolutely no food in the house. They would take all the leftovers from dinner with them to sustain themselves while they were out on the water, leaving us with nothing to eat in the house at all.

They didn't think we needed food to eat, too, somehow believing we could get by without sustenance. After feeding us just one meal for dinner at six in the evening, we were forced to wait until the next morning, and sometimes even the afternoon hours, before we could manage to put something else into our mouths. And there was certainly never any food left over for us to scrounge up, which only added to our despair.

It was during the fourth week of that very same summer that I discovered, to my dismay, that sucking my fingers was no longer effectively chasing away the gnawing hunger in my stomach. The more sports I played and the more energy I expended, the hungrier I became. I just couldn't seem to find satisfaction, no matter how hard I tried. Of course, with only a single meal each day and the rare cup of tea accompanied by a piece of bread in the mornings, my hunger had only gotten progressively worse, leaving me in a state of constant craving.

One day, during that unfortunate summer, we found ourselves under the bed reading books. Our chores were finished, but there was still nothing to eat at all. It was well past ten in the morning, and Janet had not yet returned from her fishing expedition the night before.

"I wonder when she a guh come back so we can eat sump'm?" Klam had grumbled. She had taken to grumbling quite a bit lately. It was her form of defensive mechanism, a way to cope with the situation. And this tendency absolutely pissed off Janet to no end whenever she did it.

"Oh, white squall a bite," Deidre moaned, her voice filled with frustration.

I was laying there, sucking my fingers while deeply engrossed in reading a Hardy Boys book. The hunger they were lamenting about was striking me hard and demanding attention, making it increasingly difficult to focus on the story unfolding in the book.

"We can guh shopping," I had suggested, my spirits lifting and brightening up considerably as I put down my well-worn book on the shiny, red, cool concrete floor and turned enthusiastically towards them.

"A wha you a talk bout? We no have no money," Klam had contradicted, her voice tinged with disappointment. She probably had loads of money stashed away somewhere, but she would never let us know, keeping it a secret because of her miserly ways.

"We can just go in a the supermarket with our bags, pack the food we want, and walked out," I said, making it sound so simple and easy, as if it were just a game.

"Mi nuh know," Klam had said, fear clearly written all over her face, as uncertainty danced in her eyes.

"We can give it a try," Deidre chimed in, her voice filled with a hint of courage.

Without thinking twice, we climbed out from under the bed and headed for Lee's supermarket before we could talk ourselves out of this risky idea. We were loaded up with a few plastic bags, ready for the adventure. Entering the small supermarket, we quickly grabbed two grocery carts— I took one, while Klam eagerly took the other. Because it was a little after eleven that morning, the supermarket wasn't that packed yet, and nobody seemed to be paying us any attention at all. I began to fill my cart with all the favorite foods that Janet never bought us—golden, sugary treats that my heart longed for, including peanut butter, crunchy cornflakes, creamy tin milk for the cornflakes, flavorful mackerel, sweet sugar, and loads of my beloved junk food. Banana chips, plantain chips, colorful cheese trix, and a variety of others awaited us on the shelves, and I couldn't help but feel a rush of excitement and nervousness lacing through us.

26. Getting Caught

I was bagging the items like I had already paid for them, feeling a rush of adrenaline as I expertly arranged everything. By the time I made it to the front of the supermarket, Klam had already taken her cart, which held just a few items, and abandoned it right in front of an idle cashier. There were four cashiers, and they were all busily engaged in loud, animated chatter among themselves, seemingly oblivious to the world around them. I hastily walked out of the supermarket, leaving the cart filled with my neatly packed bags alongside the other empty carts lined up outside.

Klam then scurried back to the supermarket as if she had forgotten something important, but moments later, she reappeared, making her way around to the front aisle where I had left the three packed bags in the cart. She quickly grabbed two of the bags, her movements swift and deliberate. Just seconds behind her, Deidre emerged and snatched up the remaining loaded bag, casually walking off as if she had placed the bag there herself earlier.

I stood waiting for them at the corner of the garage next to Lee's Supermarket, my heart racing intensely as if it might explode from my chest at any moment. Our first supermarket hoist felt absolutely brilliant, sending waves of excitement coursing through me. I couldn't help but smile as I watched my two sisters approach, each struggling slightly under the weight of their heavy bags while trying their best to maintain an air of calmness. They looked as if they had just spent a small fortune on groceries, completely unfazed by the theft.

We were so incredibly nervous that we didn't even consider walking all the way to the entrance of Bower Bank. Instead, we took an unorthodox shortcut through Doncaster Drive, desperate to shake off anyone we imagined might be following us. Once we reached Bower Bank, a surge of exhilaration propelled us as we sprinted the rest of the way to Janet's house, giddy with the thrill of our successful escapade.

We were a bundle of nervous wrecks when we finally stepped inside the house. Every movement outside left us anticipating the moment someone would come banging on the door, ready to take us to the police station for our misdeeds. Klam kept one of her fingers pressed thoughtfully against her lips, reminding us in a hushed tone to stay quiet and still. After five intense minutes of waiting in silence, feeling the weight of our anxiety, we realized that nothing was happening, and our hunger became overwhelming. We delved into the food like ravenous animals, the thrill of our heist igniting our appetites. That morning had brought us our first big feast ever, filled to the brim with junk food, and although we were elated, a lingering sense of nervousness kept creeping in as we chomped down on our stolen loot. The rest of our pilfered treasures we carefully stashed away in plastic bags, snugly tucked under Janet's bed for safekeeping.

When Janet finally returned home, dragging along the empty fishing cart around one in the early evening, we were so filled from our feast that we felt utterly unable to move. We chose to stay hidden under the bed, pretending to be fast asleep, while our hearts raced with guilt and anticipation.

Despite discovering that nothing had come of our supermarket heist, our reckless spirit pushed us to do it again and again on several more occasions before our inevitable capture.

The day we got caught was particularly memorable; Deidre had meticulously made a shopping list of items we should grab, including fucking chicken. Instead of waiting for the morning hours when no one would pay us any mind, she insisted on heading out in the early evening when the supermarket would be bustling with shoppers. Her reasoning was that we could gather more goods and slip away more easily amidst the chaos, and we all agreed that it was an incredibly clever plan.

With the shopping list in hand, we all ventured into the cramped and overcrowded supermarket. I found myself pushing the cart while simultaneously packing it full of goodies, all while glancing over the list. Little did I know, I was being carefully watched from the sidelines. During those days, the residents of our neighborhood didn't usually stroll into the supermarket with shopping lists; they simply grabbed whatever they wanted off the shelves, paid for their items, and went about their business without a second thought.

Once I had finished loading the cart, I slipped into the darkest corner of the bustling supermarket, hastily stuffing items into the plastic bags as quickly and quietly as I could. Afterward, I cleverly maneuvered the cart over to where a couple of other carts were lined up, then casually walked out of the supermarket, pretending that I had simply forgotten my money. Just a few moments later, Klam followed suit, grabbing up two of the bags just like she always did, and casually made her way outside.

It was while Deidre was doing the same task, less than a minute later, that they firmly held onto her. Klam and I anxiously waited for her by the garage and felt a deep sense of unease when we didn't see her coming toward us. We ran swiftly to Janet's house, taking the shortcut through Doncaster Drive, our footsteps quickening with each passing moment. When we finally got to our home, we saw Janet's fishing cart parked neatly in front of the veranda. Klam hurriedly shoved the grocery bags under Betty's cellar, and we both walked into the house, attempting to act like nothing was occurring.

Inside, Janet was not looking too happy at all. Her lips were pushed out in irritation, making the sunburnt skin appear taut over her prominent jawbones. It was her unmistakable "me not going to take no fuckery" face, and we all knew to tread carefully around her.

"A where the gal Deidre deh?" She demanded, her voice sharp and filled with impatience.

"She probly a use the toilet," Klam said, casually pointing her chin next door in a dismissive gesture.

"Me no bloodclaat tell oonuu not to use people pussyclaat toilet?" she barked angrily, her frustration bubbling over.

Just then, two men came up onto the veranda, trailing a very nervous-looking Deidre behind them.

"We catch her a steal from the supermarket, and she told us that her other two sisters have the other two bags," one of the men said, his tone matter-of-fact yet accusatory.

"A what the bloodclaat a go on yah?" Janet shouted in disbelief, her eyes wide as she struggled to comprehend the situation.

"A truth them a tell?" she demanded as she turned her gaze directly at Deidre.

Deidre looked at her with a face flushed bright red, huge teardrops cascading down her cheeks, making her distress clear.

"A Swofiyah make we do it, Janet. A she tell we to go thief from the supermarket cause she hungry." She was pointing at me as she spoke, her finger trembling slightly with fear and shame.

I was looking at her with such disbelief, I didn't see Janet as she suddenly grabbed me harshly by the neck, her grip tightening mercilessly. The two men nearby watched in utter surprise as Janet nearly choked the life out of me, clearly taken aback by the violence unfolding before them.

"You no have to do that, just give we the bag them and everything would be awright," the other one said with a mix of concern and frustration.

"Where the bloodclaat bag them deh?" Janet shouted, her voice roaring loudly enough to echo in my ears.

I was shaking now with fear and anxiety. "Dem under Betty cellar," I quickly blurted out, pointing shakily toward the cellar.

Klam sprinted to the cellar, rummaged through the dark space, and retrieved the two bags before running back and handing them to the men with a shaky hand. They took the bags and reassured us that everything would be okay.

"No bother beat them. Just give them a bligh this one time," they glanced at my mother and said casually, but they had no clue who they were dealing with.

Janet was still gripping my neck tightly when the men finally left.

"The two a oonuu go in a the house," she ordered Klam and Deidre sternly, while dragging me inside like I was a rag doll, still clutching my neck.

She picked up the baton stick, which was reserved specifically for this purpose, then tossed me down forcefully onto the cold concrete floor as if she were fighting a formidable enemy she couldn't stand. She placed her heavy foot directly in my stomach, using it to pin me down and prevent any chance of escape while she relentlessly pummeled my body with the baton stick. No part of me was spared from the assault. Klam and Deidre, overwhelmed with fear and sorrow, began to cry as they insisted desperately that it was me who had told them to go steal from the supermarket.

My head had taken the brunt of the beatings. When she finally stopped, I was swollen and bruised all over, with blood trickling from my head down my face. I felt utterly unfocused and disoriented as the pain reverberated throughout my body. I received such severe beatings for supposedly turning Deidre into a thief and for her getting caught stealing. It took a full two weeks for me to recover and for my head to feel even slightly normal again.

"You dutty bloodclaat lesbian, look how you a guh go a prison guh rub crotch," Janet warned me angrily, her voice dripping with disdain.

That fateful day marked the last time I would ever steal anything. And in the process, the once close connection my sisters and I had built together vanished forever, leaving an emptiness that would linger long after.

27. My Friends

For every good choice I made in my life, there were always six bad choices lurking just around the corner. I think that was largely because I never really had a truly positive role model in my life. An intelligent figure to influence me, someone to challenge and stimulate my young mind in a constructive and uplifting way. I was far too naive to figure out that I could have been my own role model, that realization eluded me.

Not even the teachers at my school in Kingston were able to serve as adequate role models. They had too many things on their own plates, and their busy lives prevented them from noticing a troubled child like me. I was constantly hungry, seriously abused, and deeply troubled by the chaos around me. I eventually gave up on sitting down in a classroom, pretending to learn when I felt like nothing was sinking in.

The truth of the matter was, I simply couldn't learn anything while living with my mother and her abusive sexual predator of a partner. Alongside the thick clouds of ganja that distorted my mind and perception, I couldn't seem to focus enough to take in any information. I couldn't force myself to go to school and sit in a classroom, pretending that everything was okay when deep down nothing felt right. My mind just wouldn't allow me to. Even when I genuinely tried my best to concentrate, I would find myself zoning out, revisiting the painful memories of the miseries inflicted on me just that morning, the night before, the previous day, or even just a few hours before I tried to sit at the desk in my classroom.

I succumbed to the negative thoughts that plagued me when I wasn't actively trying to escape into every school activity that involved a ball and allowed me to run, jump, and sweat out my frustrations. When school wasn't an option to evade the molestations, the beatings, and the verbal abuses, I would take to walking for hours and hours under the blazing sun. My long, exhausting walks would sometimes lead me all the way to Spanish Town, where my grandmother lived. I would seek solace and spend the night with her, and she would send me back the next day, providing me with the transportation fee to return to my mentally ill mother and her child molesting common-law-husband, only to face more abuse, molestation, and violative searches.

There were times when I would walk for what seemed like an eternity, completely absorbed in my thoughts and not paying the slightest attention to where I was going. This would often lead me to some strange and faraway places, places filled with towering trees and vast stretches of land devoid of any houses or signs of human life. When I arrived at these serene locations, I would take a moment to rest my weary body, seeking solace by sitting under one of the many majestic trees. It was here that I could pause and gather my thoughts until I could muster the energy to find something to eat, usually foraging from whatever fruits were in season. After satisfying my hunger, I would relax a little more, embracing the solitude and surrounding quiet as I talked to God, sharing my deepest concerns and longings, until it was finally time to make the journey back home to face the monsters.

I was never afraid when I found myself in these unfamiliar situations. My daily existence was already shaped by a reality that obliterated any fear I might have had of strangers lurking in those distant woods. Strangers were never the true enemies in my eyes; rather, the actual threats were often the people I lived with. Those who were supposed to provide comfort and safety, yet somehow didn't. People I didn't truly know never ventured close enough to hurt me. It was typically the individuals who occupied my life, those over whom I had no real control, who posed the greatest danger. So, I continued to walk with my head down, my lips moving silently as I engaged in sincere conversations with God, pleading for a way out of the situation I found myself in. He never seemed to listen to my heartfelt prayers, though. Despite my efforts to reach out to Him everyday, three times, or as many moments as I could carve out, I begged for His intervention to free me from my suffering. But there was never any answers. God was never present in my tumultuous and abusive world to offer the protection I so desperately sought. If He truly was, I would never have endured the trials I faced. I wished that He would have at least sent someone to rescue me from my plight, but, regrettably, nobody ever came.

~~~~~

It was in the middle of the last term of my first year at Vauxhall Secondary School, during a time filled with new experiences and friendships, that Blossom and I became best friends. Blossom and I found ourselves sitting next to each other in the same seventh grade class. She had started attending the school at the very beginning of the second term, and her vibrant personality quickly drew me in. She loved drama, which was a passion I had also taken up since it was a mandatory part of our curriculum.

We were not allowed to keep friendships with anyone from Bower Bank, but Janet never explicitly told us that we couldn't have friends at school. Another girl who soon became very dear to me was Heather Martin. She got enrolled in our school at the end of the second year, and much to my delight, they placed her in my class. Heather was stunningly beautiful, with striking hazel eyes, and long, thick, curly, honey-blond hair that she always kept elegantly in one long plait that cascaded down to the middle of her back. She had exceptionally light skin and a proper way of speaking that made her seem quite sophisticated. I couldn't help but feel she did not quite belong in our school, and I had a sinking feeling that she wasn't going to stay long.

Heather and I also participated in the same dance group together. However, I noticed that her right leg was growing faster than her left leg. Because of this, it made dancing a bit challenging for her, yet she never gave up on improving, and the dancing instructor remained patient and encouraging throughout her struggles. It was within this dance group that I also met Edmorine, along with her triplet-like friends. She was the smallest and cutest person I had ever encountered. The other two girls, who seemed to be so similar to her, were just over an inch taller, or perhaps a little heftier than Edmorine.

Edmorine had charming blond, permed hair that was as straight as it was bright, and the same shade as her complexion, but instead of detracting from her youthful appearance, it actually added an air of maturity, giving her the impression of being a little woman. She invariably became the center of attention wherever she went, drawing people in with her infectious smile and vibrant energy. Edmorine and her triplet-like friends seemed to dominate the dance group effortlessly with their flawless movements and their light-colored beauty that stood out in the crowd. They were in the eighth grade, poised to advance to the ninth grade, and their dancing outfits always appeared to be new and incredibly fashionable, setting trends among the rest of us.

Heather also seemed to possess the same keen sense of style when it came to selecting dancing outfits, which further fueled my desire to want to fit in. Initially, I felt like I was genuinely out of my realm, overwhelmed by the remarkable skill around me, until I finally stepped onto the dance floor. To my surprise, my jump and split appeared to surpass those of my peers, impressing the dancing instructor enough that she offered me a permanent spot in the front of the line, signifying my newfound status.

Overtime, I had grown to truly love Vauxhall Secondary School and the friends I had made there. Most importantly, I cherished the art of dancing. It felt like a vibrant escape, distinctly different from all the other activities I had chosen to engage in at school, each lacking the same exhilaration.

My passion for dancing became a central part of my mental imagery, allowing me to transform my experiences. I discovered that I could effectively use it to block out Janet whenever she unleashed her verbal tirades. Her words morphed into mere background noises within my mind the more I immersed myself in the rhythmic dancing that filled the vast space of my imagination. There were moments when she spoke directly to me, and I found myself unable to comprehend her at all, completely absorbed in the dancing that played out in my head. This mental escape was vital; it enabled me to manage being around her, even when I had no other choice.

As I matured, I also learned to control my facial expressions, refining my ability to mask my feelings. Through experience, I discovered that when I appeared unaffected by the chaos at home or the harsh words tossed my way, Janet would often lessen her attacks on me.

While I was successfully creating this mental barrier, I still did not want to come off as rude. Such behavior would have likely sent her into a frenzy, provoking the infamous baton stick that she reserved for Klam and me. So, when she talked and I failed to hear her, I would simply stare at her with a puzzled expression, the look that had earned me the nickname "demons," interpreted as me acting superior to others.

I still endured the beatings and the feeling up, those I couldn't easily block out with the vibrant imagery of dancing. To make matters worse, Deidre and I continued to have regular fights. She had grown bigger and stronger over time, but I now had my long nails as my defensive arsenal. So, the moment the fighting began, my nails became my weapon of choice, fierce and formidable in their own right.

The deep-seated rage, which I found myself unable to completely expel from my mind, would often manifest itself brutally in the manner in which I raked my fingernails violently over her tender skin. It drove her absolutely mad whenever she caught sight of the persistent nail scars marking her body. In an attempt to cope with this torment, she made up for her pain by weaving an elaborate web of lies to tell Janet, who, without a second thought or any hesitation, would simply allow the baton stick to reverberate mindlessly over my body, while she watched and gloat with satisfaction.

Deidre, along with Janet and her reprehensible child molester of a partner, had become permanent fixtures lodged deep within my psyche. I felt utterly powerless to expel them. They were like relentless ticks, draining the very essence of goodness from within me and driving me to the brink of madness every single day. I had ultimately stopped using my training on her to exert control, realizing I would most likely be in prison by now if I had. And the truth was, I knew I wouldn't have stopped at just her; the others would have been included.

~~~~~

I had found a wonderful helper in my friend Edmorine. I soon learned that she lived at the bottom of Doncaster Drive, nestled within the middle-class community located on the other side of BowerBank. Occasionally, she would invite me over to her lovely house, where we would joyfully practice gymnastics together. The more flexible we became, the better dancers we were able to turn out to be.

Edmorine resided with her aunt, whom we affectionately referred to as Aunty, and her cousin in one of the nicest houses I have ever had the pleasure to visit. Aunty was a successful Higgler, traveling frequently to various small islands in search of unique and beautiful clothing to sell in her thriving clothing store. Because of this, Edmorine would often wear the most exquisite designer outfits that seemed to sell out instantly as soon as she donned a sample piece.

From time to time, she would graciously give me some of her clothes, an act of kindness for which I was immensely grateful. Most of the clothing she wore happened to be a size larger than she needed, which meant they fit me perfectly. The dancing outfits that were too big for her would find their way to me, and I was always happy to receive such generous gifts. Although her shoes were a little tight for my feet, that did not deter me from squeezing them on anyway. Thanks to Edmorine's thoughtful generosity, I felt fortunate to be saved from the embarrassment of walking around naked and barefooted.

For three long years, I wore the same green uniform, which became quite familiar to me. However, during the tenth grade, I was fortunate enough to be saved from the necessity of turning my old, worn-out, and torn full uniform—one I had been wearing since the seventh grade—into a skirt that was now required for the tenth-grade students. Edmorine provided me with two of her rather expensive and finely pleated gaberdine skirts that she had worn during her own tenth-grade experience, skirts that were the envy of nearly every female student at our school. Now that she was moving up into the eleventh grade and no longer had a need for them, I was incredibly thankful for these thoughtful gifts. The beautiful uniform skirts fit me perfectly due to my very small waistline, although her white blouses were a little too snug because of my larger upper body.

She also generously gave me a couple of pairs of black school shoes that her aunt had originally planned on throwing out. To my surprise, they turned out to be an unusual mismatched pair, as they were not the same shoe for either foot. To my novice eyes, they did not appear to look any different from one another. They were made of real leather and seemed quite comfortable to wear. I took them without hesitation, and thankfully, no one was the wiser about my unique footwear situation. Additionally, another school friend of mine kindly brought me a half-white blouse that matched perfectly with my new skirt, and with that, I was all set for my tenth-grade that year.

I couldn't confide in some of the friends I had made in school. Especially the ones who came from good family backgrounds and seemed to lead perfect lives. They simply wouldn't understand the turmoil I was experiencing. My overwhelming sense of shame wouldn't allow me to speak up about my situation. To tell anyone that I was being sexually molested by my own parents, that my mother was so brazenly opening my legs for her boyfriend to look down at my vagina, was something I felt I could never bring myself to articulate. It felt too horrifying to even consider sharing those details.

I wanted so desperately to tell someone I could trust, someone who could possibly help and provide me with the guidance I longed for, but I couldn't find that person anywhere. However, as I spent more and more time with Edmorine, it became increasingly difficult to hide the bruises and cuts that marred my skin. She would ask about them with genuine concern, and I would share some tales about my mother's harshness, but there was still a wall between us when it came to discussing the more intimate and traumatic experiences, like the feeling up and the searching that left me feeling so violated.

When her aunt traveled, she and her cousin would graciously allow me to stay in the extra room at their home until late at night, but even in that safe space, I couldn't bring myself to sleepover fully. I felt a deep compulsion to return home to ensure that Leo would be able to get his finger on me before they left for their late-night fishing trips. I knew all too well that if

I wasn't there for that purpose, he would stir up a fight with Janet, accusing her of allowing me too much freedom and insisting that I had a man in my life, hence my late hours. After his accusations, he would demand that she search me, further tightening the grip of fear and control he had over my life.

~~~~~~

Blossom eventually became one of the very few individuals whom I had chosen to confide in about my deeply personal situation. We finished the seventh grade in the same class, and we continued through the eighth grade and ninth grade together, sharing many experiences. She had a great passion for music and drama, often expressing her enthusiasm for both. I, on the other hand, had made the decision to drop drama at the end of the seventh grade after a particularly hurtful incident with the music teacher, who also held the role of our drama instructor. He made an unfortunate comment about how some of our mouths resembled a vagina, and he directed this remark specifically toward me. This occurred while he was teaching us the music notes on the piano he was skillfully playing, all the while demonstrating how to properly shape our lips to produce specific sounds. Living with such derogatory statements from my mother was already a heavy burden for me, so I had no desire to endure similar criticism from anyone else. This led me to stop attending both music and drama classes altogether. Blossom, however, found the teacher's comment humorous and laughed it off. Naturally, she thought I was overreacting, especially because she had developed a huge crush on him at that time. Despite the challenges I faced, Louise Bennet remained one of my favorite Jamaican poets, and I still performed her work whenever the school allowed me to, particularly during competitions that showcased my love for poetry.

The first time I confided in Blossom about everything that had been happening with Leo, she looked at me with wide eyes and said, "If I was yuh, I would a scream bloody murder so that my mother would hear and wake up right away."

With a heavy heart, I replied, "That's what me do the first time him do it, and she never hear," feeling the weight of my frustration.

"Scream louda," she advised firmly. "See if she a go be a dead sleepa."

Taking her advice to heart, that night I followed her suggestion. However, it only woke up Klam and Deidre, and by that point, Leo had slyly gone back to bed, pretending to be deep in sleep. I looked over to my sleeping mother, and even though her eyes were closed, I could see her rapid eye movements, confirming she wasn't dreaming. The next morning, I gathered the courage to tell her the truth, only for him to deny it once more. She didn't bother to search me thoroughly; instead, she just grabbed the baton stick and rammed the bottom part forcefully into my left eye, starting to beat me on the head as if it were a drum. That morning when I arrived at school, I felt like one of the mentally ill patients wandering the hallways at Bellevue Hospital. My lips were grotesquely swollen, and my eyes were black and blue, the left lid entirely closed over as if it were never going to open again. It felt like my eye was going to drop out at any moment. To make matters worse, I also had a cracked skull with dried blood that had formed a crust over the crack, gluing my strands of hair together in a tangled mess. When Blossom caught sight of me, she took one look and immediately dragged me to the school nurse, who then sent me to the clinic. Unfortunately, nothing came out of the visit, and from that day on, I never took another piece of advice from her again.

~~~~~

Life continued in much the same way for me as the days passed. I found myself in the last term of the third year at Vauxhall when Blossom, my friend, gently encouraged me to speak up and tell someone about my situation. I decided to confide in my English teacher, who then took it upon herself to inform some of the other teachers about the troubling issues that were taking place at home. Unfortunately, their reactions were far from supportive; they merely shrugged their shoulders, showing indifference as they continued on with their lives without offering any assistance. None of them tried to help me or provided any guidance or counsel that I so desperately needed.

I didn't even have to tell my netball teacher about my struggles, as she had noticed the bruises that marred my legs from the very first day of netball practice. There were moments when I caught her staring intently at the cuts and marks that adorned my skin, which were indeed very hard to miss. I would arrive at school with the pink, raw flesh exposed, and occasionally, she would attempt to pull me away from my troubled home life by inviting me to functions she organized, hoping to provide me with some respite.

Among the three of us being molested, Deidre was the only one who rarely complained. Even though I often woke up and found him hovering over her, invading her space, and stuffing his finger up into her vagina, it seemed like she accepted her fate. There were instances when she would lie with her legs opened a little wider, allowing him to stay longer than usual. However, the moment he laid a hand on Klam, she would abruptly wake up, startled, and he would quickly retreat back to the safety of his bed.

In time, I started to become acutely aware of his dark energy surrounding me, so I learned to be vigilant; whenever he approached, my eyes would spring open, meeting his gaze. Seeing my watchful stare, he would retreat to his bed, only to wait for me to drift off to sleep once more, and then he would sneak back, determined to try again. He was a relentless molester, and the only reason he felt empowered to behave this way was that Janet, my mother, allowed it to continue unchecked.

During those nights when he was present, I learned the hard lesson of not sleeping. Yet there were some nights when the exhaustion would take over completely. Especially after a particularly demanding day of netball training or competition, I would find myself succumbing to sleep, only to wake up in a startled panic, discovering him trying to force his finger up into me once again.

28. The Promise Of America

The very first time I began walking with my head down, deep in conversation with God, pleading fervently for Him to help me find my way out of the overwhelming situation I was facing, was the moment I first truly believed I might end up in our neighboring mental institution, a terrifying thought that loomed over me. Each and every day, as I made my way to Vauxhall Secondary School, I walked alongside God in my thoughts, praying earnestly and begging Him for assistance, day after relentless day. Passersby would often glance my way as I walked past the Bellevue Mental Hospital, thinking it somehow appropriate for someone like me. After all, I lived in such close proximity to it, and given my erratic behavior, it seemed almost inevitable. I left my home many times on an empty stomach—not that there was ever anything substantial to eat, anyway. Sometimes, I simply couldn't get out of there fast enough. I found myself walking, lost in prayer, barely realizing that I had already arrived at school, my mind so consumed with talking to God and pleading for His guidance, yet it felt as though He never truly listened to me.

Deidre confided in Janet about the unsettling experience she had with Leo, explaining how she felt his hand creeping over her the very first year she entered secondary school. In response, Janet promptly called Leo to question him about the situation. He adamantly denied any wrongdoing, insisting that he had barely even left the bed and went so far as to tell Janet to search Deidre herself. Janet complied, though her approach was less forceful and harsh compared to how she dealt with Klam and me. As we observed, I noticed that Janet didn't linger as long as she typically did with us. Deidre, following instructions, removed her underwear and climbed onto the bed, spreading her legs as she was told, a scene that felt profoundly uncomfortable. Klam and I watched in silence as Janet scanned Deidre's body for what I quickly realized was an unnecessary intrusion; she barely touched Deidre's private parts, glancing for only a brief a second before telling her to get up, preserving her modesty just in time to prevent Leo from getting a good look.

It was later, It dawned on me that Deidre's father was already contributing to her home economics, which meant she was more than capable and did not deserve to be exposed for such a purpose. In her own unique way, Janet was acting to protect Deidre from the prying eyes of Leo. Still, she was careful to ensure that her efforts did not appear too conspicuous. Meanwhile, Klam and I felt a pressing need to contribute in our own way, especially given that our father seemed to care so little about our lives and well-being.

Janet was going through the challenging and often emotionally charged process of taking my father to the family court in order to secure children maintenance. At the family court, my father shockingly disowned Klam, her first child whom she had tried so hard to bring into this world for him, and having him deny that she was his flesh and blood drove her mad, or rather, made her even more unhinged than before. He callously remarked that she was too black and ugly, claiming she could never possibly be his child. The judge ultimately ordered him to pay child support for both Deidre and me. Although Janet received some financial recompense with Deidre, her persistent anger and frustration, paired with what my father was required to pay, made her believe it wasn't remotely sufficient to support us. Consequently, we also felt obligated to pay our dues in some way. Allowing Leo to look down upon us became her strategy for ensuring that we were contributing financially to the household.

~~~~~~

I was in my third year at Vauxhall Secondary School when my father took my birth certificate, firmly declaring that he was going to send me to the United States of America. All my uncles and aunties —his many brothers and sisters who had ventured abroad—were living there. He was determined to get me settled in with one of them, as he believed it would provide me with better opportunities and open doors that would help me improve my life significantly.

It was, without a doubt, the best news I had ever received in my entire life. I felt a surge of excitement and couldn't wait to rush home and share the wonderful news with my family, envisioning their joyful reactions. However, the only problem with that was, my family didn't seem to care much about what I considered wonderful news. I realized that I would not be there for Leo to feel up. One of Janet's stress management options would be gone, and Deidre would no longer be able to shine as the smart one with the money father.

With all the nasty and hurtful things Janet said about my "rotten, worthless" father, the very act of him doing this would turn every word she ever spoke about him into a blatant lie. It was after my so-called wonderful news that she started beating me more frequently, sending me off to his house to live, fully knowing he had put out his other six children along with their mother for his new wife. She was painfully aware that my father's wife would never welcome me into their home, but it didn't stop her from being utterly cruel towards me.

"Since your nasty father and his stinking, mangoose-colored gal a guh send yuh a foreign, why you nuh go and live with them?" she would say to me, the madness shining fiercely from her eyes.

After the first six long and arduous months of waiting to finally go to the USA and receiving absolutely nothing in terms of communication from my father, I had taken the thought from my mind and buried it deep within. When Janet saw that not even the crushing disappointment of not being able to visit America could alter my unwavering perception of my father, she became increasingly infuriated and insulting towards him. It didn't phase me in the slightest, because I was still able to mentally block out her relentless verbal abuse.

In the meantime, Deidre was looking at me with that infuriating smirk she had acquired, a smirk that seemed to suggest she knew something we didn't. It was at that moment that the troubling thought had crossed my mind that perhaps she had done something underhanded to prevent me from going to America, but I had long since taken the idea of traveling to the United States of America out of my mind entirely.

~~~~~

I never questioned Janet's motive for wanting all three of us in the house with her, especially after she had been so happy to ship the rest of us off to different families to be raised elsewhere. I knew that if there was someone out there who truly wanted me, she would have likely shipped me off to them as well. It was increasingly clear that she had little interest in keeping us all bundled up together in the same small space for extended periods. Out of necessity, I had become accustomed to being the only child in the house. With just one child to care for, she was somehow able to control her madness and her cruel tendencies to a certain extent. However, with all three of us present, she seemed to lose her grip on her own sanity. So, it left me pondering why she would choose to have us all in the house together, and why she included Leo in this unsettling arrangement.

Her motive for having all of us in the house was questionable at best, leading me to wonder if she was aware of Leo's disturbing past as a child molester before bringing him into our lives. Did she have any knowledge of his unsettling attraction to little girls? She always seemed to have some notion of things happening around her, so it made me curious if she discovered his intentions and purposely used us as a means to secure his support for her own needs.

Another question that plagued my mind was her assertion of being a light sleeper when he was engaging in those nightly actions right before they would go fishing. Shouldn't she have realized something was deeply wrong the very first night if she truly was a light sleeper? They would leave the house for their fishing trips, and on those occasions, he would attempt to feel us up before they left, ensuring we were tucked into bed before a certain time.

There were times when the weather outside was so relentlessly bad that they couldn't go fishing at all. During times like that, he would feel us up every single night, and she never got up from her place to monitor his questionable movements. Yet, she would constantly claim that she was a light sleeper. The moment we complained about the unsettling situation, shouldn't she have at least tried to monitor the disturbing events unfolding? Instead of doing the right thing that a normal mother would have done in that scenario, she would beat the living daylights out of us, while he would angrily shout at her to search us thoroughly.

It was a deeply ingrained routine. Going to Edmorine's would effectively save me from those long, torturous nights of being fondled. Sometimes, I would return home so late that they'd be gone. Although, it didn't spare me from being unceremoniously searched the very next day. They would return home the following morning, only to have him quarreling vehemently with her, accusing her of allowing me to have a man.

Janet, for her part, knew Edmorine's aunt quite well. She was fully aware of where they lived and their connection. They were one of the many fish customers she had developed relationships with throughout the years. The things she saw me bring into the house to wear were unmistakable to her; she knew precisely where I obtained those items. With all of this information at her disposal, she would still act as if everything he said was undeniably correct, treating us according to the way he dictated, without question.

I also couldn't help but wonder about my role in all of this chaos. Would it have been better for everyone if I had simply died? Sometimes, I wanted to—very badly. I would find myself staring at a fast-moving trailer or a looming bus, imagining running straight into it, wondering how it would feel to have my bones crushed into pieces. It was a dark thought that frequently crossed my mind. Sometimes, after she finished beating me in the head in a fit of rage, I would quietly pray that I would simply drop dead.

~~~~~

Having Edmorine in my life made me realize that it was often better to go home late, desperately trying to eliminate the unsettling feeling ups. At least with the searching, he could only look—that was—until she started allowing him to put his hands on my vagina, the way she did, pulling it apart with a disturbing sense of entitlement.

Madness and rage, coupled with the overwhelming need to cut myself all over, would consume my mind to such an extent that I would find myself walking for hours, tugging at my hair, acting like a person caught in the throes of meth withdrawal. To have him putting his hands on me at night while lying to her about it felt so much different than having him put his hands on me under her watchful gaze; in fact, it was another thing altogether that drove me almost to the brink of madness. The very thought of it would send a surge of rage, madness, and an unrelenting urge to harm myself coursing through me so profoundly that I was left questioning how I could ever hope to survive it all.

29. Klam's Torture

At the tender age of sixteen, Klam suffered the unthinkable when she was raped by a big, hefty man. The impact of this horrifying experience was nothing short of a devastation to us. It was the very first time that I had ever witnessed my mother, Janet, display any genuine kind of attention or concern for her daughter's well-being.

Determined to seek justice, Janet took the initiative to go to the police after she discovered the man's house and even dragged the authorities there to confront him in his yard. Unfortunately, nothing meaningful came out of that encounter. The man vehemently denied the allegations, claiming he had not raped her. As a response, the police took Klam to the hospital, where medical professionals gave her precautionary treatment to ensure she was not pregnant. The only silver lining arising from the traumatic event was that Leo, did not approach Klam again.

However, as the painful truth settled in that Klam had been raped, Janet's already abusive language towards her only escalated further. She hurled accusations at Klam, labeling her a whore and suggesting that she had somehow invited the attack because she wanted it, that was why she had ended up in the man's path. On other occasions, her rage would boil over, leading her to physically harmed Klam, desperate to force her to admit that she had willingly engaged with the man and was terrified of the possibility that she might be pregnant.

Klam possessed a remarkable ability to forgive and forget, which had allowed her to overcome many of life's challenges. Yet getting raped was a different kind of burden, one that she could not simply leave behind. With Janet there, relentlessly drumming her cruel words into Klam's mind day after day and forcing her to relive those traumatic memories, Klam struggled to move past the horrifying experience. There were moments when I would find her curled up in the dark chicken coop, desperately trying to hold herself together amidst the emotional turmoil.

After enduring months of Janet's escalating madness, Klam came to the difficult conclusion that it was preferable to live with my grandmother and endure the physical beatings from my cousin than to remain in that toxic environment. At least with my cousin, there was a chance for her to defend herself. Escaping to my grandmother's house ultimately proved to be a wise choice on Klam's part, providing her with a much-needed respite from the chaos and abuse she had faced.

After Klam moved out, Leo started to be significantly more bold and reckless with the feeling up. It was during this unsettling period that I became convinced that our sole purpose in the house was to accommodate his unsettling desires. I didn't understand the full gravity of the situation at the time, but as I matured and began to reflect on Janet and my life, I ultimately discovered that she had known all along that he was a child-molester, and that he was indeed molesting us. But it was the only way she could see to keep him in the house and to ensure that there was food on the table.

With this painful knowledge weighing heavily on my mind, I decided to give running away another earnest attempt. I was sixteen years old then. This time, I went to my father's house in hopes of escaping. I mustered the courage to tell him what was happening behind the closed doors of our home, and he listened, but only offered that I could stay there for the day, under the condition that I would have to leave the next morning.

I should have started harboring hate for him in that very moment, too. But I found myself overwhelmed by the anger I held for so many other individuals in my life that my mind simply couldn't take on another target of resentment.

My father was a Jehovah's Witness, a fact that added layers to my situation. He had started teaching me the Bible and taking me to the Kingdom Hall with him regularly. However, none of that seemed to matter to him when it came to my dire needs. It became painfully clear to me later that he didn't possess the attitude or capacity to be truly responsible for his actions as a parent.

For him to blatantly disregard the fact that I desperately needed help, a safe place to stay—to protect myself, both mentally and physically, from the insidious abuse—should not have been an acceptable reaction. He resided in a large house with many unoccupied rooms, which could have easily provided me with the refuge I so urgently needed.

I should have started hating him, as well, but instead, I felt an unsettling mix of confusion and resignation. That day, I learned it didn't matter to him what happened to me. I was just a result of an unfortunate accident that he begrudgingly had to saddle himself with. Yet, remarkably, he still expected me to come along with him, studied the Bible diligently, and attend the Kingdom Hall without question. At the Hall, he pretended to be the best father a girl could ever hope to have, putting on a façade that concealed the truth.

It should have made me think twice about the denomination I was getting myself involved with. A church that excused a father who so blatantly shirked his responsibilities should never be allowed to function and grow within the community. Many of the elders knew about the hidden sins he committed against his innocent children with the woman he had lived with for almost twenty long years, yet they chose to overlook it all. Just because he married another woman and pretended to settle down in a new life, shouldn't have excused the consequences of his past actions, which left its mark on all those children.

It never dawned on me to look at the bigger picture; I was too wrapped up in my own suffering. All I was consumed with was the chaos and neglect that was happening in the house I lived in. I wasn't a smart person, and I didn't take the time to think critically about my circumstances.

Although he was never the one directly administering these abuses, the fact that he had a hand in siring me should have made me realize that some of the responsibilities for what was going on in my life rested squarely on his shoulders. He should have been more accountable and responsible for the well-being of his children.

He knew about my struggles all too well. I had told him some of the things that were happening to me many times, yet he never protected me as a father should. He didn't care enough to provide me with the security and protection I so desperately needed. He should have been prominently featured on my hate list. But I wasn't thinking like this at the time.

I was too young and innocent to fully grasp that he had chosen a wife who didn't want to compete with his children for his attention and affection, a woman strong enough to turn him away from his responsibilities as a father and a man. A wife he used as a convenient excuse to hide the true nature of the person he really was. He was a weak, careless man whose only desire in life was to spread his seed around wherever he could. A mere sperm donor. A typical Jamaican man trapped in his own web of self-interest.

I was lucky that he had even given me that one day. However, it only reinforced the deep and unsettling knowledge that I really and truly had no one to lean on during these difficult times. The next day, after I had spent hours cleaning his house and meticulously washed his sheets that had piled up—

because that was the only reason he had allowed me to stay for even that brief moment—he nonchalantly gave me twenty dollars and sent me back home without a second thought.

When I got home, feeling utterly disappointed and consumed by thoughts of despair, Janet just looked at me with that familiar disdain and said, "Yuh fucka yuh. Yuh think him did a go take yuh in?"

In that moment, I hated her more than anything else in the world. If she wasn't such a cruel, heartless person, or if she had the sense to take better care of herself, or was sensible enough to use some sort of protection, I wouldn't be suffering this horrific life.

~~~~~

Life continued on its unrelenting path, and I was barely managing to pass my grades. As soon as one season for an activity wrapped up, another would promptly begin, filling my schedule to the brim. I was good at all of them, but when there was a break from school, I would find my way to the chicken coop or sneak beneath her bed to immerse myself in my beloved Mills and Boon novels.

I had successfully graduated from children's books to exploring the captivating world of young adult novels that arrived with the library van. It was the only reminder of past times that was still coming like clockwork to Bower Bank.

Those books were the only source of escape for me, offering me a different life that I craved. I had reached the pivotal age where I could fully dive into young adult literature, savoring the world and experiences within those pages.

30. Making Promises To Myself

The day I turned sixteen was the day I truly looked at myself in the mirror, and for the very first time, I saw me. I examined my reflection as though I were looking at myself through other people's eyes, and the conclusion I reached was that I was indeed the ugliest thing I had ever encountered. My skin was painfully sunburned, flushed and very dark. My teeth seemed to be too big for my mouth, and filled with plaque that only seemed to amplify my insecurities. Some parts of my gum lines had receded so severely that I could, with great discomfort, see the exposed bones underneath. They were all pushing out, uncontrollably shaking. I possessed the worst overbite imaginable. And the habit of sucking my fingers had obviously exacerbated the problem significantly.

Janet had constantly called Klam and me "black and ugly," but until that moment, I could not see what she was talking about—not until now. That day I truly looked at myself for the first time, and in my realization of my ugliness, I felt the tears begin to fall. I was indeed ugly, and the truth hurt. It was also on that exact same day that I decided to stop sucking my fingers. Remarkably, the moment I stopped that childish habit was the day I finally stopped wetting the bed as well.

Unfortunately, I didn't have a toothbrush or toothpaste available to clean the extensive buildup of plaque off my shaking teeth, so I made a solemn promise to myself that I would get braces once I managed to move out. I also vowed to return to school, a simple yet profound goal, when I finally left my current situation.

I had reluctantly come to terms with my life as it was. Deep down, I understood that this would be my existence while living with Janet. But I promised myself to strive for a better life because I owed myself at least that much.

~~~~~

I graduated from Vauxhall Secondary at the young age of seventeen. In a moment of determination, I went to my father and urgently demanded that he put money in the court, as I was in urgent need of a graduation gown. It was a unique situation for me, as I had never spoken to him in such a direct manner before, but this graduation held immense significance for me and my future.

Unfortunately, he didn't provide enough money for a proper gown, but he did manage to send just enough to purchase a piece of cloth, which I had taken to a dressmaker who crafted me a lovely dress. However, once the dress was completed, I found that I hated it.

It simply wasn't nice enough to celebrate such a monumental occasion. Thankfully, one of my favorite cousins, Pamela, generously offered me a dress that was absolutely stunning; when I put it on, I felt as though I was preparing to attend a wedding, rather than just a graduation.

Additionally, I was able to buy a decent pair of white heels—my very first pair—which perfectly matched the dress. Pamela, who was quite talented as a beautician, even offered to perm my hair. This was an entirely new experience for me, as it was the first time I had ever gotten my hair permed, which left me feeling quite excited.

On the day of my graduation, I truly believed I looked lovely. With the new perm, my hair cascaded beautifully down my back, making me feel radiant and confident. As I stepped out of the house for my graduation ceremony, I quickly noticed that Janet couldn't seem to take her eyes off me. I felt a rush of nerves and hurriedly exited the house before she could find a reason to stop me.

The night before, Klam had come to help me get ready for my special function, and Deidre was also accompanying me to my graduation. This outing marked the second occasion we had ever dressed up and gone out together. Klam had graduated just the previous year, and we all celebrated her graduation together.

After graduation, I found myself in a difficult position as I couldn't find a job. During the tenth and eleventh grades, I enrolled in the business education program the school offered. This comprehensive coursework included crucial subjects like marketing, accounting, typing, and a variety of other business-related disciplines. Surprisingly, I had somehow managed to get into one of the most sought-after vocational programs at school, but I was still uncertain how I had done it. Despite my struggle to maintain focus due to my challenging circumstances, I was able to achieve average grades that reflected my efforts.

Now that I was out of school and facing reality, I desperately needed to find a source of income. I honestly couldn't recall how I began cleaning houses, but it quickly became my primary means of survival. With no school to attend as a refuge from my difficult living situation in Janet's house, each day felt like increasing torture. I would have done just about anything to escape that environment, so I resorted to cleaning people's dirty houses and washing their piles of dirty laundry, I had become a domestic worker like my mother. While I despised this work, I acknowledged that it provided me with some much-needed money and a sense of freedom.

Janet, in her increasingly cruel demeanor, had taken to telling me to, "Guh fuck! Yuh have a pussy, guh use it, yuh bloodclaat lesbian," she would sneer at me, her voice dripping with venom.

Meanwhile, Leo persisted in crossing boundaries, continuing to feel us up. We were lost, unsure how to escape the predicament we were in, and I had begun to shut out any interest in the opposite sex.

Many times, I overheard him telling my mother, "I want a virgin to fuck."

Her silent response always left me in a state of confusion and worry. I found myself engulfed in fear, and I didn't know how to break free from that fear. Nonetheless, I resolved to continue washing people's clothes and cleaning their houses until I could find a better option that would lead me toward a brighter future.

At eighteen and a half years old, a month or so after Deidre's graduation, we found ourselves reluctantly forced to go to Dunkirk because of the devastating arrival of Hurricane Gilbert. This unexpected turn of events changed everything for us. We received the directive to evacuate our home at Bower Bank. My mother, in a moment of quick thinking, sent us to stay with her cousin and his wife, who we affectionately called Sister Joyce.

She, along with her common-law-husband, joined the other vacated neighbors at Holy Rosary Catholic Church, seeking refuge from the chaos outside. Hurricane Gilbert wreaked havoc on the island, but in a paradoxical way, it also turned out to be a blessing for me in more ways than one.

During the tumult of Hurricane Gilbert, Deidre unexpectedly started her period, and I was tasked with the urgent mission of retrieving her underwear and sanitary napkins. I had to venture out into the ominously darkened sky, contending with the furious wind that screamed like an angry alien from another world.

Fortunately, I had lived with the screeching sound of storms all my life, which instilled a certain resilience in me. The eye of the hurricane swirled around me, dark, lonely, and extremely dangerous, reminding me vividly of my own turbulent feelings at that moment.

It became my only companion on the arduous journey to Holy Rosary Catholic Church. That day, much like the tumult of my life, I had to battle against the might of the winds to reach my destination—

gathering the things my deceitful sister, with her lying tongue, had requested.

Why did they have to send me out into such peril? Then it struck me; they were only following the instructions of Janet, who had directed them clearly.

"If you need anything at all, just send Swofiyah for it," she had told them matter-of-factly.

I almost got sliced in two on numerous terrifying occasions by flying aluminum zinc sheets that the brutal storm had sent whirling through the air. Time and time again, I felt the impact of fallen trees, as well as other hazardous flying objects that the unforgiving wind hurled in my direction. The crazy howling wind seemed intent on picking me up and sending me crashing elsewhere, but my feet remained steadfast on its angry path. Just when I thought I could persevere alone, Banana, who was the father of the boy whose head I had nearly chopped off in class so many years ago, came to intervene just as fate intended.

I was almost at the entrance of Bower Bank when he finally spotted me. He was valiantly warring against the wind as he made his way towards the church with determined effort.

"Jesus Christ likkle gal, a what yuh a do out in a this? A no yuh a Janet daughter?"

Not pausing to wait for an answer, he swiftly picked me up and ran with me as though I weighed no more than a mere paperweight, all the while battling fiercely against the wind and the relentless rain, which hit my exposed skin like a flurry of needle pricks.

Part of me felt a little disappointed that he had scooped me up so quickly. I found myself battling not only the needle-pricking rain, but also the wild wind that hurled everything it could towards me, and this struggle was doing something profound to my spirit. I had begun to fight back.

The fear that coursed through me was a different kind of fear altogether. It pushed me to stand firm on my two feet. It fortified my mind and revealed to me that if I was going to survive this tempest, I needed to fight with all my might.

Engaging with Hurricane Gilbert was surprising and invigorating. It was an exhilarating confrontation, worthy of all my resolve, and I almost found myself tempting the very death it wished to bestow upon me. I craved its challenge, but that fateful end never approached, as Banana flung open the church door and called out Janet's name with urgency.

Inside the church, I saw that it was packed with people from various communities, seeking refuge. My gaze landed on Leo, the child molester, sitting uncomfortably among a group of innocent children, and an uneasy feeling washed over me. I felt an overwhelming urge to alert the parents, to warn them that a child molester was lurking among their midst, but I hesitated with dread.

The words never came out of my mouth, because he was looking at me with an intense gaze that I have only seen mirrored in Janet's eyes. The unsettling look of madness was deeply embedded within him, and I had only just caught a glimpse of it. I turned my head slightly to the left, trying to adjust my angle to get a better look at this alarming sight. I wanted to make absolutely sure that I was truly seeing what I believed I was seeing. How had I never noticed it before in all the time we had spent together? I had heard people say that mental illness was catching, and now I was left to ponder the implications of that statement. He suddenly cast his eyes downward when he realized I was finally starting to see him, really see him.

Janet did not even attempt to stop me from going back into the powerful grip of the hurricane. Instead, she diligently packed up Deidre's unmentionables in a black plastic bag and sent me back out into the danger, showing no sign of concern whatsoever for my safety or well-being. It was then, amidst the chaos, that I promised myself that should she die, I would never shed a single tear for her passing. Not one tear drop would I allow to escape for her.

I found myself crying in the eye of the storm as our fierce battle against nature continued to rage on. In that tumultuous moment, I made another solemn promise to myself. That if I were to survive this harrowing ordeal, when brighter days returned to my life, I would go back to a good college and pursue the education I had been unable to focus on while living under her roof.

That day, as I returned to Dunkirk in the ferocious Hurricane Gilbert, I fought against the intense winds, suffered through the needle-pricking rain that threatened me with temporary blindness, and dodged an onslaught of flying debris including zinc houses, uprooted trees, bicycles, aluminum fences, car parts, discarded clothing, and many other hazardous items with both bravery and a renewed hope for my future.

I was completely alone in the world, but I understood that shit happened, and one had to get used to the unexpected traumas of life. There I stood, isolated in the fierce wind and the ravages of the deadliest hurricane to ever hit the island in many decades, and strangely enough, I felt a profound sense of empowerment in that very moment.

I knew that day that my life would change forever. How, exactly? I didn't know yet. One thing I was certain of, though, was that nobody else was going to change my life for me. That responsibility rested solely on my own shoulders.

I prayed fervently to God that they would discover the molester lurking in the church, should he ever be so bold as to target another innocent child among so many people gathered together. I finally stopped hating myself for not being brave in those moments of fear. I cast aside thoughts of the two monsters cuddled together inside the church, banishing them from my mind for the next three weeks.

During those three weeks I spent with Sister Joyce and her husband, I chose to imagine that they were the loving parents God had never given me. They cared for me in ways that my own mother never had, with a warmth and attention that was both comforting and healing.

Deidre would disappear every chance she got, seeking solace from the chaos around us. Sometimes, Sister Joyce would issue a quiet warning to her to be careful, almost as if she knew something we didn't.

The Dunkirk Community was big and sprawling, filled with life and activity. The houses here were actually apartments housed within ten-story high buildings, with some reaching only five or eight stories tall. The sturdy brick apartments contained all the necessary amenities, providing a comfortable refuge. Sister Joyce lived in a two-bedroom apartment that included a kitchen, a bathroom, and a cozy living room.

In the heart of the community was a massive football field accompanied by both a basketball court and a netball court. There were numerous shops and various places to buy things to eat, making it a lively hub. Many of the netball players from my school team, who had since transitioned to the club team, also called this vibrant place home.

Having enough to eat during the first couple of days after the hurricane had caused me considerable worry, but thankfully, their son Paul, who was serving in the army, brought us an abundance of food, so much that I literally began to put on weight while living with them.

Living there was also a wonderfully peaceful experience. Throughout the three weeks we spent there, I had not heard a single bad word or curse uttered in any context. Sister Joyce's other children came to visit after the devastation of the hurricane, eager to see how she was holding up and feeling. It had been quite a long time since I had seen them.

Susan had become a doctor with a promising career, while Muffet had found her path as both a pharmacist and a dietician. With such supportive and sound parents like theirs, it was clear they were bound to achieve great things in life.

I had begun going back to the Kingdom Hall regularly. My father was, unfortunately, a difficult person, but I desperately needed the presence of God in my life. It had been a struggle attending services when I was living with Janet, as she despised what she referred to as the "Jehovah Wickedness." However, I found genuine comfort in attending those meetings. Now that I had the opportunity to stay at Sister Joyce's house, I was able to go without any worries and with a true sense of peace of mind.

It was three weeks after Hurricane Gilbert when we finally returned to our home in Bower Bank. I felt a heavy reluctance to go back, but Janet came for us, insisting we leave with her. That night, after we returned home, Leo wasted no time in falling back into his normal, troubling routine.

The next morning, when I told Janet about his actions, he quickly dismissed me with accusations, claiming I was lying. To my astonishment, Deidre suddenly intervened and confirmed that what I was saying was indeed true. I was completely shocked.

Throughout the years he had been feeling us up, she had never once admitted to it—except for that one fleeting moment—but that morning, when she finally revealed the truth, my mother decided it was time for him to stop sleeping in our house altogether.

A month later, Deidre began experiencing bouts of nausea that led her to vomiting in the early morning hours, and it was during this tumultuous time that Janet discovered the life-changing news: Deidre was pregnant. The three weeks spent in Dunkirk had resulted in her finding a boyfriend, and this relationship ultimately led to her unexpected pregnancy. This revelation was the only reason she felt compelled to admit to being fondled. Deidre had come to realize that she didn't need Leo anymore. She had remained silent about the whole situation, primarily because of the various things Leo had been providing for her.

When Janet learned about Deidre's pregnancy, she reacted with a fit of rage, and for the first time since she had witnessed us teaching each other the art of French kissing, she physically retaliated against Deidre. However, this beating was, in truth, not as severe as it would have been had it been Klam or I who had gotten pregnant.

Deidre chose to remain indoors throughout her entire pregnancy. She was overwhelmed with shame and felt too embarrassed to go out. The only time she ventured beyond the confines of the house was for her regular check-ups at the clinic.

Sometimes, her boyfriend would visit, but Janet could not hide her disdain for him. She made it clear she thought he was "too black and skinny," expressing her prejudice openly.

In the final month of Deidre's pregnancy, she made the decision to move in with her mother-in-law, as the living situation in Dunkirk where they had been staying was perceived to be much more suitable.

As a result of Deidre's relocation, I found myself alone with Janet once again, but this solitude did not last for long. After two weeks of Deidre residing at her mother-in-law's home, Leo reappeared. It was becoming increasingly clear that Janet was beginning to accept the uncomfortable truth that he was indeed a molester, and consequently, he no longer attempted to feel me up me at night as he usually did.

Now at nineteen years old, I still harbored a deep-seated fear of both Janet and Leo. Although the molestation itself had ceased along with the searching, I continued to receive unsettling looks and endured the beatings that seemed to come without warning.

I hadn't gotten a proper job yet, a situation that filled me with frustration and disappointment. I was still doing domestic work, tasks that felt beneath my potential and aspirations. I hated myself for it, often questioning my decisions and life choices. Every time I lifted a mop to wipe the floors, my mind would drift to thoughts of Janet and the unsettling possibility of me ending up like her, trapped in a cycle I desperately wanted to escape. But for now, despite my dreams and ambitions, I had no other choice but to continue with this work.

31. My Employment

I finally found a job working in the Kingston
Central Constituency office as a clerical
assistant to Mr. Benson. The office was conveniently
located over at Alpha Primary School. With this new
job opportunity, I grew a little more confident in
myself and my abilities. I was ecstatic when I was
finally able   to stop doing domestic work.

On my first day, Mr. Benson came in to show
me exactly what was to be done as part of my role.
The job was not demanding as the business education
classes I had taken at Vauxhall Secondary School
equipped me with the necessary skills to tackle task.
Been there by myself was good. I did my tasks then I
would buy myself lunch, which was usually a very
busy time since all the students of the primary school
were also out for lunch. I didn't mind, I get to watch
them and see if there were anyone looking abused or
self absorb the I used to look when I was their age.

Mr. Benson did not return to the office again until
after the fourth day. He had mentioned previously that
he would only be in the office once a week, so I was
surprised when he unexpectedly stopped by for the
second time that week.

The workplace had two offices—one that was
designated for me and the other, larger office that

belonged to Mr. Benson. After getting him up to date on all that I was doing and receiving further instructions from him, I went about completing the tasks he had outlined. About half an hour later, unexpectedly, he came into my office and stood quietly behind me. Just seconds later, without warning, I felt a hand cupping my right breast. I jumped out of the chair, my heart racing as my insides felt like they were turning themselves inside out.

"What, a what yuh a duh?" I asked, shocked and bewildered by the situation. He looked like such a distinguished gentleman, with his fair white skin and his black, shiny, straight hair. He was impeccably dressed in a tailored black suit with a crisp white shirt and a striped tie. I certainly didn't expect that kind of inappropriate behavior from someone who appeared to be so professional.

"What am I doing? I didn't do anything," he said, sounding so remarkably much like Leo, which only added to the surreal nature of the overwhelming moment we were stuck in. Is this truly what I had to look forward to in men? Was there really no one out there who possessed good morals and values? He was such a significant disappointment in my life. Frustrated and disheartened, I left the job and went back to scrubbing floors, a task that offered little satisfaction. I didn't say anything to Janet, because I had stopped confiding in her long ago.

Mr. Benson had lied so smoothly that even I, despite my better judgment, started to believe it was all just a figment of my imagination. It was two long weeks later when he unexpectedly came to Janet's one-room house to see me. With a sense of guilt on his face, he apologized and promised that it wouldn't happen again, while raising my pay by a hundred dollars.

Despite my initial hesitation, I decided to give it another chance, hoping for the best. With the extra hundred dollars, I was finally able to start saving. Over time, I sent myself back to evening classes, yearning for knowledge and growth. While I enjoyed the experience of going back to school, I soon realized that mentally, I wasn't quite ready yet. I ultimately stopped after the first semester, feeling overwhelmed by the demands of my life.

I was still living in Janet's house, enduring both physical and verbal abuse. She believed that I was going to bring all my pay to her, which added to the strain of our living situation. When that didn't happen, she transformed into someone I hardly recognized, becoming more evil in her demeanor.

Sometimes, to avoid her wrath, I would go home late, hoping to dodge her anger. However, when I did finally get home, the door would be locked tight against me. I often had to wait for her to return, enduring the dark nights. At times, I would resort to sleeping on the veranda until she eventually came back to open the door.

It had never truly occurred to me that I could begin saving my money and seriously contemplate moving out of my childhood home. In fact, it really didn't cross my mind that I was now an adult, fully capable of making my own decisions, and that I didn't need to live there anymore if I didn't want to. I had become so very accustomed to having it as my only home that it simply never dawned on me to start saving up, to gather my belongings, and to finally make the leap and go.

Deidre came back to Janet's small one-room house, bringing with her the baby who was just two months old. He was undoubtedly the cutest baby I had ever seen, with soft cheeks and bright eyes, and I loved him immediately. Three months after she moved back in, her father, wanting to ensure her future, signed her up for college.

The moment I reached the age of eighteen, my father made the decision to stop giving us any financial support.

When Deidre moved back in, I quickly learned that I was no longer allowed to sleep on the bed. That space was now reserved solely for Deidre and her little baby, Tailor. As a result, I began sleeping on the floor, which I had gotten used to over the years.

At this point, I had started using my hard-earned pay to buy small things for little Tailor. He had quickly become the love of my life, and I took great joy in taking him with me wherever I went whenever I managed to find the free time.

Six months into her college journey, Deidre unexpectedly found herself a married man who was willing and able to help her financially. The very first thing she did with her newfound support was to buy a brand new bed. The old one, which was extremely worn and tattered, was thrown out promptly. Unfortunately, my pay still wasn't nearly enough to afford a new bed, so I was forced to continue sleeping on the cold, hard floor. When the new bed arrived, I couldn't go near it at all, much less brush up against it or even sit on it.

They began to treat me as if I had some kind of contagious disease. Sometimes, little Tailor would try to sleep on the floor with me, seeking comfort in my company, but his mother would shout at him to get back up on the bed, firmly insisting he stay away from me.

I had stopped using the chicken coop for quite some time now because the scorpions had become increasingly prolific. I was constantly getting stung by them whenever I ventured inside. Over time, the coop had turned into nothing more than a junk storage area for all the woods Janet picked up off the street.

~~~~~

I felt impoverished and poverty stricken, living on the thin, hard floor of my mother's cramped one-room house, even though I had a job. Deidre and I still cursed and fought—more frequently now than ever before. Since she returned with the baby, I had become the unwanted presence in the house. I was considered the "nothing," a label my mother had always classified me as.

Both Deidre and Janet were now cursing me incessantly and telling me to get out. Although I had a job, it still wasn't nearly enough to fully support myself or contribute meaningfully. If I wanted something as simple as a snack or a small item of clothing, I had to save for months and meticulously budget to buy it.

With her attending college, she seemed more convinced than ever that she was better than us, soaring above the rest of us in stature and worth. My mother had now begun looking at her like she was the superior one in their eyes. Sometimes when we fought, it was over the smallest of infringements, like when I had taken a little of her food, or a simple squeeze of her toothpaste. She absolutely hated it whenever I touched her things, but the moment I had something she wanted, she would use it until it was finished, then she would promptly go out and buy her own, issuing a strict prohibition against my usage. When I did, the inevitable fighting would start without fail.

Deidre had grown as hefty as Janet, both of them seeming to find strength in numbers. Whenever she felt like treating me like her own child, or perhaps the unwanted dog they took me for, she would hit me with a force that felt so strong it would seem as if it were Janet delivering the blow. This treatment would incite waves of incensed anger within me. As a result, I would dig into her skin deeply with my long, sharp nails. Anywhere my nails could find a place to grip, I would leave huge, glaring red scars that would be hard to ignore. When Janet returned home and Deidre showed her the scars I had left, the baton stick would come down hard on my head without mercy.

That was the only place she aimed for now with the baton stick; my head was the unfortunate target of her wrath.

"Bloodclaat lesbian, go fuck and come out a me house!" Janet would shout at me with a fierce intensity, sometimes when she wasn't satisfied with the beating she had just inflicted, or I had managed to escape her wrath before she was fully satisfied. When those moments occurred, she would act like a relentless parasite, until she got her satisfaction.

My job with the Kingston Central Constituency had granted me the opportunity to work at the Head Office located on Duke Street. The pay was consistent, amounting to four hundred and eight dollars every fortnight. Although it wasn't nearly enough to make ends meet for a full two weeks, I was still managing to make do with what I had. While I was working at the Electoral Office, I discovered that the other employees there were earning significantly more than I was. Eager to improve my situation, I tried to apply for a job in that office, but, unfortunately, I was turned down.

Each day, in order to get to work at the Electoral Office, I had to take the bus, except for the weekends.

This stood in stark contrast to my previous situation, where I would simply walk to Alpha Primary School each morning. Back then, I didn't have to worry about bus fare, but now I found myself increasingly anxious about the daily expenses. In light of this, I made the decision to search for additional work on the weekends to supplement my income. Eventually, I secured another job working as a data entry operator, which was scheduled to start at ten in the night and concluded at six in the morning. This arrangement really helped since it meant I didn't have to sleep at home, enabling me to earn some extra money that could be put aside for future needs. Yet, in that moment of decision making, I didn't truly think through the consequences.

Janet, with her erratic and hateful behavior, would inevitably start her chaotic chanting whenever I was trying to get some much-needed rest in the early evening hours. On particularly desperate nights, I would hide under the bed, but even then, she would somehow figure out that I was there, and her chanting would only escalate, growing even louder. As a result, I was not getting the amount of sleep that was necessary for me to function normally throughout the day.

With the relentless beatings she would administer, the incessant noise, and the profound lack of sleep, I started to feel an unsettling strangeness creeping into my head and body, making it difficult to grasp the reality around me.

Six weeks into the grueling night job, I experienced a complete mental block. Recognizing the lack of sleep on my well-being, I knew I had to quit it for the sake of my health. A month later, after leaving the night job behind, I made the difficult decision to resign from the Electoral Office as well to accept a position ffrom Ammars on King Street, conveniently located across from Woolworth. It was during my time there that I unearthed an unexpected talent for sales. Just three months later, I received a promotion and was transferred to Ammars' uptown branch located in The Village Mall on Half Way Tree Road. My pay increased significantly with this new role, allowing me to save my money, this time in a real bank account. Though I contributed to the house expenses, it always seemed like it was never quite enough.

Over the years, I had endured so much that it became almost secondary to my existence. The ceaseless cursing, the frequent fighting, the physical confrontations—the psychological damage I sustained was deep and profound. I found myself at a loss, unsure of how I was going to embark on a journey to heal myself. However, I realized that if I intended to function normally in the years to come, I would have to actively seek out a way to mend my mental scars. At almost twenty-two, I finally came to the enlightening conclusion that I could begin purchasing items in small quantities for the new apartment that I was increasingly obsessing over in my mind.

I had finally made a firm decision: I would not be living the life of poverty any longer, trapped in a cycle of sleeping on the floor and allowing my family to hold me down with their biting words for the rest of my life.

The first sets of things I bought were beddings for the double bed I haven't purchased yet. Along with the beddings, I acquired knives, spoons, curtains, and a variety of other small items that I considered absolutely necessary for my future living situation. I bought them at my job, where I happily received a ten percent discount for being an employee. I kept all these items safely stored at Bobby's house, a friend I had met some time ago and had grown quite fond of.

Bobby lived up Jackson Road, just off Windward Road. His mother, who was of Asian Jamaican descent, baked delicious treats every day. His grandmother was Afro Jamaican, which added to the cultural tapestry of their home, while his father was Indian Jamaican. Bobby bore a striking resemblance to his father, which often caused me to feel a sense of connection to his family. He and I shared a bond that felt like an escape I often craved. Sometimes, I would spend hours at Bobby's house, simply to stay away from the tensions found within my own home. I even entertained thoughts of running away to live there permanently, an idea that felt both grand and liberating. His mother ran a successful bakery in the back of their house, which brought in steady income and made their home a cozy haven.

At one particularly difficult point, I began to question whether they truly liked me, until a dramatic incident unfolded. One day, my mother chased me all the way up Jackson Road, trying to do me harm on the rare occasion I mustered the courage to stand up to her. In a moment of defiance, I had told her that my father was a much better person than she ever was. She became incensed at my words. In the heat of the moment, I made my escape into Bobby's yard, only to have Janet, my mother, follow me there unleashing a torrent of curses that echoed through the neighborhood.

I thought his mother was going to tell me to go away and fetch my crazy mother from her gate. But instead, surprisingly, she went outside and firmly told my mother to get as far away as possible from her gate.

I was crying so hard that Bobby was frantically trying his best to console me. He knew well that I was getting abused, but unfortunately, he didn't know how to help me in any meaningful way. Many people were aware of my situation, but they too didn't know how to help me. That day, when Bobby's mother ran my mother off from her house, I suddenly realized that they didn't actually mind me being there at all.

As I started buying more and more things for the small apartment I had in mind, my confidence in myself became more and more manifested. I was slowly becoming a woman, and I had exciting goals to strive for. It was truly the only thing that was carrying me through those difficult times, the idea that I had something better to look forward to in the near future. I was still continuing to play netball on Saturdays for the Vauxhall Club team, but now that I had to work on Saturdays at Ammars, I was missing both training sessions and netball matches. I also found myself losing interest in the game and its excitement.

My primary focus had shifted towards getting out and starting my new life. I was genuinely looking forward to the next phase of my life. I could feel this current phase coming to an end, yet I had no clear idea of how the next phase would actually begin.

32. Roller Skating

A new skating rink recently opened up on Windward Road, bringing a fresh wave of excitement to the area. It quickly became another beloved nighttime escape from my daily life, providing a temporary respite from my worries. I had fallen deeply in love with skating, pouring my heart into it, and I became quite skilled at it over time. However, I faced a dilemma, as I couldn't afford to spend all my hard-earned savings on what was meant to be pure fun. I wasn't that frivolous, and I had to be mindful of my finances.

I decided to take the advice of my penpal, a good friend I had found some time ago. He was from Ghana originally but had made a life for himself in Japan. He encouraged me not to be afraid of reaching out to him for assistance. The only thing I wanted very badly at that moment was a pair of proper skating shoes. Unfortunately, they were well beyond my budget, so in a moment of vulnerability, I asked him for help.

When he graciously sent me a hundred United States dollars along with three hundred thousand Japanese Yen, I was overjoyed and felt as if I had struck gold. I was already making ambitious plans to move out the following week to embrace my newfound freedom, until I visited the bank and discovered with shock that the Yen was only worth Jamaican one hundred and forty-five dollars. I couldn't shake the feeling that I either had been misled or worse, had been robbed at the bank. My disappointment was profound, but short-lived, after I finally purchased my very first pair of skating shoes. They were a beautiful white leather, which I decorated with ambient lighting that glowed enticingly in the dark.

From that moment on, I was at the skating rink every single night, practicing diligently and honing my skills. As a result, I began to gain recognition among the owner and the staff who worked there. They started to trust me, allowing me to enter without having to pay a fee, which was a rare privilege I cherished.

Over time, my skills improved significantly, enough to attract a crowd to the skating rink. Young people from various neighborhoods, many of whom had parents that would not have normally allowed them to attend, were now frequenting this vibrant place. The prevailing belief was that if nothing bad had ever happened to me while I was there, then surely nothing bad would happen to them either. This sense of safety and community led to more parents feeling comfortable sending their children to learn how to skate, creating a positive atmosphere for everyone involved.

On the weekends, the Rink opened very early in the morning, much to the delight of eager children. It would quickly become overcrowded with enthusiastic young skaters who had recently begun taking skating lessons to improve their skills. There were several dedicated workers employed to teach them the fundamentals of skating, ensuring that each child received the guidance they needed.

By this time, I had completely stopped playing netball, choosing instead to use skating as a means of exercising, recreation, and finding an escape from my home life. The less time I spent at home, the fewer chances my mother had to see me, which, in turn, seemed to lessen her craziness and abusive behavior. I had come to learn that something intrinsic about me drove her to the brink of insanity, and in her turmoil, she directed that insanity toward me in various harmful ways. When she saw me less frequently, she appeared to manifest less of her erratic behavior.

Meanwhile, Ben, my pen pal from Ghana who had relocated to Japan, suddenly stopped writing to me. I was utterly devastated by this unexpected silence. After nearly a year of exchanging heartfelt letters and him even proposing to me, it felt like an emotional blow. He was the first man who had ever proposed to me, making our connection uniquely special. He was the only person who had ever allowed me to dream of a life beyond the harsh realities I faced. When my letters started returning to me, unopened and marked, I knew in my heart that this was the definitive end of our once vibrant correspondence.

~~~~~~

I was almost twenty-two when I met Ony for the first time. I had known him from Vauxhall Secondary School, but during that time, I did not dare to look at or think about a person of the opposite sex. I felt like I had too much on my plate to even be thinking about boys. I remembered him from school quite vividly because he was one of the few students who kept giving me those playful horse whistles when we were training on the netball field, which was both amusing and a little embarrassing.

Washington, the owner of the skating rink, was hosting a much-anticipated dance at the skate land that night. The place was perfect for an event like this. It was packed to the brim with people that evening. The music was loud, pulsing through the air, and the rink was flooded with skaters from all corners of Kingston. The energy in the room was high, and happiness radiated all around me.

Many guys had tried their best to get my attention over the many months I spent practicing to skate there, but I consistently ignored them all, determined to focus on my own passions. On the night of the dance, Ony tried everything he could think of to get my attention, but I ignored him along with everyone else, as I usually did, stubbornly occupying my own little world.

During my skating lessons, I had made a few skating buddies—three girls and one guy, who was gay—over the past few months of learning to skate, and I guess Gary became my friend because he was no threat to me and we shared a comfortable friendship.

I was skating with joy, having a really great time that night, but my mother's venomous words kept ringing loudly in my ears, refusing to let me fully enjoy the moment.

"Why yuh nuh guh fuck and come out a me house?" she had snapped at me, viciously, after I told her not to go through my things. She had taken to searching my belongings relentlessly, trying to find where I had hidden my money. I had learned my lesson long ago when she had found my money and used it up.

That night, I skated so intensely that I didn't care if I fell a couple of times while others watched me. I chose to focus entirely on the music and the art of skating itself. It had become my passion, my escape, my constant companion. When I finally took a break from skating, I was breathing heavily and sweating buckets. I opened the bottle of water I kept tucked in my waistband and took a long drink while watching the others glide gracefully on the rink. Just then, Gary, my cheerful friend, skated up to me looking very happy, as if he had just won a small victory of his own.

"Swofiyah, me always love to see yuh skate," he said, his voice filled with excitement as he laughed heartily, gracefully skating around me while moving his body rhythmically to the lively music.

He was, without a doubt, a very good skater, gliding effortlessly across the surface. His jovial personality shone through; he was a playful and happy person by nature. Yet, I sometimes couldn't shake the worry that I might never have the chance to see him again. His sexual orientation often put him at risk, especially in a society where many Jamaicans didn't readily accept gay people.

"Thank you, my dear," I replied, returning his infectious laugh while shaking my upper body to the beat of Beenie Man and Lady Saw.

"Me friend want to meet yuh," Gary shouted, his voice rising above the loud, pulsating music.

"I don't want to meet anybody right now," I told him firmly, trying hard not to let his insistence spoil the joyful mood I was in.

"Come on, Swofiyah, just come meet him. Make him buy we a drink," he begged, giving me a cheeky wink that made me laugh again.

With a playful tug, he grabbed my hand and pulled me over to a dimly lit corner of the rink. This area wasn't as bright as the others, but it was filled with life; people crowded together, some watching the skaters while others danced passionately to the infectious reggae tunes.

In the corner, a very familiar-looking guy stood out. He was tall and strong, with a round face, alluring oriental eyes, and lips that were beautifully sculpted.

"I know you," I said playfully, shaking my finger at him, intrigued by the sense of recognition.

"I kno, kno, know you, too," he stammered, glancing nervously at me with a mixture of excitement and apprehension.

"Why yuh no go fuck!" Janet's voice slammed into my head, echoing sharply for the second time.

I quickly shook her intrusive words out of my mind and focused intently on the music and the boy standing right in front of me.

"See, so it's a good thing yuh come then," Gary bragged, his voice full of pride and satisfaction as he beamed at us.

Matchmaking was his undeniable talent, something he loved to boast about whenever someone tried to get him to be quiet, much to the amusement of the group.

Ony and I hit it off that night in a way that felt special. It was the very first time in my life that I experienced the warmth of someone walking me home to Bower Bank. Because of his stammering, he didn't talk much that evening, which only made him seem more captivating and mysterious. Later, I learned that it was only when he was extremely nervous that his stammering became more pronounced. I also found out that he was a highly respected tailor and an incredibly talented designer of men's clothing. Our friendship blossomed and grew until it transformed into something deeper and more meaningful. I began visiting his house regularly, where he warmly introduced me to his ninety-eight-year-old grandmother, the woman who had lovingly raised both him and his brother. His brother, I had previously met once at the skating rink. I observed the two brothers together and saw their unique behavior towards each other. I felt a pang of envy as I noticed the deep respect and affection they held for one another. They were especially loving, kind, and gentle when it came to their grandmother, a bond that warmed my heart and left a lasting impression on me.

~~~~~~

Sometimes Ony would come to my job after his own day was done and patiently wait for me, sometimes for what felt like an eternity. He would take me to the movies, or we would stroll for long hours together, enjoying each other's company under the stars. I genuinely liked that time spent with him.

The first time we kissed, all I could see was Leo's face, the memory vivid in my mind.

"What's wrong?" he had asked, concern etching his features.

"Nothing, I just have bad teeth, so I don't like kissing," I had told him honestly, my insecurities surfacing.

"I don't care 'bout yuh bad teeth. I love yuh. Yuh a the first girl me ever feel like this 'bout," he had replied with sincerity that caught me off guard.

"But yuh don't even know me. How yuh can love somebody yuh don't really know?" I asked him, my voice laced with confusion. It was the first time anyone had ever told me that they loved me. I didn't trust it.

There were times when I would not see him for days, and I would still continue going to the skating rink, hoping to lose myself in the gliding motions of the concrete surface. He would always be there, watching me from the sidelines. After a while, I stopped ignoring his presence and gradually allowed myself to feel the connection that was developing. Eventually, we grew closer, and I started spending more time at his house, feeling more comfortable with each visit. I began substituting my frequent trips to the skating rink for those moments with him in his very large room, filled with warmth and laughter.

They lived in a big house, only a ten-minute walk away from the skating rink. Over time, I learned to adjust my thinking and feelings whenever we kissed, embracing the warmth that blossomed between us.

I had grown to like Ony very much, perhaps even more than I initially realized. At his house, he was patiently teaching me to sew, a skill I was beginning to truly appreciate. I was learning how to cut and stitch on his sewing machine with great enthusiasm. I discovered that I was quite good at it, surprisingly so.

I remembered fondly how, in the ninth grade, I had made a fish tail skirt during sewing class. It was a project I had poured my heart into, and I had loved that skirt so much that I used to wear it constantly to the Kingdom Hall. However, that beautiful piece of clothing was taken from me in the chaos of hurricane, or so I was told.

Having Ony as my teacher, guiding me to sew properly, made me imagine that perhaps I could one day become a fashion designer. For a moment, I was able to forget about all the pain and brokenness I had been feeling. The time spent with him seemed to be helping me heal. It was allowing me to piece together some of the shattered fragments of my life.

The first time that we were intimate, I told him plainly that I didn't want him to put his hands on my vagina. It was a difficult ordeal, one filled with mixed emotions and uncertainty, but it was also a moment I was glad was over with. Now, at least, Janet could finally stop telling me to "guh fuck."

Did I really use Ony to get rid of my virginity? I wasn't entirely sure anymore. As time went on, I had grown to genuinely like him. However, after that intimate moment we shared, I quickly realized how much I had cherished my innocence. Now that I was no longer the same, my world seemed to become more cumbersome and complicated. I found myself playing a grown-up role, but the condition I was living in proved to me that I was inadequately prepared to take on such a heavy task. Because I was not yet my own woman, I was still searching for my identity and independence, I couldn't completely give my heart over to him.

Moreover, the outcome I had expected after Ony's grand declaration of his undying love simply didn't happen. The fact that he noticed the bruises on my skin yet chose to say nothing substantial about them left me feeling incredibly turned off and disenchanted.

I truly longed for someone who would genuinely care for me, someone who would say, "You don't have to go back there, you can stay here with me; we will figure everything out together." Because he didn't take that initiative or offer any words of comfort, it made me wonder if he truly understood the depth of what I was going through. Was he really going to be man enough to help me in my time of need?

33. The Baton Stick In My Belly

T he last time Janet told me to "go fuck," I took Ony by the arm and introduced him to her without hesitation. She looked at him, her eyes narrowed, and asked him, "Oonnu a fuck?"

To which he replied with a chuckle, "Yes."

He laughed in a way that suggested he thought it was all a joke. Little did he understand the monster he was truly dealing with. What he witnessed was just her mild side, the side that only appeared once in a blue moon, and even that was only because she was under the influence of a severely potent strain of marijuana that had mellowed her out significantly.

Later that very same day, after Ony left and the atmosphere settled back to its usual tension, Janet turned to me and expressed her approval, saying she liked him, but added with a pointed tone, "But yuh should a never guh fuck." Her words were laced with an unspoken warning that hung heavily in the air.

Two months after my very first sexual encounter, I began to experience bouts of vomiting that mirrored the way Deidre had suffered in the mornings once she became pregnant. It was then that Janet, brandishing the baton stick in her hand, cornered me behind the house, where I was desperately trying to rid my stomach of its contents. She pressed the baton stick forcefully into my belly and demanded with an unsettling intensity, "A breed yuh a breed? A how yuh a vomit up so?"

The pain shot through me, and I hunched over instinctively, wrapping my hands protectively around my stomach, trying to shield myself from the brutal reality of her question.

It was striking to recall, as she tormented me, that she had never once directed the baton stick toward Deidre's belly, even during her pregnancy, a fact that reinforced the horror of my current experience. In truth, she had never used the baton stick on Deidre at all.

"No," I told her, feeling a wave of fear wash over me. "A stop playing netball, so me period a make me sick." I was holding myself tightly around my belly, as if trying to soothe the anxious knots of uncertainty stirring within me.

She believed the cramp story I told her, nodding in understanding, and released me with a cautious warning. "Don't bloodclaat come in a me house a breed. Yuh not Deidre, so don't even think bout it."

That evening, the heaviness in my chest compelled me to visit Ony at his house, where I mustered the courage to tell him. "Me think me pregnant."

"What, yuh sure?" he asked, his brow furrowing in disbelief, as if the mere idea of me getting pregnant had never even crossed his mind before. We had never used condoms, a fact that now loomed large between us.

"I was vomiting this morning. I never vomited like that before," I assured him, feeling the weight of my words. "Janet see me and rammed the baton stick in a my belly and tell me not to come in her house if me a breed," I continued, the urgency of my situation bleeding into my voice.

"I don't have anywhere to put yuh," he said, his response hanging heavily in the air like an unanswered question, an invisible weight that made it hard for me to breathe. I could feel whatever feelings I had slowly growing for him crashing to the ground and drying up with that devastating statement. It was not in me to suggest that I could come and live with him, as the idea seemed to hold too much vulnerability. I wanted him to make the suggestion himself, to take the lead and reassure me. I wanted him to be a strong man, to look into my eyes and confidently say, "It's okay, yuh have me, just bring yuh things them and move in with me." But all he uttered was, "Go to the clinic tomorrow and make sure."

The next morning arrived, and I went to the clinic with Blossom and her friend, where I reluctantly confirmed the reality that I was pregnant. My already fragile world, which felt like it was barely holding together, was crashing down around me. I imagined the terrifying image of Janet ramming my innocent baby out of my belly with that baton stick, and the thought alone made my body tremble uncontrollably.

Blossom, my best friend who knew the depth of my situation, quickly said, "Come home with me. We can raise the baby together."

But in my mind, I couldn't bear to inconvenience her and her family like that. She didn't have the space to accommodate both me and a child. Though her mother, whom I had met so many times and found quite nurturing, was one hundred percent better than mine, I had learned to distrust any kind of mother figure. I couldn't bear the thought of saddling them with my presence and my psychological problems, along with a baby on top of it. But what choice did I truly have? So I stored her generous offer away in my mind as a faint possibility for the future.

That evening, while I sat in Ony's room, the weight of the moment felt pivotal as I told him that I was confirmed pregnant.

"What yuh want to do? Yuh want to throw it way?"

"What? No!" I exclaimed, utterly shocked that he would even put such a thought in my head. "A what yuh a ask me? Yuh don't want it?"

I was devastated by his reaction. It was not what I wanted to hear, nor was it something I ever expected. The disappointment weighed heavily on my heart.

The thought of abortion had never crossed my mind, never once had it dawned on me as an option. But now, when he suggested it, I felt like a drowning person grasping desperately at a flimsy straw. I simply wasn't ready to bring a child into the chaotic mess of my current problems. And in all my life filled with dreams and hopes, I had never seen a child in my future.

Yet suddenly, the idea of having a baby—someone to love me unconditionally and to whom I could give all that love I had bottled up inside, began to take root in my mind. It filled me with something very different to think about: hope. I instinctively hugged my belly, imagining the tiny person I could nurture and grow with. A little person emerging from my body, someone to develop an intense and beautiful bond of love with. Someone to live for, and yes, even to die for. The thought was both daunting and exhilarating at the same time. I yearned for this baby with all my heart.

But as I allowed my thoughts to flow, I couldn't help but imagine all the terrible things that Janet might do to us—me and my baby—and the fear threatened to overwhelm me. I dreaded the thought of my child being raised under her roof, knowing all too well the chaos she brought with her. No! It was simply not going to happen.

I even considered the possibility of going to stay with Blossom's mother, but I quickly dismissed that idea. With her living so close on Langstand Road and not very far from the turmoil of Windward Road, it just wasn't a practical solution to my predicament.

My tormentor would have hounded me, relentlessly, without any mercy. She would have found me and forcefully dragged me back to Bower Bank just so she could fulfill her cruel desire to torture the baby out of me. I simply could not take it any longer. It took me only a week to do what I considered the cowardly thing. I went to Ony and told him in a shaky voice that I would be having an abortion. There was no way I was going to tolerate someone like her hurting both me and my unborn baby.

He reluctantly gave me the money, and I went back to the clinic to ask for guidance and support. Two weeks later, I found myself baby-free. I stopped seeing Ony after that, mentally writing him off as my first and biggest mistake. I stayed away from the skating rink for a while, needing to distance myself from it all.

As my body began to heal, I started attending church regularly and prayed to God for forgiveness for the terrible choice I had made, for what I perceived as the murder I had committed. But amid all the guilt, I also felt a strange sense of relief. The cruel future that Janet had been planning for me, one that involved being burdened with a child, did not come to fruition. She didn't get that satisfaction, and for that, I was grateful.

My friend Blossom, moved back to her hometown in Hanover, leaving me alone to navigate my days. After an entire three months of adjusting to her absence, I found myself returning to the familiar and comforting environment of the skating rink. It was, after all, the closest place available for me to go in order to clear my mind and de-stress from the whirlwinds of life. I truly needed that outlet; I needed the exercise to rejuvenate my body. More importantly, I craved the mental escape it afforded me. The rink provided the recreation that my spirit sought desperately.

After returning to the rink for three solid months, I unexpectedly saw Ony again. However, I realized with a tinge of disappointment that my feelings for him had faded. I was still at my job at Ammars, though I began to limit my skating sessions to only three nights a week, as I started to feel the rink was becoming an increasingly dangerous place emotionally. I tried to stay away from it as much as I could, hoping to protect myself.

It was during this time, when I was nearing my twenty-third birthday, that I made the decision to give romance another genuine try. I felt that I owed it to my younger self to seek out love and connection, although I was careful to lower my expectations after my experiences with Ony.

One evening at the skating rink, I encountered Michael. His skating was absolutely phenomenal, showcasing skills that I had rarely witnessed before. Yet, it wasn't just his impressive abilities on the concrete rink that captivated me; it was the way he affected me, stirring feelings I hadn't experienced before. I couldn't seem to tear my eyes away from him, drawn inexplicably to his masculine presence.

While he wasn't conventionally handsome, he exuded a raw masculinity that was magnetic. Every time he offered a smile in my direction, it felt as though my heart would stop. I beamed with warmth. I found undeniable happiness in being around him, a sensation I had never felt before, not even with Ony. I made a conscious decision to grab hold of this newfound happiness while I still had the chance, fearing it might slip away too quickly.

During our very first skate together, I felt an exhilarating sense of isolation from the outside world; it was as if we were the only two souls present, gliding through time. The music resonated with an energy that was perfect for the moment. In his company, I found that I didn't care that I wasn't my own woman. With him, I felt every bit the woman I aspired to be, strong and free.

He was twelve years older than I was, a significant difference that brought with it a sense of maturity and wisdom. He possessed a thoughtful demeanor and was always respectful, truly embodying the essence of a gentleman in every interaction we shared.

During one of our conversations, he revealed that he had an ex-wife living in Canada, who had borne him two children. He generously handed me a picture of his two children, something I cherish deeply, as I still carry that picture in my wallet even to this very day.

As he spoke about his ex-wife, I could feel my heart split in two, grappling with a mix of emotions.

Yet, he quickly reassured me that there was nothing to be jealous about, calming my fears with his words.

He introduced me to his family, and among them, his aunty was someone I already knew well. She held the esteemed position of Captain of the Jamaica Netball Team and had been a part of the 'A' team at the Vauxhall Netball Club. I had always admired her talents and accomplishments, which led me to believe that he came from a genuinely good family with strong values.

A significant trial in our relationship arose one day when he caught sight of my bruised-up legs for the very first time. With a serious expression, he asked, "Swofiyah, what do you want me to do? Do you want me to give her a taste of her own medicine? Just tell me, and I will deal with it for you."

I was fully aware of the seriousness of his tone, but I firmly believed that this was ultimately my battle to fight. The notion of being involved with a woman-child—or, from his perspective, a woman who was not permitted the freedom to be a woman—only fueled his anger the longer we were together.

Although he was always kind and gentle, it became increasingly clear that he was deeply troubled by my ongoing struggles. I could see that he genuinely wanted to help me and put an end to my hardships.

Yet, I understood that this fight was not his to conclude; it was mine, and I had to summon the strength within myself to find a way to bring it all to an end.

The more he noticed the baton stick marks on my body, the angrier he became, his frustration at the situation palpable in the air around us. Unlike Ony, who saw me as a target, he viewed me as an angel deserving of protection, and he firmly believed that nobody should ever be treating me in such a cruel manner.

"Me mother is my battle. I will deal with it," I told him, trying to project confidence even though I had absolutely no idea how I was actually going to manage that. Deep down, I could feel that the end of this struggle was drawing very near, like the frightening approach of a storm.

"If I had the money, I would snatch you away in an instant and place you upon a pedestal, because that's where you truly belong," he would tell me, his tone filled with all the seriousness he could muster.

"You're so corny," I had joked once, playfully dismissing the sentiment. Yet, he had no idea just how deeply his words resonated with me and how good they made me feel inside.

On the weekends, when we weren't out skating, I would watch him play football with rapt attention. Just like his impressive skating skills, he took my breath away, completely captivating me as I observed his movements on the field.

"How comes you're not on a national team, been famous somewhere?" I had asked him once out of pure curiosity, genuinely wondering why someone so talented wasn't in the spotlight.

"Here, I'm too old and in Canada, I wanted to make fast money. I wasn't serious about joining any team," he admitted, sounding a little sheepish about his past decisions.

"Fast money?" I asked, wanting to understand more about his choices.

"Yes, I was very rich in Canada, until I got deported. My ex-wife took everything," he said, his voice heavy with the weight of his past.

"Oh, are you angry at her?" I had asked, not knowing what else to say in the moment, my curiosity piqued by his story.

"I was, but not anymore," he admitted, as he playfully grabbed me and began tickling me in spots I didn't even know were sensitive to tickles, bringing unexpected laughter to the room. We were in his room, filled with remnants of his family's life. He lived on his family's property, where memories lingered in every corner.

"Don't worry about anything, Swofiyah. I'm going to take care of you," he promised me, his expression shifting to one of earnest seriousness that gave me a sense of comfort. He was saying all the right words I had once imagined Ony saying to me, words that felt like solace during turbulent times. Sometimes, I stayed with him for days on end without even thinking of going home.

"So yuh find new man! A when yuh a go move out? Yuh a fuck now; a time yuh move out," Janet would say, her tone sharp and laced with the madness lurking behind her eyes, reminding me of the true reality I often wished to escape. With Leo there, watching quietly, his usual smirk playing on his lips while she sprouted her craziness, I found myself at a loss for words and didn't know how to respond to her taunts. So I simply remained silent.

34. Losing It

As my relationship with Michael steadily strengthened and my feelings for him continued to grow deeper, I found myself unable to envision a future where he wasn't a part of my life. I spent every free moment I had with him, enjoying his company and the connection we shared, while I gradually spent less time at Janet's place. My visits there became infrequent and were limited to only when I needed to pick up something important.

"What's the point of going back there, anyway?" Michael had asked me, his eyes filled with concern and understanding. "Just bring your things and stay here, with me. You don't need to go back there!"

Despite his compelling words, I couldn't bring myself to completely cut ties with her. As time passed, and almost half a year into our relationship, Michael took the thoughtful initiative to have his mother bring me some clothes, all without my prior knowledge or expectation. She was making a trip to Jamaica from Canada to spend a couple of weeks visiting, and when she arrived, she brought an abundance of things for me. Among the items were beautiful earrings that I could wear to work, a few stylish pairs of sneakers, and various other essentials that I never really considered buying for myself, which truly made me feel appreciated and cared for. I was so incredibly happy to receive them.

At that moment, I wasn't buying anything for myself to wear, as I was far too busy purchasing items for my future apartment. When Michael introduced his mother to me, I liked her immediately. She was small in stature, well-spoken, and had an air of properness about her. She struck me as a mother who had seemed to come to terms with her son's unfortunate deportation. She stayed for a couple of weeks, and during that time, I tried to give him more time to be with her, understanding how important that was for them both.

The last weekend she was there, Michael and I made arrangements to go skating, an outing I was genuinely looking forward to. We had not skated in a little while, and the very thought of us enjoying our favorite past time together had me feeling exuberant, like a child filled with excitement. I went home to bathe and changed into one of my new outfits. As I arrived at Janet's one-room house, I heard her saying to Deidre, "Hurry up and gwon before Swofiyah come," with a sense of urgency in her tone.

I had arrived just in the nick of time to see Deidre, my bothersome sister, getting ready to leave, and she was well suited up in my new clothes. Her oversized, hefty body stretching my clothing into dimensions I never thought possible. In that moment, the rage I had been containing over the years erupted uncontrollably. Before I even fully grasped what I was doing, I was on her like a rabid animal, ripping every piece of my brand-new clothing from her, driven by a fury that had been boiling within me for far too long.

"Yuh think a me and yuh a bloodclaat fuck for this?" I asked defiantly, not caring at all that Janet was standing there, her presence irrelevant in that moment. Janet, in a sudden burst of anger, grabbed me tightly around my long neck and swiftly flung my skinny body to the hard ground, then knelt on my virtually nonexistent stomach with a weight that felt unbearable.

"A my bloodclaat house this," she spat out slowly, emphasizing each word with a dangerous tone. "Yuh nuh bloodclaat come in a me house and act so."

In that moment, she would've killed me then and there, if I had not instinctively stopped breathing to escape the situation. Before I closed my eyes, I caught a glimpse of Deidre, wearing that nasty, smug smile she always wore whenever she was pleased to see my mother beating the living daylights out of us. I watched her put on one of her short mini dresses that she had hung up, then grab her matching purse and start to transfer her personal belongings into it with a casual indifference. Finally, she walked out, leaving Janet still kneeling in my stomach while choking me in a cruel attempt to dominate me. As the tears began to roll down my face, I squeezed my eyes tightly shut, wishing for it all to end. I felt my mother's merciless grip on my neck loosen slightly, just enough for me to gain my bearings. I turned my body a little and she lost her balance unexpectedly. Seizing the opportunity, I sprang up like a cat, propelled by pure instinct, causing her to fall over clumsily. I rushed towards the door, not caring at all that she had fallen down on the floor behind me. She was absolutely livid.

"Come here, dutty bloodclaat gal," she called out breathlessly, her voice filled with fury. Her face was flushed with rage, a wild madness infusing her features as she struggled to formulate her next move.

It was at that very moment that I began to wonder why I had never taken the drastic step of chopping her up like I did the chickens I used to practice on in the backyard when I was much younger. I felt an intense urge to rid myself of my mother with her idiotism that had plagued my life for too long. I wished the dark thought had occurred to me to dismember her before I made the decision to put that badness business firmly away from me. It would have been so incredibly easy to carry out such a plan and place the blame squarely on Crotchless Wayne, but the notion had never even entered my mind. What kind of killer did I truly want to be? As I stood there staring at the thing that was never actually a mother to me, I was struck by the relentless question of why had I allowed her to abuse me for so long. I was left feeling even more mentally unstable than she was for having endured her torment over countless years. WHY? WHY? I picked up the only thing I could find, my skating shoes, and hurled them at her in a fit of rage, before I ran out of the house in a desperate rush. Unconsciously, I found myself pulling at my hair with a frenzied intensity, yanking it out in large, painful bundles. My body shook violently with the energy of my mental turmoil, and despite the chaos, I felt utterly unable to stop myself. I was filled with confusion, my body trembling with agitation. Unaware that my shaking hand had been forcing strands of hair from the roots of my scalp, I could not even begin to feel the pain that my scalp was enduring.

The skin on my face suddenly felt uncomfortably taut, and I instinctively opened my mouth like a fish gasping for air, only to close it again moments later. All the while, I found myself pulling at my hair and raking my nails frantically over my skin, glancing anxiously over my shoulders as if expecting her to emerge. The madness that had been creeping up on me was inevitably overcoming me, and I knew deep down it was only a matter of time before I slipped completely.

I was at Michael's house, yet I had no clear recollection of how I had arrived there or when I had made the journey. He opened the door after the very first knock, almost as if he had been waiting for me.

"A caan duh it nuh more," I said, my voice above a whisper, trembling with barely contained desperation. "A caan duh it nuh more." My body was shaking violently, and I continued to pull at my hair in a frantic manner. "I caan duh it nuh more."

Michael watched me intently, with tears rolling down his cheeks, his heart visibly breaking. He understood this moment was the end for me. He recognized that the inevitable madness I had feared was finally here, manifesting in my disheveled state.

"Swofiyah, yuh can't continue like this. Them a guh mad yuh," he said softly, pulling my trembling body close to him, trying to provide some semblance of solace.

"A caan duh it nuh more," I continued to repeat, trembling and mumbling in sheer panic.

He tried to gently stop my hands from pulling out my hair, but each time he successfully removed my fingers, I would resume the frenzied pulling as if it were the only thing I could control.

"A caan duh it nuh more," I kept mumbling under my breath, a mantra of despair.

"Baby, tell me what yuh want me to do?" he whispered urgently in my ear, his cheek moist from the tears he was shedding for me. "I will do it for yuh, just say the word."

But I couldn't comprehend what he meant. I was too far gone, lost in a swirling chaos of overwhelming emotion. I had finally snapped, and the reality of my situation was beyond reach.

I withdrew myself slowly from him and walked away, still mumbling under my breath. "A caan duh it nuh more."

He was feeling my deep pain, but he was utterly hopeless to fix it for me. It wasn't just about moving out of her house; I realized that profound truth in that very moment. It was about escaping her, altogether, in every possible way. To move out and live so close to her was simply not what I really wanted. It was not far enough. I could clearly see that now.

Even when he made the suggestion for me to come and live with him, I had finally figured out that was not what I truly desired, not deep down in my heart.

I left Michael behind. He didn't even try to stop me as I walked through his gate and began my trek up the street towards Windward Road. I walked and walked until I got to the junction of Jackson Road. I was still pulling out the little hair that remained on my head, feeling frantic, and mumbling the same words over and over, "A caan duh it nuh more."

As I turned up Jackson Road, Blossom's friend spotted me and hurried towards me with concern.

"Jesus Christ, Swofiyah! A what wrong wid yuh?" She asked, panic evident in her voice as she noted my distressed condition. She had never witnessed me in such a state before; the sight left her frightened and uneasy.

"A caan duh it nuh more," I mumbled again. "I caan duh it nuh more."

"Come, Swofiyah," she said urgently, gently leading me further up Jackson Road.

I continued to mumble, "A caan duh it nuh more," while desperately pulling out my hair in frustration.

When we finally reached Bobby's gate, she called out to him in a tone of urgency. "Bobby!" Tears were streaming down her cheeks, reflecting the depth of her concern for my well-being.

Bobby came out to the gate and quickly took in the scene, and immediately opened the gate.

I think I was suffering a mild case of catatonia, mumbling softly to myself, "A caan duh it nuh more."

"Make she stay with yuh until tomorrow, Blossom's friend urgently begged, her voice tinged with anxiety and a hint of desperation.

But it really didn't matter in the long run, because Bobby was my friend and he would take care of me, no questions asked. He opened the gate with a gentle, almost cautious motion, pulling me inside the yard and leading me toward the cozy little house where his kind grandmother was sitting on the patio, observing us with palpable concern and curiosity.

I was still pulling out my hair in frustration and mumbling incoherently to myself, thoroughly lost in my inevitable madness.

"Me a guh call Blossom in a Hanover and come back," Blossom's friend shouted to Bobby as she rushed out the gat and up Jackson Road, clearly worried about my condition and uncertain about how to help me.

But Bobby was far too busy leading me into his house, feeling broken inside and on the verge of a complete mental breakdown. His grandmother noticed my distress almost immediately and hurriedly went into the kitchen. She made some sweet sugar and cool water to help me recover from this tumultuous state. They gently sat me down on the plush sofa, the softness of the cushions contrasting sharply with my frazzled mental state, and insisted on forcing the sugar and water down my throat with a gentle but firm insistence. I started coughing suddenly, a reflex that caught me off guard. I don't know if it was the coughing fit or the sweet sugar and water they had given me, but in that moment, I finally came back to myself, tears streaming down my cheeks as the harsh reality of my situation began to set in.

"Bobby, a caan take it nuh more, it too much now," I said hoarsely, my voice trembling with deep emotion and uncontainable vulnerability.

"Don't worry, me dear, go on in a Bobby room and rest yuhself and get some sleep. We will deal with this tomorrow," his grandmother encouraged soothingly, her voice filled with warmth and reassurance, creating a small beacon of hope amidst my turmoil.

35. The Out Of Body Experiences!

The next morning, I slowly woke up beside Bobby, the sunlight streaming into the room, but my headache was so maddeningly intense that I could hardly focus my vision on anything around me. I instinctively held on tightly to both sides of my throbbing head and curled myself into his warm back, letting out soft grunts from the pain that seemed relentless. To my surprise, he turned and enveloped me in a comforting cuddle, his presence providing a momentary sense of relief. Gently rocking myself back and forth while being held close to him, I eventually drifted back into a light sleep, hoping the pain would ease.

When I next opened my eyes, it was already twelve noon, and I found myself alone in the bed. The sound of voices filtered into my awareness, and I could hear Carlene—Blossom's friend—along with Bobby and his grandmother engaged in a hushed conversation.

"She can't continue like this," Carlene said with a hint of concern in her voice. Instinctively, I knew they were discussing my situation.

"I don't mind her coming here to live," Bobby replied earnestly, his tone warm and inviting.

"Yuh too near, that's why she never take yuh offer," Carlene responded, reflecting an understanding of my complicated circumstances. "Her mother would be here a knock down yuh gate everyday."

Seeking a moment of privacy, I got up from the bed and made my way to the bathroom. On a whim, I decided to take a shower while I was there. I focused on the refreshing cool water cascading down and hitting my skin, momentarily distracting me from the throbbing in my head. I used my flimsy undies as a makeshift washcloth, soaping them up to scrub my body, trying to feel more human. After my shower, I returned to Bobby's room, feeling somewhat revitalized, and rummaged through his drawer to find a pair of his underpants that I slipped on. I then pulled on my familiar jeans shorts and a green floral T-shirt that felt like a comfort blanket against my skin. Finally, I applied some of his fragrant lotion on my exposed skin, all the while avoiding the mirror, I wasn't yet ready to confront my reflection—to see the damage I had inflicted on myself.

"Swofiyah, me a come in," Carlene said softly, knocking gently on the door, her voice barely above a whisper.

"Awright," I replied, my voice hoarse and ragged.

She pushed the door open slowly and stepped into the dimly lit room.

"How you feel?" she asked with genuine concern etched on her face.

"I feel like shit," I admitted, the weight of my emotions heavy in the air.

"Yea, madness will do that to you," she stated, having experienced a similar descent into mental herself not too long ago.

My lips twitched for just a brief moment at the shared understanding between us, but soon I found myself crying, my body shaking violently from the pain that seemed to overwhelm me.

"It's okay, Swofiyah," she said softly, pulling closer as she came to sit on the bed beside me, rubbing my back in a soothing motion. "It awright, me talk to Blossom and she said you can come to Hanover. We can leave later."

"A have to go for me things them at Janet house," I told her, my voice still struggling to regain its strength.

"Awright, me a guh come with yuh," she assured me, determination shining in her eyes.

It was Monday, and I had unfortunately missed going to work at Ammars, which left me feeling a bit unsettled. I realized that if I was truly going to leave Kingston for good, then thinking about work and my responsibilities right now was not as important as it once seemed. However, despite that realization, I couldn't shake the urge to go there one last time, to leave the right way. At the very least, it felt necessary to talk to my supervisor about my departure.

I knew I was only fixating on work as a way to distract myself and prevent my mind from wandering to other matters — matters that weighed heavily on my thoughts, matters I desperately didn't want to think about. My headache had just started to ease up, which was a relief in the midst of everything else.

Carlene and I walked into the living room where we found Bobby sitting with his grandmother. As soon as we entered, Grandmother looked up and said warmly, "Bobby, go and share out some breakfast for Swofie," as if she had been expecting us.

I hadn't even realized she was aware of my name, which surprised me. "Thank you, but me just want some tea," I informed them politely, feeling that with the high stress I experienced the previous night, I didn't think my body could accept any sort of heavy breakfast at that moment.

Bobby soon returned with two cups of steaming mint tea, one for me and the other for Carlene. As I took a sip, Grandmother turned to me and asked, "So, have you decided yet what you want to do?" Her voice was gentle and sincere. "Because you know you are always welcome to stay here," she continued, her eyes filled with kindness.

"Thanks," I replied, trying hard to keep my expression neutral and avoid blowing air in my cheeks or pouting my lips. "A think a going tuh guh a Hanover. The farther away I am from her, the less likely I will see her." I said this quietly, as if to no one in particular, letting my words hang in the air between us.

Grandmother pushed out her lips and slowly nodded her head in understanding. For a brief moment, her expression mirrored that of my own grandmother, evoking a surge of nostalgia within me.

"Awright, but remember, you will always have a place here to stay whenever you need it."

This heartfelt assurance brought more tears to my eyes, blurring my vision for a brief instant.

"I'm going tuh guh for my other things them and whatever I can't take with me, I'm going to leave them here until I can get back on my feet," I said, glancing over at Bobby, whose steady presence comforted me.

"Yes mon, yuh know yuh things them safe here, no worries bout that."

It got quiet for a moment, the sweet sounds of slurping tea and the cheerful singing of birds filling the space around us. I was trying very hard not to dwell on the memory of Janet and me hitting her last night with the skating shoes, willing the thoughts to vanish.

"Yuh done?" Carlene asked, stretching out her hand expectantly for the tea cup. I handed her the cup and watched her as she walked over to the kitchen, putting it in the sink with a soft clatter.

"Just leave them there. I will wash them later," Grandmother said, her voice gentle but resolute.

"Bobby, yuh have a scarf or something yuh can give her to tie up her head with?" Carlene asked, her tone pleasant and helpful.

Bobby got up and went to his room, his footsteps light on the floor. He came back out with a large white floral cotton scarf and handed it to me with a smile.

"A me cousin give me this in America. It never wear yet, but me glad it's finally a guh find some good use," he joked.

Carlene took the scarf from him and expertly tied it around my head, placing the knot just over my right ear with care.

"Now yuh look fashionable instead of distressful," she said, putting much emphasis on the word "distressful" while admiring the vibrant scarf that was tied expertly around my head.

It didn't matter to me whether I appeared fashionable or completely crazy; I just wanted to get this painful ordeal over with and be gone from this place. I took a deep breath, trying to steady myself, and looked over at them both. "Thanks," I said shyly, my gaze briefly darting from Grandmother to her grandson.

"Don't worry yuh self bout nothing me dear. It will only make yuh end up in the grave sooner," she kindly advised, a hint of warmth in her voice.

Carlene and I stepped out of the door together, the weight of the moment pressing down on us. We walked down Jackson Road in palpable silence, every single step I took felt heavier with each passing moment as I approached Bower Bank. My heart thumped louder and faster, reverberating in my ears—I was a nervous wreck by the time I arrived at the community that had never once tried to protect me all these long years.

Carlene knew exactly where I lived, having been there a couple of times before with Blossom. I didn't want her to witness the confrontation that was about to unfold, or worse, to get caught up in Janet's madness and be hurt in the process.

"Carlene, stay here suh, me soon come back," I instructed her, trying hard to control my shaking hands.

"No, me a come," she declared stubbornly, determination etched on her face.

"Please," I said, my voice trembling slightly as I pleaded with her.

She looked at me with her striking eyes and took a deep breath, as though steeling herself for what was to come. For she had seen the shaking in my hands that I was trying hard to control, though it was becoming increasingly difficult. I nodded at her, a silent acknowledgment of the weight of the moment, and then turned to walk away, feeling the air grow heavier behind me.

Everything in Bower Bank looked eerily normal, almost too normal, as if each day was just a repeat of the last. At the entrance, the bustling marketplace had long since disappeared, leaving only echoes of laughter and conversation. In its place, more wooden houses had been constructed, and a few unemployed residents had taken to planting banana trees that lined the sidewalk, reaching down towards the bottom of the street like sentinels.

It was very quiet, an unsettling kind of stillness that wrapped around me. I walked towards Janet's house, fully aware this was the last time I would ever return to this familiar place. I stepped onto the so-called veranda, feeling the hard concrete beneath my feet. The door was half-open, stuck by a piece of cardboard under it. A gentle gust had begun to blow, and I welcomed its cool touch on my clammy skin, a momentary relief in the rising tension. I slowly approached the door, my heart pounding. Inside, Janet was sitting on her stool beside Deidre's bed. Her lips were pursed, the skin stretching tautly over her jawline, an all-too-familiar expression of rage. It was her fierce, infuriated look, and I was bracing myself for whatever might come next. I knew this was going to be the last time.

"Afternoon," I managed to say, taking off my shoes just inside the doorway and stepping into the room with a sense of finality.

She didn't respond, her eyes locked onto me with a mix of emotions that made the air thick with tension. I reached into my pocket, retrieving the large black bag I had received from Bobby. With deliberate movements, I went to the large cardboard box where I kept my clothes and began the painstaking task of transferring the contents from the box into the plastic bag, each item representing a piece of my past that I was preparing to leave behind.

I was calm, almost unnervingly so. So calm that when Janet suddenly got up with the mop stick, brandishing it like a weapon, and began beating me mercilessly with it, I didn't jump from the fright at all. In fact, I was expecting it. I didn't make a sound or plea for help; I just continued methodically stuffing my belongings into the bag, focusing on that task.

Then, with a powerful swing, the mop stick broke in two, splintering in her hands. Undeterred, she quickly reached for the baton stick. At that moment, I felt my spirit unsettlingly slipping away from my body, and I stood to the side, a silent observer, watching as she continued to rain blows down upon my back with the heavy stick. Strangely, I couldn't feel a thing. It was as if I was both there and not there, detached from the painful reality, merely an onlooker to the harrowing ordeal unfolding before me. I felt nothing at all.

The first time this peculiar phenomenon occurred, I was just fourteen years old, and I genuinely thought I was finally dying. The experience used to terrify me each time my soul left my body like this, leaving me in a haunting state of unfeelingness.

There were also those other times, unsettlingly frequent, when it would leave me while I tried to sleep. During those instances, I had to lay there calmly, waiting until it finally decided to return to me. Only when I laid down would it stay out for an extended period, a disconcerting release that sometimes prevented me from even turning over in bed.

Many times, over the years, while she unleashed her fury upon me, I would watch in a dispassionate manner as my spirit slowly left my body, standing aside as a mere witness—just as it was now. I was not able to feel anything as she mercilessly administered the beatings. Because I couldn't feel a thing, I couldn't cry out for help or protest against the unyielding suffering.

This was yet another reason she cruelly called me "demons."

I knew deep down it wouldn't stay out of my body for too long while I was forced to move about. I also fully understood that the moment my soul returned, the pain would become far more excruciating, more shocking than before.

A question consistently nagged at me: why did my spirit never choose to leave when Leo was in the house with Janet? It would have made everything—if only just a little—so much easier for everyone involved, wouldn't it?

Suddenly, Pamela, my favorite cousin who had been occupying Aunty Norma's house for some years now, burst into the house with Janet's friend, Theresa, trailing closely behind her. They witnessed the alarming moment when Pamela raised the baton stick high above her head and brought it crashing down onto the back of my own head, striking me forcefully like a baseball. The instant they entered the room and the baton stick made contact, a surge of energy flowed through me, and the spirit I thought had left my body returned with a jolt. The shocking impact of the baton stick connecting with my skull caused me to collapse to the ground, trembling uncontrollably like a leaf caught in a fierce wind.

"No!" Theresa screamed loudly at Janet, her voice laced with disbelief. "Jesus Christ! A mad yuh mad?" She found it hard to comprehend the shocking scene unfolding before her eyes.

"Aunty Jaa! A wha wrong wid yuh?" Pamela cried out, rushing to my side and instinctively blocking my body from Janet's furious view, determined to shield me from any further harm.

"Move out a me way, mek me blood har up," Janet demanded of Pamela, her voice tense and breathless, filled with the anger that radiated through the room. The atmosphere was thick with tension. They knew

Janet was beating the living daylights out of me, but they had never actually witnessed it before—not until this very moment.

"How yuh must beat yuh pickney suh?" Theresa questioned loudly, her voice ringing like a warning bell. "A Bellevue Hospital yuh want her to end up?" Her alarm was palpable, as she worked at Bellevue Hospital for the Mentally Ill, primarily caring for mentally ill children. She had been one of the few friends that had steadfastly stayed by Janet's side over the years, enduring the complexities of their friendship. In addition to their ties, she was also the only person whose laundry Janet still took on as a chore.

They had often talked about having me marry her son someday, but it wasn't something I had ever truly thought about or envisioned for my future. I pondered on why I had never confided in Theresa over all these years. Perhaps it was because she was one of the longest-standing friends Janet had ever kept in her life, and that made the dynamics between us all the more challenging to navigate.

Through it all, Pamela remained at my side, still fiercely trying to protect me from the very woman who had brought me into this world.

My body was convulsing intensely, the movements uncontrolled and badly disorienting. My head felt as though it was experiencing a fierce seizure, overwhelming and chaotic. I was profoundly relieved to see Carlene entering the room, her presence a ray of hope as she picked up the discarded bag from the floor. Tears were streaming down her face, glistening in the light as she fought through her emotions. She was trying very hard not to look directly at me lying there on the floor, trembling and shaking in distress. Noticing the opened box beside me, she began to chug clothes from it into the plastic bag with a sense of urgency, casting me sideways glances filled with concern.

Once she finished packing the bag, she tied it securely and laid it on the floor nearby. Then she came and knelt gently beside my head, her voice cutting through the chaos.

"Swofiyah, yuh have to get up know," she said, but I couldn't grasp the meaning of her words. I was seeing everything around me and hearing every sound, yet nothing was truly sinking in, as if I were in a fog. In the deepening darkness that was enveloping me, I was trying with all my might to remember the beautiful sound of Chopin's music. Finally, it came to me, softly at first, then louder as I rose up on my toes, preparing to dance.

A wave of happiness washed over me as I glided elegantly to the music, losing myself, if only for a brief moment, in a world that I often escaped to find solace and peace. The familiar notes flowed through me, filling my spirit with warmth as I rose on my toes, gliding gracefully. Yet, the reality remained that I was still lying on the floor, in front of the box where I had fallen. I knew I should get up, but I desperately needed my body to stop its relentless convulsions and for the seizure-like weirdness to finally release its grip on my head.

My eyes were starting to roll over, a sign that fatigue was creeping in, so I focused even harder on the vivid mental imagery of me gliding effortlessly through the air with grace, executing the most perfect side split imaginable. I knew deep down that this moment could very well be the end for me. Surrounding me, everything was fading to black, and I was struggling mightily to maintain the vibrant images in my head. If I surrendered to the suffocating darkness that was overtaking my senses, I would not escape the clutches of death—an end I had so desperately desired all these years. I wanted to just give up. What was the real purpose of holding on anymore?

Hanover!

The mere thought of Hanover, along with the promise of a brand new life, sparked a flicker of hope within me. It represented a different kind of escape. A new life, filled with new experiences, new possibilities, was now within reach, and the idea of never having to face my tormentors again felt like a dream that was somehow becoming possible. I was genuinely looking forward to that promise of relief.

The very moment Carlene mentioned "Hanover" last night, a palpable shift occurred within my mind that enabled me to firmly latch onto that glimmer of possibility. I wanted Hanover more than anything, so I kept it anchored in the back of my focus while I danced on my toes, striving to chase away the encroaching darkness that threatened to consume me entirely.

Epilogue

O n life's journey, we often find ourselves
unexpectedly thrown onto various pathways
that can lead to profound healing, or, conversely,
sometimes even greater tribulations. The choices we
make along the way, then, ultimately rest in our own
hands. On that fateful day, my mother's fierce
determination to put an end to my existence was
unexpectedly thwarted by the sudden arrival of her
friend, who worked at the Bellevue Mental Hospital,
located near our community. She was accompanied by
my cousin, a presence that added to the tension in the
room. Their unexpected appearances made Janet livid,
and I could feel the air grow thick with discontent.
What could have possibly prompted them to stop by—
together—on that particular morning? Only God knew
the reason for their visit. The overwhelming darkness
that sought to engulf me eventually began to dissipate,
and I found the strength to rise and follow Carlene
into the unknown. Was it truly the right decision? You
better believe it; in fact, it was the best decision I had
ever made. Any decision that involved me getting out,
and away from my abusive mother, was undoubtedly
the right choice. Getting as far away from her as I

could was a dream that I had longed to see come true. At last, I was free from the grips of my tormentors.

It took me a considerable amount of time to truly realize that I was genuinely free from the oppressive chains of my tumultuous past. My mind was like a bird that had become so accustomed to being caged for far so long that it didn't even want to venture out into the inviting and expansive open skies, even when the cage door was left wide open for me, beckoning me to take flight and embrace my newfound freedom.

For months on end, I found myself looking over my shoulders, anxiously expecting to see her looming ominously behind me with her baton stick, ready to impose her control and fearsome presence once again. It was an entirely different kind of mental torture, one that I had to learn to combat diligently and ultimately overcome if I was truly going to live my life fully and attempt to be as normal as possible, whatever that might mean for me.

My dear friend Blossom, along with her incredibly supportive family and the many other unfamiliar strangers who had, over time, transformed into close friends, all played a vital and indispensable role in my long and challenging healing journey—if you could really call it healing at all. There were moments when I would find myself curled up in my small apartment, huddled in a corner on the floor, much like I had once discovered my sister, curled up tightly in the shadows at the back of our house when she was much younger. My arms were wrapped tightly around my middle, as if trying desperately to hold myself together, while my body shook uncontrollably from the overwhelming and excruciating pain of those haunting memories that refused to let go, clinging to me like a persistent shadow.

THE END

Acknowledgement

I want to sincerely thank Michelle Ross of Tampa Career College, located in Tampa, Florida. You were the very first person in Florida who genuinely and selflessly endeavored to assist me...a complete stranger from off the street, whom you had never previously met. The exercise book you generously gave me sparked a newfound motivation within me to embark on my second attempt at writing while traveling on the Greyhound bus, journeying back to my feelings of hopelessness.

I am truly grateful to Kim Hamilton, who has been more than just a sister to me over the years, and continues to be a steadfast support in my life. Thank you for always being there.

To Juhi Roy, my university friend, who provided me with an abundance of encouragement throughout our time together. Your support means so much. Thank you.

To all the wonderful people who took the time to read my blog and encouraged me to finally finish my book, I deeply appreciate your belief in me. Thank you.

Lastly, a heartfelt thanks to all my beautiful customers who purchased a copy of my work; I sincerely hope you enjoyed reading it as much as I enjoyed writing it...well not really. It was torture all over again.

GLOSSARY

Duppy.	Ghost
Dutty/dooty	Dirty
Idiat.	Idiot
Cho.	A Jamaican Expresion
Bloodclaat.	Strong Jamaican bad word
Pussyclaat.	Strong Jamaican bad word
Bumboclaat.	Strong Jamaican bad word
Raas.	Mild Jamaican bad word
Mi.	Me
Dem	Them
Dem	Plural you
Neva	Never
Yuh	You
Oonuu/onu/oonu.	Plural you
Dat	That
Puppa Jesas	Father Jesus
Jesas Chrise	Jesus Christ
Guh.	Go/to go
A guh.	Is going to
Wha.	What
Weh	Where/what/why
Wope	Hope
Nuh.	No/not
Nyam	Eat/ to eat

Nyame.	Name
Sup'm.	Something
Sumpting.	Something
Sista.	Sister
Scueem.	Scream
A-sack.	Stool
Dis.	This
Brekfuss	Breakfast
Yah.	Here
Inna	In a/inner/in the
Falla	Follow
Si	See
Earliyah	Earlier
Tek	Take
Not'n/nut'n	Nothing
Har	Her
Fi	For/to
Dah	That
Deh/dey	There
Duh	Do
Attaclaps	Armageddon, the end The big finale
Pickney	Child: son or daughter
Pumpum/punaney/chocho	Vagina
Renk.	Smelling of urine
Gwon.	Go on/going on
Grine	Having sex

ABOUT THE AUTHOR

T anya R Chambers was born and raised in Kingston, Jamaica. Her journey led her to the United States, where she pursued higher education with determination and focus. She earned an Associate degree in Liberal Arts, along with a certificate in

Interior Designing from Monroe Community College in Rochester, New York.

After her time at Monroe Community College, Chambers transferred to the University at Buffalo. There, she excelled academically and obtained a double bachelor's degree in Psychology and Global Gender Studies, graduating magna cum laude. Her educational background reflects a deep commitment to understanding both individual and societal dynamics.

In addition to her academic achievements, Chambers has a passion for traveling. She embraces a nomadic lifestyle, cherishing the diverse experiences and perspectives gained from her journeys. Through her travels, she continues to expand her horizons and deepen her understanding of different cultures.

OLD MAN TREE PRESS